ABOUT THE BOOK

This book – the nearest the Sex Pistols got to telling their own story - was first put together at the height of the punk rock explosion. The authors had unique and continuous access to all the band, to their families and friends, to Malcolm McLaren and all the members of McLaren's Glitterbest office. The book got rave reviews, was translated into several languages and itself became part of the Sex Pistols legend.

- The authentic story of all the key people.
- Told in their own words as it happened.
- Explosive extracts from the Sex Pistols' secretary's secret diary.
- Now completely updated.
- With background notes and exclusive McLaren biography.
- Complete discography.
- The truly inside story of one of the most extraordinary sagas of rock 'n' roll.

THE AUTHORS

Fred Vermorel was McLaren's friend and confidant from earliest art college days and introduced him to Vivienne Westwood. Judy Vermorel met and married Fred when they were studying mass media at the Polytechnic of Central London. *Sex Pistols: The Inside Story* was their first book. They subsequently co-wrote several outrageous pop anti-biographies and *Starlust* (1985), a source book about pop fans' hidden desires and obsessions with an introduction by Pete Townshend. Fred and Judy also co-write songs and are signed to Chappell Music.

MALCOLM McLAREN: 'Destroying record companies is more fun than making it.'

JOHNNY ROTTEN: read Keats and *Brighton Rock* for 'O' level.

SID VICIOUS: 'I shall die before I'm 21.'

PAUL COOK: his school report warned of 'bad influences'.

STEVE JONES: 'Give my love to mum.'

GLEN MATLOCK: too posh for the Pistols.

SOPHIE, THE SECRETARY: opened her secret diary for this book.

VIVIENNE WESTWOOD: from schoolteaching to Sex fashions.

JAMIE REID: from politics to punk.

The story is told at first hand through interviews, diary extracts, quotes and documents. A checklist of people interviewed appears on page 234.

ve THE QUEEN
PISTOLS

WHAT THE CRITICS SAY:

'Easily the best book about punk. The only one to articulate the mania of that moment.'
– Simon Frith, *New Statesman*

'Reads like a thriller.'
– *Centre Press*, France

'Here at last is a truly solid and perceptive study of a group whose sensation reeking activities have so often resulted in perverted and overly biased viewpoints . . . Superb editing work . . . a constant fluidity which like any "good read" draws one instinctively into the action . . . Sheer revelatory potency . . . stands in a category rare in the rock 'n' roll stakes: the in-depth biography.'
– Nick Kent, *NME*

'An entire epoch is distilled in this book.'
– *L'est eclair*, France

'Absolutely astonishing . . . a real work of history . . . This book shows how much we live in a present continually overtaken by events. A shattered present . . . The Sex Pistols as expressed in this book illuminate the last quarter of our century.'
– Maurice Achard, *Les Nouvelles Litteraires*

'The Pistols as anti-Beatles was the last innovative shot the rock industry would get, and Judy and Fred wrote the definitive book about it.'
– Jane Solanas, *NME*

'Talk about a nose for a story! – they don't leave one skeleton unturned or one stone in the closet.'
– Julie Burchill, *The Face*

'Very comprehensive and very readable . . . It is definitive.'
– Peter Owens, *The Hot Press*

'Everything is revealed, scrupulously and with precision.'
– Alain Wais, *Le Monde*

'The Bible of Punk'
– *Shinko Music*, Japan

THE INSIDE STORY

Book Designed by Undercover, London

ISBN 0.7119.109.1
Order No. OP 44213

Exclusive distributors
Book Sales Limited
8/9 Frith Street, London W1

Music Sales Corporation
225 Park Avenue South
New York, N.Y. 10003, U.S.A.

Music Sales Pty. Limited
120 Rothschild Avenue,
Rosebery, NSW 2018
Australia

To the Music Trade only:
Music Sales Limited
8/9 Frith Street, London W1

Photographs
Bob Gruen P8, 39, 43, 47, 53, 104-5, 119, 121, 123, 125, 137, 149, 153, 157, 168, 171, 173, 191, 201, 209
D Morris P8
Barry Plummer P13, 81, 91
Ray Stevenson P5, 21, 23, 33, 46, 194
Fred Vermorel P187

Typeset by MC Typeset, Chatham, Kent
Printed in Great Britain by Scotprint Limited, Musselburgh, Edinburgh.

CONTENTS

THE GREAT
ROCK 'N' ROLL
SWINDLE

PART I
THE STORY
YOUR
NEVER MIND
THE BOLLOCKS
HERE'S THE
SEX
PISTOLS
Wanna
Be Me
Sex
Pistols
EMI
South Kensington
A322
CHEYN

EARLY DAYS

ALAN EDWARDS: Rock 'n' roll had got very boring. I hadn't been listening to it or going to concerts for my own amusement for a long, long time. And I used to, just for drinks and just for fun, go round to places like the Nashville – in fact, the Nashville was my local pub. And I used to go to the Marquee and the 100 Club. But I think it was at the Nashville I noticed the first changes. The Sex Pistols played there, the Stranglers played there. And they were radically different to anything that I'd ever seen.

In fact, when I went to see the Pistols it made me feel like a really old man. I mean I was only 20 at the time, it made me feel like I was 50. And I was shocked. And I just hid in the corner, literally, drinking Double Diamond, wondering what was going on – all these people with amazing make-up, fights and God knows what. And I completely rethought my whole attitude after seeing them. It called for a total revising of one's opinions on music and it made one feel that maybe music had some sort of relevant part to play in one's life, which in the last couple of years it hadn't really at all.

And so I got involved with the Stranglers, started doing a few bits and pieces of publicity from last summer. And then suddenly in October the whole thing exploded and a complete scene came out of almost nowhere. And there were bands like the Vibrators, the Damned, the Clash, they were all formed within a matter of weeks of each other. And suddenly it was 50 punk bands playing in London which had happened overnight. But it hadn't actually happened overnight. All those people were kids who had been hanging around, really bored, feeling there was nothing to do . . .

Q: When did you first become aware of punk?
TRACIE: Well, I used to live in Bromley and I used to go round with Siouxsie and Steve, Simon, Berlin, people like that, and Simon went to see the Sex Pistols at a college in Bromley when they played. It was about one of their first gigs, and he just sort of like came back and said: 'Oh, I've seen this group and they're really good and they're different and that,' you know. So we started going to see them at places like the Nashville, and then they played the El Paradiso Club, which started off as a strip club in Soho. Then my friend Berlin had a party last May and he invited the Pistols. By then we'd seen them quite a lot and they had started to get to know us. And they all came along. I suppose that was the first time I got to know them like on a social level, not just like seeing them as a group on stage and that.
Q: Can you remember what your reactions were when you first saw them?
T: I don't know. I just kept looking at Steve Jones and he had these two nude women on his guitar and I just thought it was a bit funny. And I just thought

John was a bit mad, you know what I mean? But it was exciting and that was what was good about it. I suppose you just sort of wondered what hit you at first because like in those days John used to do things like he used to swear a lot at the audience. The equipment used to pack up and stools used to break and all stuff like that, and so he used to stand there and swear at the hall and throw beer at people and tell them they were stupid and things like that.
Q: What did it make you feel like?
T: Well, I just thought it was good. I thought: Christ, someone's actually doing something that's a laugh, you know what I mean? It's just good fun. I mean I liked other people before but you could never go and see them. I used to like people like Alice Cooper when I was about 13, and you could never get to see them because you didn't really have much money and they played the big places in London and it cost loads of money to get in. So, you know, that's what was good about the Pistols. You always knew they would play in places that didn't really cost much to get in. You could go along, you could say what the hell you wanted, dress how you wanted and no one cared.

At the beginning you used to get a lot of hassle, like those old hippies that used to hang around with things like 'drugs destroy flowers' and 'stop people living on planets', things like that, on their T-shirts, and they used to say that the Pistols were horrible and destructive and you shouldn't really go and watch them. They tried to convert you into peace and love and all that, which made you just like them all the more. But I suppose it's just because they were different, different from everyone else. They were the first proper punk band. There was no one like it before the Pistols.

Q: Can you tell me a bit about how you and Steve started the group?
PAUL COOK: It wasn't our doing really. It was this bloke called Wally. Like he used to go to our school – he was in the same year as us. And we didn't used to play anything when we was at school or anything. He was interested in it and we just used to go round to his house, towards the end when we was just leaving school. And we used to bunk off, go round his house and sit in his garden like. See, his mum and dad were out and they didn't care anyway. In the summer we just used to go round there – cos it was near the school – and sunbathe and that. And at the time – we didn't know John – there was me, Steve, this Wally geezer and a couple of our other mates. And I think it was after we left school, Wally – he used to play guitar – he said let's start a group.

We decided our own little things, what we was going to do. I wasn't going to be in it at first cos I wasn't all that interested, but Steve, he got a drum kit first, and Wally was on guitar. There was a different bass player, and someone else. After a while they said Steve will be the singer like and I'd play drums. So I said all right. And Steve had learnt to play a bit by this time so he taught me what he knew and I carried on from there. And he was going to be the singer and he started playing about with guitar. Then there was just the three of us: me, Steve and this Wally. And then we got Glen through the shop, cos we knew Malcolm by this time.

GLEN MATLOCK: I'd worked in Malcolm's shop for about a year and then Steve and Paul started coming in. Malcolm introduced us really. Steve and Paul had all this equipment around and they didn't know what to do with it, so they might as well learn to play it. So that's how they started. Then they started to get a little bit more serious. Then they had this bass player who was married and had a wife and kid, you know, never turned up for rehearsals and all that. About that time I met them. I was learning to play bass. So that was it really. It was about four years ago we started rehearsing, in '73. It's in the last two years though that we really got serious.

Q: I'm interested that all of you went in the shop and that it was in a sense a focal point. Can you tell me what attracted you to it?
STEVE JONES: What, the shop? It was just different from any other shop down the King's Road. You felt, you know, you could go in there and stand there and no one would sort of bother you. But if you went in Take Six down the road as soon as you'd go in you've got five blokes on you like that to start with, saying: 'Yes, can I help you?' 'Do you want a suit?' And like it was nothing like Take Six anyway, the clothes in the window. We used to go in there because it was like Teddy boy clothes. It was just like being not in a shop but a sort of a hang out, you know what I mean? Somewhere to hang about for half an hour, just watch people really.
Q: Did you used to buy those clothes or did you used to nick them?
SJ: No, I bought a few things. The first thing I bought in there was a pair of pink trousers. I'll never forget that. I didn't know if to buy them or not because they had like tight bits at the bottom, because like at the time everyone was wearing sort of flares and that – that was about five years ago. Anyway I bought them. I thought: I'll be a bit of a lad and buy them. Ever since after that I was getting a lot of clothes like that. I never bought a drape jacket or anything like that, but like I bought them Teddy boys shoes and that.
Q: What did you feel like when you wore clothes like that?
SJ: I thought I was something different. Thought [*American accent*] I was a man now. [*Normal voice*] I don't know. Just didn't want to be like all the others. It's always the same, isn't it, when you're young.
Q: Did it used to annoy people to see you dressed like that?
SJ: Yeah, jealous.
Q: What sort of people do you think that that shop attracts now?
SJ: It's mainly punk rockers. At one time it was called 'Sex', and they used to get a lot of businessmen in there, perverted businessmen, you know,

1976. Four boys on a street corner.

touching you up and all that. It was a laugh too. I used to like going in there and just watching these blokes trying on things like. And then they'd get all their orgasms in the dressing room. Used to come out of there and you'd try a pair of trousers on and they'd be soaking wet. It was really funny like, the people you used to get in there . . .

And we asked Malcolm, we told Malcolm that we was messing about with the group and we was looking for a bass player. And he must have asked Glen if he could play the instrument, and Glen says: 'Yes, I play the bass.' And we got him as a bass player. So we started to rehearse and this went on for about six months I think. We had this studio – Wally's dad had this studio. It was a big – you know Hammersmith Bridge? – the Riverside Studios. It used to belong to the BBC but they had it rewired or redecorated or something. It had closed down anyway. We had this fantastic room where we used to rehearse like. And we used to – well, we stole most of the equipment because we didn't have any money, we just used to go round . . . well, we used to steal most of our equipment. Well, I did – Wally didn't steal anything like that. I just got excited by stealing anyway . . .

So we used to rehearse at this place, for about six months I think. And Malcolm he comes out to see us a few times. Like we was doing Small Faces numbers and like sort of dressing up and sort of getting that image, and Malcolm suggested that I should start playing the guitar, and I thought yes, that was a good idea, because I fancied the guitar more than the singing because I didn't really have the confidence for singing, you know.

PAUL COOK: We used to rehearse for a while, the four of us. Then we sort of slung Wally out cos we weren't really happy.

Q: I seem to remember something about Wally being married.

PC: No. Married to his dad, yeah. He was one of them sort of kids. We knew Malcolm by this time. Used to hang about with him and that. And then we slung Wally out. This was two and a half years ago now. And we said to Steve: 'You carry on playing guitar and we'll look for a singer and we'll start from there.' We thought that was the best way to do it.

Q: How did you get to know Malcolm first?

PC: He had his shop and we used to go in there, round about 1970, 71. I was about 14, 15 then – no, about 15 I suppose. Used to buy all our clothes, cos we were mad on clothes, Steve and I. It was called 'Let it Rock' then. Used to sell all Teddy boys clothes and that. We used to go in there round about 1971, every week like. We didn't talk about anything to do with music – we'd just go in there and talk to him. And we knew all the people who worked in the shop – we were friends with them, cos we used to hang about the King's Road a lot. And we heard that Malcolm was looking for groups like to do something with and – this was when we was with Wally – we said: 'We're

getting a group together.' He said: 'I'll come and listen to you.' He just used to come down, hang about and listen us to. Give us his 'bad advice' about what to do.
Q: Such as?
PC: I don't know. We was just sort of a bit naïve at the time like. Was playing all these old numbers, you know, Beatles. He just said stop playing this shit and write your own stuff or get something together so you definitely know what you're doing. You know, we didn't know what we was doing or anything. We just used to pick stupid random numbers and play them. But then we decided to play all the stuff we liked, like early Small Faces numbers and early Who, like so it's all directed into one channel. And we picked up from there, writing our own stuff. You know, we done them as a sort of guide, but we done our own stuff.

And one of the first bands to influence us like, well me anyway and Steve, coming out of that old stuff, was the New York Dolls. Saw them by accident cos we went to see the Faces at Wembley and the Dolls were supporting them. It was about the time their first album was out. And then I saw them on the old telly like and I was fucking really knocked out by them. It was mainly their attitude I think. It was this really conventional BBC – you know the Old Grey Whistle Test, like everyone's really straight – and I couldn't believe it: they was just all falling about all over the place, all their hair down, all knocking into each other. Had these great big platform boots on. Tripping over. They was really funny. And they just didn't give a shit, you know. And Bob Harris at the end of it went: 'Tut, tut, tut, mock rock,' or something. Just cast it off in two words. I thought it was great though.

GLEN MATLOCK: I wanted to be in a group because I'd never heard a band that I thought was exactly right, what I thought a band should be like. I wanted to do it for myself, so I could hear my own records on the radio sort of thing. Not because it's me but because it's what I always wanted to hear. And the same like kind of image-wise. You know, everything was so laid back at that time. Anything that was slightly exciting was a very contrived, very poseurish way of going about things, very arty. As though someone sat down and thought out an idea and thought, oh, I'm going to be like that. All like David Bowie and Roxy Music which are very contrived things. And it was just good to just go out and like rock out. Cos there was no rock 'n' roll then at all.

STEVE JONES: So Wally got the boot and I started practising guitar. I could play – I knew a few chords – and so we just started looking for a singer. And Malcolm kept his eyes open at the shop and we tried one bloke but he was a dead loss, he was worse than me.

So just by John like coming in the shop . . . I'd seen him about six months ago. I thought he looked pretty good and I said to Malcolm to look out for this bloke, he's got green hair and that – because he had green hair at the time. And he come in the shop and then Malcolm must have asked him: 'Do you want to sing?' And he said: 'Yes, I don't mind,' or something. So we arranged to meet him in the pub round the corner from the shop.

So we went to see him and like he was really like piss-taking, you know, and we was piss-taking back because like we thought he was a bit of a bowser, you know, and like he was really flash. Like he come with his mate and we was talking for about an hour and he said all right, he'd audition it. And he said: 'OK, when?' We said: 'Tomorrow night.'

And then we had this idea of taking him in the shop and making him sing to the juke box. So we told him that and we went back to the shop. He put the juke box on and put on these Alice Cooper records and things like that. He was just piss-taking all the time – like out of us and everything else – and he was just pissing about, trying to make out he was singing. And we thought he was really funny. I thought he was hysterical. And he probably thought we was a bunch of idiots. So we went on from there. We just started rehearsing.

Q: What made you decide on John in particular?
PAUL COOK: We thought: He's got what we want. Bit of a lunatic, a front man. That's what we was after: a front man who had definite ideas about what he wanted to do, and he'd definitely got them. And we knew straightaway. Even though he couldn't sing. We wasn't really interested in that cos we was still learning to play at the time, so we wasn't really worried about whether he had a great voice or anything.

Q: How did the rest of the band react to John when he first joined you?
GLEN MATLOCK: Steve and Paul looked on him as a kind of a joke really. You know, cos he was like taking the piss out of them and they took the piss out of him. They just thought he was like a kind of a puppet character. I just thought: Yeah, he's kind of like mad enough and now we can get on with the band. We can start gigging straight away. Cos we'd been rehearsing for a year and a half, two years by then. Not rehearsing solidly, but learning to play, you know . . . Yeah, we'd been like stuck away for years and we just wanted to get on the stage and play. And when John came along he seemed the right guy to do it. Yeah, everything seemed to work.
Q: Why do you think it is that he has become so much the focus in the group, that he's the one that everybody talks about?
GM: I don't know. I mean he's obviously got a lot going for him, he's pretty mad and all that.
Q: What do you mean, mad?

GM: Well, a bit nutty, and kind of like looks a bit kind of psychotic. And he stares good, you know, he's got a good stare. You know, Robert Newton kind of stuff. He looked exactly like what was needed. I mean that's why we picked him to be the singer because he looked like what our ideas were in the back of our heads for somebody to look like. So he embodied the whole thing. He was just the right guy at the right time. He's got the right face.

Q: Do you remember the first gig that you did?
PAUL COOK: I remember it well, actually. It was in St. Martin's College, in a little room upstairs. Glen used to go there, right, and there was this group playing and we said: 'Can we come over and support you?' And they said: 'Yeah,' like they were acting really flash like. And we went over there and big hassle about whether we could or not. They didn't really want us to support them. They was just a sort of rock 'n' roll band, revival and that, sort of sub-Teddy boys like, and all their mates and stuff were in the audience. We went on and it was really loud, it was deafening like. And we was going really mad cos this was our first gig and we was all really nervous. And suddenly you had this great big hand pop out, and someone pulled the plug out like. Someone switched the power off. Well *they* did, the other band, I think, cos they wanted to go on. They was getting all annoyed and that. We had a load of our fans there and they had a load of theirs and it nearly evolved into a big fight, you know. We just went off then . . .

Q: At the early college gigs, where you gatecrashed, what was the audiences' reaction to you?
GLEN MATLOCK: Disbelief. There were people who were very snide. They always used to take us off halfway through. A guy would come rushing up and say: 'Hey, it's your last number', and then he would say: 'Thank you very much the Sex Pistols and their wall of sound,' in a very piss-taking kind of way.

DAVE GOODMAN: Every time the Pistols played they got some reaction from the audience. They created a lot of violence. Their gigs used to stir up this venom inside people. Like the bouncer, for no reason at all, beats up one of the audience. The music got them. It would happen if someone's holding a beer and they get pushed; they either turn round and push back or they let themselves get pushed and they push someone else. The beer goes over someone's shoulder and they turn round and that's it.

Colleges were where the big fights used to happen. There was Coventry, and a big fight at Hendon Poly which involved Paul and some Teds. He was outside with a chick and these Teds walked past and said something to him and he wouldn't leave it at that, cos Paul's always wanting to have a go.

Anyway about four Teds chased him back into the College. As they came through the door the bouncers hit the Teds. Paul ran off and the Teds ran through and tried to get back out of the College. The police arrived. Paul was hiding over the top of this doorway. They were running to and fro looking for these Teds. And there's people outside throwing stones at the windows for some reason. And it went further than that. Like the guy on the door who'd hit one of the Teds got in another fight with someone else. It was like a bloodbath really. There were about five or six different fights going on.

But I suppose you get violence anywhere. I never used to directly associate it with the Pistols. Coventry, one time, someone in the students union heard the word 'fascist' in 'God Save the Queen' and because of this they refused to pay the band. So there was this big argument between the band and these students union guys and other organizers and Malcolm and me and anyone who was involved about the lyrics of this song. It was really crazy.

They were getting between £60 and £200 at the time. Depended how Malcolm could work it. But they just used to take as many gigs as they could. They would be on the road seven days a week if they could, just to get around England.

Q: What sort of people were following you then? Were they just people that you knew or was there already a kind of identity?
PAUL COOK: No, in the early days the first couple of gigs was just our friends and their friends, you know. It grew from that really.
Q: What was the second gig that you did?
PC: Second one was supporting a group called Regulator who're still going now, and we played at some art school. And that was really good. That was in Holborn. I was expecting another disaster, but we played good, and we really went down well. That was when we started getting a following, playing around, getting a bit of press. It gradually started building up till we played the 100 Club and the Nashville. It was getting quite big by then. It was really good the early gigs though.

DAVE GOODMAN: I started a PA company, and that's how I met the Sex Pistols. They just phoned up and asked to hire a PA, which was for the first gig they did at the Nashville, supporting the 101ers. And they was getting £25 and we were asked to do it very cheap for £20. And we said: 'OK, fair enough. It's a new band, they need a break.' It was Albion Agency that asked us to hire it to them and when we got there it was a typical Albion trick, cos it was for the 101ers as well.

Joe Strummer of the 101ers, when he saw the Pistols that night, he just freaked and left the band immediately after the gig and formed his own punk rock group.

I was totally shocked by the band. I had to think about it for a bit. Because the Pistols definitely had more to offer than the other band. But musically awful. I mean their 'Substitute' is so bad, but very exciting. So I went up to Malcolm in the dressing room afterwards and said: 'If you want any more help or a permanent PA to hire out, we'll help you out.' We were the first people that really offered any sort of help in that sense. They thought everyone was against them.

The audience used to vary. At the 100 Club it started off with about 50 people, and it ended up we used to have 600 or more. They had to finish then. The 100 Club was the first place where they had a really punk-type reaction, where everyone came dressed for the occasion. And they'd all start doing this dancing – pogo dancing. And they were so fierce, right? Band there, the audience here, and they'd be pushing up on the stage and the band were pushing them back again. Jumping up and down.

But say up North somewhere, like Wolverhampton or somewhere like that, you'd get just a few people that were into it – two or three with the safety pins. And like there was one girl that had 'I wanna be me', the title of a song, written on the back of her jacket and we couldn't even work out how she knew about the song then. And some of them had been down to London to check it out and they'd travelled hundreds of miles. If they lived, say, in Leicester and the band were playing in Manchester, they'd go there.

Q: People have told me that you really stuck your neck out to have the Pistols at the 100 Club. Why did you do that?
RON WATTS: Well, first of all I'd seen them before most people. You've got to bear in mind that I'd seen them at the Valentine's dance at High Wycombe College which was the second week in February. So I'd seen them at a much earlier stage than almost any other promoter. They just turned up and played along with – Screaming Lord Sutch was top of the bill and he lent them his equipment. I think unwillingly. There was some sort of argument about the equipment at the end, in fact. I wasn't involved in that, don't know what it was specifically. I noted them and I thought: Yes, great. They're wild enough, they've got enough anarchy in them, they're different enough. They'd taken a different attitude by just turning up to play irrespective. And lo and behold about two weeks later – I was trying to get hold of them, didn't know how to get hold of them, in fact – Malcolm McLaren turned up down here. He said: 'Hey you, you Ron Watts?' 'Yeah.' 'What about putting the Sex Pistols on?' So I said yes immediately and we sorted out a date there and then.
Q: What was it though particularly that excited you about them?
RW: Rotten's attitude to the audience. He was playing to a lot of – let's face it

– hippies. I mean hippies have got pretty boring. I think they've got really boring. I try and stay away from what I call progressive rock altogether. So they quite excited me, though obviously they were rough. And they insulted the audience well enough and pulled back just in time to let me know they were in control of what they were doing. They did have a definite idea of presentation.

GLEN MATLOCK: One of the things I always remember was when I was playing at the 100 Club. It was the first time I'd played at the 100 Club. There was only 50 people there I would have thought. And me, Steve, Paul and Malcolm was trying to get John to come out with us – till it was time to go on. And John was with his mates that night and it was all like: I'm in charge of the group and I do exactly what I want to do. So he stayed in the bar and he got well pissed with his mates.

By the time he got on stage he was like falling arse over tit, couldn't sing the words of the songs properly and kept coming in at the wrong time. And it was making us look cunts as well because we was playing all right but it sounded like we were coming in at the wrong time and all. And he just kept glaring at me like that all the time. And he smashed up glasses on the floor. And there was one of the songs he come in completely wrong. I was just pissed off. I said: 'What a cunt,' I was like singing that instead. And he was all glaring and in the middle of the song he says: 'Do you want a fight?' I said: 'No, I don't think so, not now. I'd rather play the bass, thank you very much.' And like he said: 'I'll fight you, you cunt.' His mates are sort of going: 'Go on, John.' And, I don't know, he just freaked after that and he run off stage and run out of the Club. And we was like standing on the stage thinking: Oh well, it's the end of the gig then, more likely the end of the band. And then Malcolm shouted at him: 'Get back on that stage or that's the end of you.'

Then John come back down and he wanted to do an encore and we didn't want to know. He'd been sitting at the top of the stairs and he'd come back down really sheepish and we didn't want to know. We didn't see him for a couple of days after that.

Q: How did the kids react to them?

RON WATTS: Oh, it was great. It was hero worship. There were a few who didn't know what was going on, just chanced in. But basically it was their crowd from the beginning. It was obvious something was happening, right from the start. No question. Well, I saw that, and so did the other people. But the business were amazing because they came down week after week and I used to take them to task at the bar. This is funny, because I was standing at the bar just watching the general scenes, and they would say the same old

Jamie Reid's Sex Pistols fanzine. Now a collectors' item.

thing, week after week: 'Do you think it's going to happen?' 'How long do you think it's going to last?' 'Oh, I don't know about it, I think it will be over by the end of the summer.' I said: 'No, this is it. This is what's going to happen. This time next year you'll be jumping on the bandwagon if not before.' Which turned out to be the fact.

The first gig was 30 March. They came in and there weren't that many people in. But there were people there to see them and a few stragglers. That was great. I immediately agreed as soon as possible to give them a residency every Tuesday. And that started in May and they started on Tuesday 11 May. They did the following three weeks, which were the three weeks which were available. And they stormed. They really stormed.

I think that was the first time pogoing happened: Sid Vicious starting jumping up and down on the spot with excitement, bashing into people, and that was the first recorded incident of pogoing in the UK. Sid started that off and John started the safety pins off and between them they're responsible for a lot, aren't they?

All sorts of unlikely people used to turn up, you know: Mick Jagger, a lot of journalists were down all the time obviously checking it out, Chris Spedding started getting involved with them . . .

Then there was a bit of a gap while other things happened. They came back on 29 June and it had grown appreciably by then. And they were back again a week later, that was the 6th [July] – and the Damned played their first gig then. That was a sort of watershed of a gig. And then other bands started to appear of the same ilk. Then there was another gap then. Then they came on 10 August and the support band then was the Vibrators. Then they did 31 August and the support bands were the Clash and the Suburban Studs from Birmingham. That was a big gig. Then there was a gap. Then we had the Punk Festival and they played on 20 September, the Monday, with the Clash and Slaughter and the Dogs.

Q: Did things get violent?

RW: There were scuffles on the night the Pistols were here [during the Punk Rock Festival], but they weren't scuffles of a vindictive nature, they were scuffles of the sort: I'm a bigger punk than you. Two or three guys had come down from Manchester and I had to keep putting them out different doors. Every time I threw them out one door, (I explained it all to them that if they went down there they'd cause so much chest slapping the other kids were going to have a go at them because they were like a red flag), they went round the front door again, paid in, and came back in again. I gave them their money back once more and put them out the front door, and, blow me, they were sneaking in the back door ten minutes later. I just couldn't get rid of them.

Q: Why won't the 100 Club let the Pistols play here any more?

RW: Well, the thing is at that time it was bad. I mean punk was getting banned everywhere for similar things. Not just here, all sorts of incidents at the Nashville, the Marquee, everywhere – Dingwalls, there was fights at Dingwalls, people getting injured at the Nashville. It was very bizarre how everyone – they didn't come to a corporate decision amongst the clubs, they just individually did it. After one particular incident at that time [a glass splinter hitting a girl's eye during the Punk Rock Festival], obviously after that we just could not continue with that sort of threat. I mean if it happened again *we* could be in trouble. There had been one or two scuffles down here before. Nick Kent got, well, he didn't get beaten up, shaken up a bit. I had to pick Sid up and hold him in the air for a little bit, till he cooled down.

EMI

At this point negotiations with EMI began, initially with EMI Music Publishing.

Q: Could you tell me why you signed the group in the first place?
TERRY SLATER (EMI Music): I'd seen the group performing at the 100 Club in Oxford Street and I just thought they were one of the most exciting groups I'd seen. And one of the key reasons I was interested in them was that they were filling the gap which the industry had created whereby when a lot of kids go to concerts today it's expensive to get in, and if there's any aspiring pop star sitting in the audience, they're looking up at the stage in most cases and they're seeing hundreds of thousands of dollars' worth of equipment, very sophisticated lighting systems, etc, etc, and it's removed from them. If someone is an aspiring pop star, so to speak, it's very removed from them because it's so expensive, it's so extravagant. And what – on seeing the Pistols – what they did for me was really took me back to the way I started where you could play a 30 quid guitar through a 30 quid amp and have a lot of fun and make music and have people right in front of you, probably about 20 to 30p to get in, have a lot of fun. So when I see the Pistols and the audience reaction, all that all came back to me and I realized then that that was going to happen and was going to develop to fill the void made by the industry.
Q: Why was it that the record business just wasn't putting money into groups? I mean there were plenty of groups who wanted to be signed up round about that time. Why was it it seems that all the record companies were holding back?
TS: What, on the New Wave type of material? Well, companies are run by people; people are people and they just didn't recognize it – a lot of people just didn't recognize it. I was one of the people that fortunately did, you know. And when I eventually sat down with Malcolm McLaren I think he was as surprised as anybody that anyone would be as keen. I'm sure he'd tell you that. I said: 'Malcolm, I really believe in what you're doing. I really believe in this group, and you're going to be big and it's going to happen.' And that's why he signed with me. And they didn't have a record and I was so confident that they would eventually obviously have a record deal and would be very successful. I mean Malcolm would be the first to tell you, I really did it that way.
Q: Why was it the Pistols rather than any other band?
TS: There was very few at that time. I mean we're talking now over a year later, when the whole business is inundated with so called New Wave. At that

time there was only a few groups around like that and the Pistols were for me the most energetic. And what they were emitting was just pure raw energy, rock 'n' roll, which again took me back to my days when I was a performer starting a long time ago in the rock 'n' roll business. It was right back to then and that's what was important. Your question: why the Pistols? They were the most energetic bunch of boys playing on stage that I'd seen for years.
Q: Could you tell me a bit what the reactions were within the company when they were first signed?
TS: Well, when I first signed them there were mixed feelings because some of the boys that work for me thought I was maybe crazy and some others, when I told them what I thought it was all about, you know, agreed with me and were excited. And then in the end, after reviews, I think everybody really got the message and supported them entirely. I still do today and I still have relationships with the boys, specially with Malcolm who I keep in constant touch with and I support him. He's come through a lot and whatever success they have now and they're going to continue to have, they deserve. I'm amazed that the industry has waited so many years saying: 'We want something new,' 'When is something new going to happen?' blah, blah, blah. For years the record companies have been repackaging this, repackaging that, breaking the odd group here and there, but really when it was something new, when it was there, very few record companies, and I really mean this and I'd been in the business 20 years, very few record companies would recognize it. It was there. Once the whole thing got going then, oh, everyone got hit. But I feel quite good that I was the one who did recognize it, proved it, by signing the Pistols.

EMI recording contract signed 8 October 1976

SEX PISTOLS JOIN 'ESTABLISHMENT'
EMI QUICK ON THE DRAW FOR SEX PISTOLS

EMI's capture of the Sex Pistols, a group regarded in various quarters as one of the most exciting to emerge from the wave of new, young British musicians who have generated public and media interest in recent months, was also one of the fastest signings implemented by the company. The act's decision to go to EMI – despite intensive competition from other record firms – was conveyed to a & r manager Nick Mobbs by Pistols manager Malcolm McLaren last Friday (8) morning, and the contract drawn up, checked and signed by the evening of the same day.

Music Week, 23 October 1976

Sophie, the Pistols' secretary, begins her diary 27 November 1976 with a few memories.

. . . Life with the Sex Pistols definitely worth recording. . . . Should've begun at the beginning. No matter. A few impressions.

Started the Thursday before 13 Sept. It was still hot then. Sitting in cafés down South Molton St, outside, while Malcolm ran round Polydor, Chrysalis et al.

A bit difficult sorting what I was supposed to do or not, not knowing much, shy of Malcolm, unconfident. Two or three weeks mostly working from the flat in Balham. The ritual quarrels between Malcolm & Viv. Endless phone calls. The band doing gigs round the country at that point & Malcolm mostly working on the recording contract . . .

. . . our evening printing & flyposting for the 100 Club.

19 Sept. We realize Ron's publicity is up shit creek. Malcolm tells me to get our artwork together which I'm quite happily doing till he drives me crazy interfering. It comes out great though. Jamie a bit peeved. Murder printing it, blue & solid. Eventually we get 'em out, find a bucket, paste & off. Run out of paste about 2 am. I'm driving, & enjoy watching Malcolm so weedy looking & leathered trousered sticking em up, ignoring passers by . . .

The last two weeks really insane. Production for tour, a million things to organize, coach, posters, PA, lights. The fan mag to get together – did some last week-end & improved it greatly. Wed. with Viv & Malcolm . . .

. . . I seem to be constantly carrying hundreds of quid around & remark to Nils [first road manager] one day how strange it is to have all that money & attempt to live on £25 pw. Nils says just living on £25 is hard. Malcolm looks up all innocence & says 'Is it?'

. . . Polydor pressing hard for a signing. Malcolm playing delays, really pushing for EMI. I thought he was wrong at the time. Now I guess he was right. EMI not at all interested at first but eventually saw them at Derby and the contract was signed within a week, I think.

'Anarchy' single released Friday 26 November 1976

He had no doubt whatever that this was mortal sin, and he was filled with a kind of gloomy hilarity and pride. He saw himself now as a full grown man for whom the angels wept.

Graham Greene, *Brighton Rock*

Mon 29 Nov

. . . 19 Nov. Fri, up to Ladbroke House to the squatters benefit – Jam Today & the Derelicts. Elaine there & millions of old faces, all getting older. They look like a lost generation – they (we) refused responsibility too long. There's something very Peter Pan about all those alternative people now.

. . . Malcolm was very clear, talking to Jamie last night, as to what he is about and it sounded o.k. to me, with some reservations obviously. He is clear anyway as to the political limitations of running a rock 'n' roll band. If they sell out, take the money and run he said. But while there is feeling going, and however obliquely, the band, like The Stones, Who, are feeding rebellious stances, making kids question to a degree I think. What worries me is fascism. That rebellious stance at this point of political time could equally lead rightwards as leftwards. Hence the importance of explicitness and I wonder if this is possible within rock n roll. But perhaps the message is not as important as the practice i.e. the gigs, the participation, the friendliness of the band and associates towards their audience???

Lots of question marks. It's all double edged but at least it's not the dead end that I feel the political parties to be. At least we have contact, I hope.

Tues 30 Nov

. . . Malcolm begins to wonder if EMI are deliberately failing to distribute the record . . . M. decides we must get money off EMI to support the tour and hassle them about distribution of record. The difficulty is that in an organization like EMI it is very hard to pin down responsibility. A guy may tell you something he believes to be true but you find out later it's someone else's department . . .

. . . Malcolm is . . . having interminable worried circular conversations and looking tired.

ANARCHY IN THE UK

I am the antichrist
I am an anarchist
I don't know what I want
But I know how to get it
I wanna destroy the passer by
Cos I
I wanna be anarchy – no dogsbody
And I wanna be anarchy
And I wanna be anarchy – know what I mean
Cos I wanna be an anarchist – get pissed – destroy
© Cook, Jones, Matlock, Rotten

GRUNDY

The Grundy Incident, 1 December 1976

Do not affect amazement, hypocrite

Keats, 'Otho the Great'

1 Dec 76

Up early, because posters . . . are supposed to arrive at 9. They turn up about 11. Malcolm seems to be running between EMI and Steven Fisher's [Pistols' solicitor] all day. Thames TV ring. Want to have Pistols on Today. It fucks the rehearsal a bit but we agree. The rest, as they say, is history. Steve swears at Bill Grundy till they're switched off. At the time it doesn't feel very important. I'm more worried about the rehearsal & meeting Johnny Thunders. Up to the Roxy with Nils in the new car. M. has slunk off with Bernardo to discuss politics. Eventually find him & drag him back to EMI's Limousine that they've let us have for the evening. A long wait at the airport. The Limo driver is a tower of strength at this anxious period. Malcolm is a bit hysterical, my throat seizes up so I can't swallow or move my neck. After some discussion, they get through, last out. Only 16 on the plane apparently. M. & Lee take a taxi, the rest of us squeeze into the Limo. My throat is agony. I can't speak. I fear it will close up completely & I'll suffocate . . .

Nils turns up with John & Steve & gives me a lift to a hospital. Of course they say they can't treat things like that. I ring home & Viv collects me. To bed with painkillers, whiskey & milk & hot water bottle over that side of my face & by morning I'm fine. NERVES.

BILL GRUNDY: I'm told that the group have received £40,000 from a record company. Doesn't that seem . . . er . . . to be slightly opposed to their [*deep breath*] anti-materialistic view of life?
SEX PISTOL: No. The more the merrier.
BG: Really?
SP: Oh yeah.
BG: Well, tell me more then.
SP: We've fuckin' spent it, ain't we?
BG: I don't know, have you?
SP: Yeah, it's all gone.
BG: Really?
SP: Down the boozer.
BG: *Really*? Good *Lord*! Now, I want to know one thing.

SP: They're all heroes of ours, ain't they.
BG: Really? What? What were you saying, sir?
SP: They're *wonderful* people.
BG: Are they?
SP: Oh yes! They really turn us on.
SP2: Well, they're very . . .
BG: Well, suppose they turn other people on?
SP: [*Mumbled*] That's their tough shit.
BG: It's what?
SP: Nothing. A rude word. Next question.
BG: No, no. What was the rude word?
SP: Shit.
BG: Was it really? Good heavens. You frighten me to death.
SP: Oh, all right, Siegfried . . .
BG: What about you girls behind . . . ?
SP: He's like your dad, i'n'he, this geezer. Or your grandad.
BG: . . . are you er are you worried, or are you just enjoying yourself?
FAN: Enjoying myself.
BG: Are you?
FAN: Yeah.
BG: Ah, that's what I thought you were doing.
FAN: I've always wanted to meet you.
BG: Did you really?
FAN: Yeah.
BG: We'll meet afterwards, shall we?
[*Laughter*]
SP: You dirty sod. You dirty old man.
BG: Well, keep going chief, keep going. [*Pause*] Go on. You've got another five seconds. Say something outrageous.
SP: You dirty bastard.
BG: Go on, again.
SP: You dirty fucker.

THE PUNK ROCK HORROR SHOW
BILL GRUNDY IN FOUR-LETTER POP OUTRAGE
TV FURY AT ROCK CULT FILTH

A pop group shocked millions of viewers last night with the filthiest language heard on British television.

The Sex Pistols, leaders of the new 'punk rock' cult, hurled a string of four-letter obscenities at interviewer Bill Grundy on Thames TVs family teatime programme 'Today'.

The Thames switchboard was flooded with protests.

Nearly 200 angry viewers telephoned the *Mirror*. One man was so furious that he kicked in his £380 colour TV.

Lorry driver James Holmes, 47, was outraged that his eight-year-old son Lee heard the swearing . . . and kicked in the screen of his TV.

'It blew up and I was knocked backwards,' he said. 'But I was so angry and disgusted with this filth that I took a swing with my boot.

'I can swear as well as anyone, but I don't want this sort of muck coming into my home at teatime.'

Natural

Mr Holmes, of Beedfield Walk, Waltham Abbey, Essex, added: 'I am not a violent person, but I would like to have got hold of Grundy.

'He should be sacked for encouraging this sort of disgusting behaviour.'

But a fan of the group, girl singer Siouxsie Sue, who took part in the interview, said: 'I don't know how people can get so worked up about something that's so natural. The boys hear words like this every day.'

Lead story, *Daily Mirror*, 2 December 1976

GLEN MATLOCK: [About Bill Grundy] Oh, I think he's very clever. I don't think he was an old cunt really. It was kind of good. Who'd heard of Bill Grundy before that? He didn't mind. No matter what he said in the paper afterwards.

ANARCHY IN THE U.K.
PUNK special
100 CLUB
100 OXFORD ST.
Monday SEPTEMBER 20
SEX PISTOLS
CLASH
STINKY TOYS
7PM LATE BAR
Sex Pistols

FOUR-LETTER PUNK ROCK GROUP IN TV STORM

Angry viewers demanded the sacking of TV interviewer Bill Grundy last night after four-letter words were used in his 'Today' programme. They accused Grundy of encouraging the group to use 'some of the dirtiest language ever heard on television'.

The switchboard of Thames television in London was jammed by thousands [sic] of calls. There were hundreds to the Daily Mail and other newspapers. One man said he was contacting his MP and others said they would complain to the Independent Broadcasting Authority.

Another said he would take legal action against the TV company, the rock band and 52-year-old Grundy.

Afterwards, a duty officer at Thames said: 'Mr Grundy was very embarrassed. These people were trying to shock viewers. Everybody was flabbergasted.'

Asked later about the swearing on the programme Grundy said: 'You'll get nothing from me so you can — off, I'm saying nothing.'

Daily Mail, 2 December 1976

SWEARING IS BANNED AT HOME, SAYS MRS GRUNDY

Mother of six, Nicky Grundy sat in the drawing room of her imposing country home yesterday and defended her husband Bill, the TV interviewer in the Punk Rock row . . .

Mrs Grundy, whose children are aged from 12 upwards, remarked: 'It's not like Bill to encourage bad language, especially at a time when children could be watching.

'I know that with the boys in the pub after a few drinks he uses some pretty strong language, but he's never allowed swearing in his own home because he hated it, and the family were never allowed to indulge.'

Daily Mail, 2 December 1976

Q: What do you think of people working in television?
STEVE JONES: Crawlers. Get in just for lots of dough and get their egos boosted by every time you see them on telly.

BIZARRE STYLE

When the group appeared – its members are celebrated for their bizarre style – the interviewer, Bill Grundy, who is not easily shocked, asked them if they would like to say something.

One parent, Mr Leslie Blunt, said: 'Our children were waiting for Crossroads when suddenly they heard every swear-word in the book. Surely a button can be pressed to stop this filthy language.'

Daily Telegraph, 2 December 1976

Q: What did you think of the Grundy interview?
MRS COOK: I thought it was wonderful. I just said: 'Oh, that's Paul.' I couldn't believe it. I said: 'That's the shirt I washed for him last week.'

TWO WEEK BAN ON GRUNDY OVER FILTHY SHOW
WERE THE PISTOLS LOADED?
PUNK ROCK GROUP 'PLIED WITH BOOZE'

TV presenter, Bill Grundy, was suspended for two weeks yesterday as a probe was started into the four-letter words used in his show.

And the row grew yesterday as it was claimed that the Punk Rock group involved, the Sex Pistols, were loaded with drink before going on the air.

Sun, 3 December 1976

Q: I'd like to hear your version of the Grundy interview.
PAUL COOK: What, how it happened?
Q: Yes.
PC: Before it happened we didn't even know we was going to go on, even on the day. We was about to set off on this tour, cos our single had just come out, and we was rehearsing in this place in Harlesden. And we got this phone call like. Malcolm said: 'Oh great, got you on the Today show.' You know, says: 'It's going to be really good. Go on there and talk about your single and that, and what's happening and going on this tour.'

So this car come round and it took us to that tower wherever it is, up the West End, Euston Road. And we went in there. Didn't sort of know what was happening. Just sat around this room. There was a few of our friends there, like we had followers who were standing at the back, was chatting to them. We had a drink and that. Didn't get drunk, that much.
Q: How much did you have to drink, cos everyone makes out you were . . .
PC: Steve had the most. He *said* the most. [*Laughter*] I wasn't drunk at *all*. I remember feeling sort of nervous of going on the telly. So I was feeling very nervous at the time – I remember that. And, er, we went into this little room – I thought it was going to be a great big room cos on the telly it looks massive – and it was this little room with all these lights. And they lined us up against this wall like for the beginning of the programme. And this woman said some corny remark like: 'Would you let your daughter go out with one of these?' That was at the beginning, and they said: 'We'll be seeing them later in the programme: the Sex Pistols.'

Then it come on. Glen started talking first – and we thought he [Grundy] was going to talk about the record and the tour. And he went straight into like: 'You've got all this money, ain't this rather against your anti-materialistic view of life?' and that, you know. Started putting us down straight away without even getting into an interview . . . [repeats the course of the interview] . . .

And that was it. It was all over so quick. And we just got up, just ran out laughing – like we ran straight out of the building into this car and fucked off. And the next day I couldn't believe it like. Me and Steve used to stay in Denmark Street. There was all these reporters knocking on the door like, bang bang bang bang bang. 'Ere what's happening?' Woke up like. 'What's happening?' you know. 'What the fuck's happening here?' 'Haven't you seen the paper?' they were going. 'Come on. What did you do? What happened?' they was going. We were going: 'What's happening?' And we looked at a couple of the papers and we couldn't believe it like. Headlines. All the press we got. For about three days, wasn't it? Non-stop.

Q: Yes, it was incredible. Everybody was talking about it.

PC: We didn't think nothing about it. I mean I forgot about it the same night, you know. I didn't think it was nothing at all. But people, they just wouldn't leave us alone after that. That was it.

AS THE MONEY ROLLS IN, ROCK GROUP FACES TOUR BAN AND TV CHIEFS SUSPEND GRUNDY. PUNK? CALL IT FILTHY LUCRE

Concerts for the Sex Pistols were cancelled and interviewer Bill Grundy was suspended last night in a row over the group's four-letter outburst on TV.

But the real four-letter word behind it was CASH. For EMI, Britain's biggest record company, has a big financial interest in the 'punk rock' men.

The firm's records chief, Mr Leslie Hill, thought the four weirdos were 'invited to be outrageous' and swear at Grundy on the Thames Today programme – and, he said, there was no question of dropping their contract.

Another official admitted: 'After this row it's anyone's guess how big they could be.' But it was denied the incident was a publicity stunt.

Yet the rewards are enormous. If, as the result of the group's behaviour, a record made the Top Ten it would sell 10,000 copies a day and gross £30,000 a week with the company clearing two per cent on every single.

. . . the group was signed in September for £40,000 by Nick Mobbs for EMI and its first record was released last week . . .

At this critical time the strength and influence of EMI's promotion and marketing ensured a series of remarkable appearances for a brand-new group – a London Weekend's London Programme, BBC TV's Nationwide, BBC Radio Four and Newsbeat, and finally, of course, Thames TV, in which EMI has a 50 per cent share.

Daily Express, 3 December 1976

Q: I would like to ask you about the fact that EMI as a company does have links with Thames Television. It owns a considerable amount of shares in it, and one newspaper in particular raised the issue that it wasn't exactly against EMI's interests to have somehow got the Sex Pistols on to the Grundy show, and then perhaps the thing went too far. But it could really have paid off. In fact, maybe it did pay off in terms of giving them a vast amount of publicity which they wouldn't have had before and maybe a publicity that wasn't really warranted by the stage that they had arrived at; I mean they were a very small concern at that time.

LAURIE HALL (Business Affairs Manager, EMI): Yes, I must say that Thames Television is an associate company of EMI Limited and is associated to EMI Records, but what happened on Thames TV was in no way contrived or planned by EMI and in fact EMI Records has no control over what Thames Television does at all. It just happened. It wasn't planned at all.

Q: How was the initial contact made? Did you contact the Today programme and suggest that they might like to consider having the Pistols on the programme?

LH: I don't know exactly. Undoubtedly it's our job in the promotion of any group to get them as much exposure in the media as possible, and I would imagine that when the possibility arose of them appearing on the Today programme we were obviously behind it; remembering at that time we didn't know at all what was going to happen. Yes, I would think we – we must have been to a lesser or greater extent instrumental in getting them on TV, as we are with any group – any publicity of this sort is good.

MICHAEL HOUSEGO (Today studio producer): . . . the object of this particular item was to find out why people put safety pins through their noses; the same as if I'd been here 20 years ago I'd want to know why people wore drainpipe trousers and had Tony Curtis haircuts or latterly why mods and rockers punched the shit out of one another on Brighton beach . . . [Concerning the 'top level probe'] . . . nothing happened that night really except we went to see Jeremy and John [bosses] together and had a discussion. Then we dealt with phone calls nearly all night, and press. The next day – no, the next evening – I was called in, and I went in with Lew Gardner, who was then our father of the chapel in the NUJ, and I was given an official reprimand but not on my record; and the same happened to Tom Steel . . . I mean if you go and find my file in personnel, it will not say: 'Put Sex Pistols on' . . . 'bad research, should have known' . . . I didn't even get a free album of the Sex Pistols. To this day [*laughing*] I've never had a free record from the Sex Pistols. Speaking with my television hat on, it was a bit embarrassing . . . Well, I'm not the sort of person who likes to be on the front page. I like to write front pages, not be in 'em . . .

TONY BULLEY [Today director]: Especially for such a shabby and inconsequential item.

JOHN PEEL: I was really frankly appalled [by the Grundy incident] because if you took any four or five lads off the street, 17, 18, 19, 20-year-old lads, made them feel important and filled them full of beer and put them on television and said to them, 'Say something outrageous,' they'd say something outrageous. I rather suspect that – as a middle-class individual of 38 – if they did the same to me, I'd do the same. So for those people then to wring their hands in horror and say, 'This is outrageous,' is just bare-faced hypocrisy, I think, and it's shocking. I was really outraged about that.

2 Dec 76
Arrive at office to find James Johnson [*Evening Standard*] etc and a million reporters on the phone. The TV is front page news. How to react? It seems so trivial. Irritated that many people think it is pre-planned . . . Malcolm dazed. I have to drag him into the café to write a press statement . . . Catch the bus back with one of the *Observer* guys who is amazed the punks are such nice guys. I tell him not to believe everything he reads in the papers.

3 Dec 76
. . . I'm upset because H — says his kids saw the programme and he's upset by that. So stupid and hypocritical. He has half a dozen mistresses himself.

Fame, like a wayward girl, will still be coy
To those who woo her with too slavish knees,
But makes surrender to some thoughtless boy,
And dotes the more upon a heart at ease;
She is gipsy, will not speak to those
Who have not learnt to be content without her;
Ye artists lovelorn! madmen that ye are,
Make your best bow to her and bid adieu –
Then, if she likes it, she will follow you.

Keats, 'On Fame'

THE ANARCHY TOUR

At this point the Pistols were on the 'Anarchy' tour with the Clash and other punk bands. Largely because of the Grundy incident, venues began cancelling dates.

6 Dec 76

. . . A slow day, pissing around – getting newspaper files together. Making a few phone calls. Getting a few. Wondering what's happened. No one bothers to ring me . . . The taxman is after us. Eventually Malcolm rings with a few orders – sue all the gigs that pull out, switch a few adverts, cancel a few. Not very friendly.

GLEN MATLOCK: The 'Anarchy' tour was just like one string of madness. Travelling about the country in this big coach. Everybody sitting in there thinking: I wonder if we'll play tonight. And staying in all these five star hotels because we're all supposed to have been making a mint because all the gigs were going to be sold out all over the place. Well, we only did about three gigs in the whole thing, and we were still staying in these hotels, right, running up these enormous bills.

THE BAD AND THE UGLY

The Sex Pistols were busy making a nuisance of themselves again yesterday.

The four-man Punk Rock group wrecked the lobby of a luxury hotel, uprooting ornamental plants, hurling plant pots around the room and scattering soil over the carpets.

The vandalism at the four-star Dragonara in Leeds was the prelude to a Punks' concert in the city tonight. Ten shows scheduled for other towns have been cancelled by worried managements since the foul-mouthed group angered millions of TV viewers last week.

A *Mirror* man who watched the group go wild at the Leeds hotel said: 'As they walked away they shouted, "Don't blame us. That's what you wanted. Send the bill to EMI" ' – their record company.

'Tonight's show will be staged at Leeds Polytechnic. The group's manager, Malcolm McLaren, said that the high spot would be a song that opens with the words, "God Bless the Queen and her fascist regime".'

Front page, *Daily Mirror*, 6 December 1976

MRS LYDON: . . . The councillors annoy me because they sit back and they don't do their job that they're supposed to do. They keep banning kids who want to see them but they won't rehouse people, they leave people homeless on the streets and they have people squatting. Then they just sit back and say this band can't play and that band can't play because of the violence. I think it's more violent people sleeping on the streets and giving them no homes.

Condemnation for 'punk rock' came today from the man they call one of the founders of rock and roll – Bill Haley.

As he left Heathrow for New York, Haley told reporters: 'I think it's carrying things too far.'

Haley's controversial film *Rock Around the Clock* had teds jiving in the aisle, and seats slashed and torn in the fifties. There's also been some trouble on his present tour.

But he can't take the bad language of punk. 'I am all for entertainment but I have got a teenage daughter and I wouldn't like her to listen to some of the language these fellows use,' he said.

Evening Standard, 6 December 1976

7 Dec 76

. . . strange and virulent remarks from Tony Collins in the *Ev. Standard.* Why? Malcolm asks me to try and arrange something. Complete helplessness. How to set about influencing people when you have no idea who/what they are? I do my best . . .

The EMI Annual General Meeting has been going on. Jack and Nora keep me informed – Sir John Read says a few things but I don't think the contract is really in doubt. One lovely quote on the 6 p.m. news about people trying to attack the system 'of course we all agree things need to change' but if it's a real threat EMI will chuck it for the public good. If he feels the Sex Pistols are that much of a threat it really gives them credibility for me.

WHAT *YOU* SAY ABOUT THOSE PUNK SHOCKERS

I am eleven years old and when I saw those people in the *Mirror* with safety pins through their nostrils it made me feel sick.

If I saw them I'd tell them how dangerous it is and how stupid it looks.

Julie Hynes, Mansfield, Notts.

Daily Mirror, 8 Dec 1976

13 Dec 76

. . . Malcolm rolls in about half one. Instant rows and sulks over money and this and that. I'm peeved because I feel I'm not being told what's going on. He's irritable because he has too much on his mind. Glen arrives. I get him some money out. We chat, between phone calls about how to get back out of the shit – the tour in ruins and EMI playing it so cool you'd hardly know they were our record company. They're all quaking under wrath from the top. Playing good boys, in fear of their jobs. M. says John Bagnall [EMI A+R man] is back in flares and sans safety pins again and no one would speak to him on Friday. Even when they do speak there's no way to get a straight answer – it was pretty hard when things were going well but now they all just say 'Personally I . . . ' and you say what's policy? and they clam up. Paul and Steve turn up and it turns into a full scale discussion – to stay with EMI or not? Obviously everyone is really confused, but at least discussion has begun. Corky and Mike turn up. Chaos. How can you do business in a 10′ × 10′ office with 7 people in it and 2 phones continually ringing? Everything except money sorted out. Malcolm goes off to see EMI and hopefully get some money out of them. I doubt if he will. I think that may have to be the criterion as to whether we get out or not. We have to have a company which will give us money.

Bernardo wants us to bounce back and take the press by the throat but they won't be interested in anything serious we have to say. We have to think of something, some way to get going again. Fears that SPs may just drop quietly, having paved the way for all the bands which are signing now.

14 Dec 76
. . . at the office we just gossip. I do a little work. A couple of phone calls to EMI. They seem to be cooling out O.K. Malcolm said this morning that they said again they would give us money for the tour . . .

15 Dec 76
. . . Malcolm came in at about 5 – zonked. Phone calls. Apparently Lisa Robinson (syndicated column in 187 papers USA and Australia) has slagged us off. I'm not worried but Jamie and M are.

17 Dec 76
. . . Roger Scott on Capital says 'SPs having troubles in studio called in session musicians. So the record (which they refuse to play anyhow) isn't even the SPs kids'. From an 'impeccable' source. Anger. Flurry of activity. In his retraction he says 'Malcolm McLaren rang up 5 seconds after I made that statement declaring it was untrue. Terribly sorry Malcolm. Smirk.' What a shit. Malcolm manages to irritate me to the point of walking out. Beautiful Steve tells him to stop slagging me off. But I go for a beer anyway. What's the use? Who do you turn to? A pint in the Ship then I fetch some beer back. Hassles with PA and lighting both wanting more money. M pays them in the end while I sit sulking in a corner not doing anything. Glen also sulking. I piss off in the end. Cycle over to Earls Court, watch King Kong with the HBs [Heartbreakers] and lend them a fiver. It's very grim down

John with Sue Catwoman (left) and Siouxsie (right)

there. Home about 9. Jamie says M rang up to apologize. He arrives. It's OK. I love him really.

20 Dec 76
. . . Ingham told me a couple of interesting things that Seymour told him – not for public consumption, but they must come out at some time. Phonogram apparently specifically said they would not back a Ramone/Pistols tour to the extent that they would a Ramones/anyone else tour. Bribery . . .

. . . I'm pissed off I've got no money. I feel like leaving.

Sleep full of dreams – spy stories mostly, same as last night, and machines.

22 Dec 76
. . . Rang M before I left [for the Plymouth Gig]. He told me not to come. But I decided I would go. So up to the office. A few loose ends left but I had to go. Got the 11.30 train and arrived Plymouth 3.30. Someone gave me a lift in to town – civilized middle class people, like my parents in a way. Very sweet. I didn't say what I was up to . . . to Woods about 9. Only about 10 people have arrived. Ergh. Manage to pacify Andy (coach-driver) over his expenses, lying constantly and to everyone that I have no money. It is clear no one will turn up so Clash go on and play brilliant. Ditto HBs. SPs play well but the sound is up the creek. Dave [sound man] apparently out of his head on pills. Nils gets so pissed off he gets Keith to take over – that's worse. Gloomily back to hotel. Bagnall gets us sandwiches. We all drink a lot and piss around. I end up having a serious conversation with Glen.

23 Dec 76
. . . about 10. Sit in lobby feeling a little paranoid and dirty. Glen rolls down looking confused. I wake Mike up slowly. Freddie ['Anarchy' tour manager and security man] begins to get people together. Hassles. The lighting guys room is a bit fucked. The swimming pool. Apparently people went out swimming late at night. Mickey [Clash sound man] cracked his head diving into the shallow end. One of the lighting guys looks really beaten up. The other cut his feet on broken glass. Mike and Freddie deal with the manager. Fortunately Malcolm didn't sign the £500 cheque.

24 Dec 76
. . . To office by 10. Nothing much to do. Bank to get to. Money for Xmas. People come and go. EMI send us a hamper. The drinking starts.

27 Dec 76
. . . Up at 9 and off towards my parents. Couldn't remember if I'd locked the

office on Xmas Eve so up there first. Broken into. Quite a relief in a way. Ring Jamie, then Malcolm. The band are doing backing tracks today. I have to wait for policeman – nice bloke. V interested by SPs. I panic because I think they've stolen receipt for car etc. but they all turn up. Only obvious things gone – Viv's jeans and boots, radios etc. Late for lunch with Mom and Dad at Elizabeth Neames in Montagu Sq.

29 Dec 76

. . . Into the office early to wait for the CID. Freezing cold. No phone calls. I do the books a bit. Malcolm arrives eventually. Much talk with Mobbs [EMI A & R manager]. Nothing resolved. The Holland trip begins to take shape. Miles [Copland] from downstairs keeps running up to hassle us about carnets and stuff. It's a bit of a last minute job. Malcolm is supposed to come over and see Jamie in the evening but doesn't make it. Jamie, Pat and I sit in the pub. The HBs shoot up and then go off to Louise's to meet Lee [Heartbreaker's manager]. Johnny gets stomach cramps and we go all soft and motherly on him. Hot water bottle sorts it out.

4 Jan 77

. . . Around 7 I go off in the dark to wake Paul and Steve – and Sharon, Tracie and Debbie as it turns out. Lovely and warm up there. They take ages to wake up. Chat with Sharon whom I like a lot. Eventually the car and Glen arrive. I phone Malcolm whose alarm mysteriously failed to work. John rolls up in an old Vauxhall with his friends, very high. Steve is in a really grim state. No shock therefore when I heard later (via news via Miles) that they shocked Heathrow by puking. Newspapers again.

THESE REVOLTING VIPs!
SEX PISTOLS IN RUMPUS AT AIRPORT

The controversial Sex Pistols punk rock group caused an uproar at Heathrow today.

They shocked and revolted passengers and airline staff as they vomited and spat their way to an Amsterdam flight.

An airline check-in desk girl said: 'The group are the most revolting people I have ever seen in my life. They were disgusting, sick and obscene.'

The girl, who would not give her name, said: 'The group called us filthy names and insulted everyone in sight.

Drinking

'One of the group was sick in a corridor leading to the aircraft. He threw up again later in a rubbish bin.

'While this was going on the others were spitting on the floor and at each other. It was a disgrace.'

A passenger who witnessed the group's 'performance' at Heathrow today, Mrs Freda van Roiden from Rotterdam, said: 'I've never heard of the Sex Pistols before but I certainly won't forget them in a hurry.

'They were the most degenerate bunch of small-minded children I have ever seen.

'I think they had been drinking and they looked as if they needed a good wash.'

Evening News, 4 January 1977

LESLIE HILL (Man. Dir. EMI): . . . in the end there were stories in the press which really, you know, [*laughs*] couldn't be justified by the facts. I mean the incidents at Heathrow, for example, the so-called vomiting and spitting, never took place. We had a man with them every minute of the day and that never happened. I mean there was supposed to be a sort of thing where they went to the ticket desk, and they upset the KLM girl by vomiting and spitting, or something. They didn't go to the ticket desk because they were late for the plane. Our guy went to the ticket desk and got the tickets for them.

MECCA BOOKMAKERS

EMI FIRE THE PISTOLS

6 Jan 77
Up late. Buy a new sweater & in to the office (late again). Simon arrives. It's all very calm & I feel quite constructive – getting on with this & that. Simon goes off to get xeroxes of all the newspapers we don't have. Someone from the Evening News rings to ask what our reaction is to getting kicked out of EMI. What?! First we've heard of it. I ring Steven who tells me to deny it – talks still going on he says – so I ring back & deny it. Then Steve Havoc rings – heard it on the news on the radio, & Tony Rose [Pistols' accountant]. Then the papers start ringing in. I'm delighted. Tom Nolan [press officer] at EMI knows nothing . . . Things got quiet & I got a bit pissed off that Malcolm hadn't rung me.

LESLIE HILL: Let me try and explain to you – it's quite difficult to understand – how we got to the point we did. When it [the bad publicity] first happened, we hoped it would blow over and that the group themselves would be less provocative. They weren't really. I mean I sat in this office with Malcolm McLaren on a number of occasions and I talked the thing through with him. I mean I talked to him about all sorts of things. I mean . . . you see the people in EMI and also outside of EMI had different kinds of objections. Some objected to the four-letter words on television; some objected to the supposedly violence aspects of the whole thing; some objected to the word 'anti-Christ' in the song. You know, there must have been six or seven different groups of objections. And . . . we couldn't promote the records in that situation.

Supposing, for example, they were doing a tour and we'd done what we usually do on tour, which is to have a press party or a party at the end of the do, or some sort of reception. You imagine what would have happened. There would have been a riot. You know, there would have been people outside protesting, there would have been photographers everywhere, there would have been press people everywhere. That's not an environment in which we can operate in a normal fashion.

So I was saying to them: 'Look, you do understand that if you pursue this line of publicity then it makes it very difficult for us to promote your records, because we can't do the normal things. I mean, how do we for example promote your records overseas, because the only thing we have – newscuttings – are all about the filth and the fury from the *Daily Mirror*. That's very difficult to hang the promotion of records on.' And that was all we had, [*laughing*] that was all we were getting . . .

So what I tried to do was to sit down with them and try to get them to understand that what we wanted to do was to promote the music and not to

News from EMI

6th January 1977

EMI AND THE SEX PISTOLS

EMI and the Sex Pistols group have mutually agreed to terminate their recording contract.

EMI feels it is unable to promote this group's records internationally in view of the adverse publicity which has been generated over the last two months, although recent press reports of the behaviour of the Sex Pistols appear to have been exaggerated.

The termination of this contract with the Sex Pistols does not in any way affect EMI's intention to remain active in all areas of the music business.

* * *

Enquiries: Rachel Nelson
Group Press Relations
01-486 4488

* * *

From the Group Public Relations Department
EMI Limited
20 Manchester Square London W1A 1ES
01-486 4488

promote all that kind of stuff. Now in order to achieve that situation, they had to co-operate really, and they had to sort of, they had to be prepared to take a slightly lower profile. We wanted publicity for them, but not of that kind and that magnitude.

And really the answer was, after a number of discussions with not just them but with the people here, the answer really was that they really wouldn't co-operate with us in that sense.

And it went on and it got to a point where I, personally, was spending half my time – I mean . . . there was uproar, you know, and the press were ringing me up. I can't spend half my days talking to the press about things like that. It isn't worth my time. You know, we've got hundreds of groups and hundreds of things to do. It got to a point where it really wasn't worth the trouble.

And they were ringing us up saying: 'Look, if you won't promote the records in the normal way, then let us go somewhere else.' So one day I rang up and said: 'Look, this situation is getting worse and not better. You suggested we terminate the contract, let us do just that.' And I said to them: 'You go to a smaller,' – in fact, I told them to go to Virgin, not A & M. I said: 'Go to Virgin or a label like that, because with a small label like that' – and, in fact, I even introduced them to Virgin, myself, at that point – 'with a small label like that, you know, it's much easier for them to handle what you are and what you want to be.'

But that took about six or seven weeks and the important point of that, and this is where we get back to the word 'consensus', is that if I had said 'out' the day after, we would have had a lot of resignations, because we had people on the first floor who were very enthusiastic about the music and about this group, who wanted them to succeed.

I mean I took everybody's views in this organization: I took views of people who work for EMI Records, I took views of people who work for other parts of EMI . . .

Q: Which other parts of EMI?

LH: Um, I really, just all parts. I just wanted people's views on it. I wanted to know what they thought about it.

I mean, one of the subsidiary companies of EMI Records, for example, took a very strong – at least certainly one or two of the senior managers took a very strong line and said, you know: 'We really don't think we should be involved with people like that.'

And because of the outrage in the press, there were ladies at the factory who said: 'We aren't going to handle the records.' And they refused to handle the records. Now that was why the records weren't available for some time. Because, you know, with a thing like a single you don't know how many you're going to sell and you have to react very quickly to demand. And because the ladies refused to handle the record, we couldn't supply it for a time and so shops didn't have it.

But then they had meetings about it and in the end they did in fact go back and handle the record. In other words, rather good example, those ladies themselves were a bit uncertain – they read about it in the paper, they were upset about it, and when they sat down and they talked about it and they thought about it, they decided well, maybe it wasn't so bad after all. And they went away and handled the record.

Now that was typical of the kind of feeling within EMI Records itself. I mean there was one instance where someone wrote to *EMI News* – a group of people wrote – and complained that EMI was involved in an act like the Sex Pistols. On the other hand, you had a lot of people internally who know and understand the record business, who were saying: 'This is no different from the Rolling Stones in the mid-sixties.' So you had a total split . . .

But that, really, wasn't the point. I mean, we did agree to terminate – which is very important to understand, that it was a mutual agreement to terminate, whatever Malcolm McLaren may have said afterwards. You know, I actually rang him in Amsterdam . . . and Laurie Hall was with me, and I said to Laurie Hall: 'I want you to say the same thing as I've just said, because I want a witness that we have actually agreed something on the telephone.' And Laurie did just that. And Malcolm McLaren afterwards chose to, to change his mind . . .

What we wanted Malcolm to do [*laughs*] was to cool it. We said: 'Look, just cool it. Just adopt a low profile. This thing will blow over and then we can concentrate on promoting the group and its music.' But it didn't happen that way. And I don't think, you know, he didn't give me the impression that he was anxious to have it that way. I mean, what he really said was: 'I don't run their lives,' you know. 'They are their own agents. I'm not going to control them, I don't want to control them and I can't control them,' and all that kind of thing, and: 'They must do what they must do. And they are where they are because of the way they've approached this thing so far.'

Q: Are you happy now about your decision?

LH: [*Pause*] That's a – you know, it's very difficult to give you a yes . . . The answer really is yes. I mean, we wouldn't have made a decision if we hadn't believed it was right. And quite honestly, when I saw what happened afterwards, um, I was even happier because I felt that at least we handled it in a sensible way, we gave it time, we didn't panic.

I mean, I was extremely pleased in a way with the way it turned out because we didn't have any resignations on our staff – people who had initially felt very strongly for. And I think that, you know, we were able to get back to normality . . .

You know, we cannot – I can't spend my time on all those sort of things.

You see, initially – this is very ironic in a way – because before we signed the Sex Pistols, Malcolm McLaren was ringing me up saying he wanted to come and see me. I said: 'I'm sorry, Malcolm, I can't see you.' He said: 'Why not?' I said: 'Because this is a big company, and I don't get involved in decisions on signing new groups. And I'll happily meet you one day, but I'm sorry, I can't set up a separate meeting.' I ended up by spending half my life with the guy. I mean, I ended up by going to Amsterdam for *two days*, you know, and spending half the night waiting for him to come and see *me*. You know, [*laughing*] I got caught badly.

Q: Was one of the factors [in terminating the contract] the imminent release of – well, the next single was going to be 'God Save the Queen', wasn't it? Did that have any part in the decision?
LAURIE HALL: None at all, none at all.
Q: Because I think, um, people do question this. It was Jubilee year and when that record finally did emerge it was the one voice which expressed any kind of resentment. And I think that in general in Jubilee year, certainly in terms of the media, that kind of resentment generally wasn't tolerated.
LH: I can honestly say in the two or three weeks immediately before the termination of the contract it was not brought into consideration at all.
Q: An element that it occurs to me might have been involved in the decision to terminate the contract is the fact that EMI is a very large concern with a great number of employees, and that Malcolm McLaren as a manager could be regarded as a bit anarchic or unusual or simply individualistic, and that perhaps it was a conflict between innovators – creators – and time-servers?
LH: I'm totally rejecting the idea that we used the powers of the great EMI to put down the small Malcolm McLaren. That just didn't happen. We have innumerable groups of managers or representatives of groups in a similar vein to Malcolm McLaren and we have no problem at all. And certainly it is our job and our wish to be involved with the people you call innovators. I mean this is what it's about. We're in the music business. Um, the Sex Pistols were just a particular situation that arose which both sides really found it impossible to live with.
Q: Was there any pressure from artists, other artists in EMI? Was that one of the factors involved?
LH: [*Pause*] I would say no, there wasn't, inasmuch as a number of artists may have expressed slight displeasure but none of them really felt very strongly. And in fact there were other artists who were right behind us and certainly felt that we should resist the media pressures and stay with the group.
Q: Did it tend to be a particular type of artist who was for it or against it?
LH: Um, I think you're putting it too strongly to say they were for it or

Sex Pistols' first recording session.

against it. If they were asked their views – they obviously had views – and, er, I would imagine the artists who were on the pop side would probably be for it and the classical side against it.
Q: I've spoken with Johnny Rotten and he thinks that the behaviour of pop groups shouldn't really be censored by record companies because he thinks it's the job of record companies to produce records. Would you like to comment on that?
LH: That's right. In no way is it our job to censor or attempt to, er, tell the pop groups what they should and shouldn't do and in no way, at no time, during the Sex Pistols period did we attempt to do that. What they do, other than record and make records for us, is really their concern. But unfortunately, like it or not, whenever the Sex Pistols did something the press picked up on it and they either exaggerated it or distorted it, and whenever they did that EMI, as their record company, was in some way held responsible for these activities, whereas in fact we had no control and never wished to control that side.

8 Jan 77
Managed to get up at 10.30 & do the laundry. Nice & quiet down the launderette while Jamie shopped. Talked to Pat about reorganizing shopping & rota. Just got into changing our rooms round when Malcolm rang with 1000 things to do – get people to the airport & the press & arrange transport. So. End of quiet day at home. I just half sorted things then rushed off – if you can call a 137 bus rushing. Knightsbridge took about half an hour to get through & Oxford St was packed as before Christmas. Where does the money come from? Did everything I could at the office. (Strange dream last night concerning me thieving from a clothes shop – lots of keys & loot/mislaid/in the wrong places. Lots of people to hide from/or friends in wrong places. End up making love on the floor, wooden boards, with Jerry. I can't remember why.)

9 Jan 77
Jamie wakes me. I crawl out of bed about 11 just as Walter & Jerry [of Heartbreakers] return. Chat over breakfast. They borrow some of Helen's tranquillizers & go to sleep while we go to the pub. Helen comes over. We drink coffee at her place – nice. Still feel dazed & fuzzy.

Everyone is bored out their heads so I drag them out to see Spiders Stratagem. Maybe we would've been less bored at home. Beautiful photography good idea. It could've been 20 mins long though not 100. Home. Pub. Bed.

10 Jan 77
Couldn't wake up. Got up the office about 10.30. Ted arrived wanting money. Eventually Viv and Malcolm arrived as well & I went off to the bank. Conversations with the music press all morning – Malcolm has flu & we aren't getting on too well.

11 Jan 77
. . . I keep thinking of that quote – situationist, I think, 'The majority of men & women live lives of quiet desperation' – my life, the Sex Pistols, the Heartbreakers maybe especially, lead lives of loud desperation. We shout it, display the wounds, shove them in people's faces.

Eventually Jamie came back. Jerry rang & I had to wake up Walter who was in a bit of a state with his cold. I found some Vitamin C pills for him. Jamie & Walter went off together about 6. I hung about, loving being alone, reading, totally unrestrained in my choice of music & volume to play it at.

16 Jan 77
. . . got to office in time for Bernie's [manager of the Clash] phone call. Both of us a little nervous. He drove off to the ICA looking for a friend of his, Mike, who has just been fired from there for being too political – he used to run the Theatre side of it – the ICA is revolting & Mike is not there so over to his place in Notting Hill . . . Mike is a guy after my own heart – a Marxist with no party or affiliation but hard & still learning & not libertarian either.

17 Jan 77
Up late again. Taxi to work. Malcolm rings from the shop eventually. Can't see or speak to anyone today. Simon gets 125 copies of the record from EMI – great. I start looking for another office & flats for the boys. A real drag. Jamie keeps ringing. The guy arrives with the Grundy video – at last. Lee & Julian turn up so I get the brandy out. They're a gas. We decide between us that Finland must go ahead despite Malcolm & plot accordingly. Over to the studio – John not arrived yet but otherwise all well. John pissed off because Malcolm says he can't live in the place he's found in Edmonton. Shitty.

20 Jan 77
Get to the office OK. Malcolm off seeing AM Records, people keep turning up to see him. Very Waterloo Station. These days when he wants to see someone he drags them off to a café & the others are left hanging . . . Sort out, first the recording with Dave, then the air tickets for him to go to Midem in Cannes. Viv pays a visit, Miles, Boogie, various members of the band, Lee etc., etc. I am profoundly relieved Malcolm will be gone tomorrow & I can get a few things done. It takes hours to get everyone out of the office.

24 Jan 77

. . . Spend most of the day doing the books & going crazy. Malcolm rang in the morning sounding half pissed but cheerful. We had one of those long pointless conversations we always seem to have when he's abroad, rambling & circumstantial . . . him telling me little things of what's going on. Nice really. The books don't balance of course but it's not too badly out of control. I think it'll be OK. I keep getting disturbed. Eventually get called off down the studio to sort out the money because the guy won't let the tapes out till that's done. He's one worried guy. Just had operations on his eyes – face lift it looks like – looks all bruised & weary. Don't really hear the tapes but Steve & Paul both seem pleased. 6 tracks completed. Pretty good.

25 Jan 77

Still struggling with the books. Boogie comes round. He spends a lot of time sitting in the office, worrying. I find it difficult to talk to him often. The tour slowly getting together – organizing numbers, ferries, talking to Ray etc.

Malcolm got back about 3. The tour is off he says. Can't be associated with Secunda. I think I agree, although it's a drag (for me, not business wise) to alienate ourselves from the Heartbreakers.

Meet Jamie & Malcolm . . . go for a meal & they talk. I listen. Malcolm thinks we can make a really big deal, get into movies etc. I think John won't like it much. M is definitely into creative management.

26 Jan 77

. . . Malcolm comes in at about 2. Apparently things went badly when the band met W. Bros yesterday. The continuing problem of Glen. Meanwhile still pestered by Miles [who wanted to delay the tour] to such an extent that it begins to be a joke. Steve comes up & has a long talk with Malcolm & with John on the phone. I shoot out for a bit of a rest. On return, M is deep in telephone conversation with Mel Bush [the promoter]. Good one? Bernie has signed with CBS. Poor old Polydor – again. Malcolm reckons dealing with Miles should toughen us up. It's true I'm really wishy washy over things like that – even though I really dislike the guy I can't help feeling sorry for him. An inherent weakness I think, that I always identify with people who get fucked up & try to soften things for them because that's always where I expect to end up myself. I attempted to get over to the studio but failed. Met M back at the office at 7 and talked a bit about possibilities. He's getting better – the other day he said to J & I that he thought one of his worst faults was never explaining fully to all relevant people what goes on with him in his head. Perhaps he finally realizes precisely how much of a king pin he is & that he can't continue being so all powerful?

27–28 Jan 77
Thursday is a bit of a blank. Things in the band are a bit heavy – should Glen go or stay? John's position is clear, it's the others who have to make up their minds. Thur & Fri I spend mostly fending off Miles & stonewalling Nils & Lee. Malcolm wisely keeping out of the office & not telling me too much of what's going on. I spent a lot of time puzzling over the books which aren't quite in total chaos & they form a good excuse for my absentness when in inquisitive company. Thursday p.m. John turns up late in the afternoon with Carlsbergs & we sit & chat a while. He asks me to his party tomorrow which is a real boost. Arrangement to meet Malcolm in the Cambridge at 8.30 – spend the intervening time eating/drinking with John who gets better & better. We both go off about 9 pissed off that Malcolm didn't turn up. Over to the Ship where I find Jamie – with Nils, Lee, Siouxsie & Steve – on the point of committing murder after his interview with Secunda who offered him a job+bonuses for each poster produced. I'm being all diplomatic & smooth!

1 Feb 77
Me looking for offices, Simon [Simon Barker – office assistant] looking for flats. After a few false starts (going through slums in Greek St etc.) I found an OK one in Regent St, 5th floor, attic. Simon didn't have any luck. By then it was quite late. Malcolm was back in the office, & John. Sat around talking over the problems. Mainly Glen who today bought a Sunbeam Alpine (yeuch) & record deals, & recording. Roger Bain who produced Black Sabbath came round to talk over production. I didn't get any work on the mag done. We went & ate, then off to meet Jamie & Grey. Terrible. Grey seemed really depressed. The juke box kept blaring slushy Irish tunes, John was being mischievous & nice, Malcolm was feeling left out & talking to Simon, Jamie was being silent & I was being irritable & just wanted to hassle everyone into moving really fast & getting it out. Eventually I left & did some typing at the office, a bit drunkenly but it was OK.

3 Feb 77
Slow day I think, can't remember much. Wobble & John came up in the afternoon & caused chaos – screaming fuck off down the phones whenever they rang & stuff. Paul & Steve finally got their holidays sorted. They leave on Saturday. Glen bought his Sunbeam Alpine – metallic blue – & was sorting out his insurance before going off for a dirty weekend with 'X'. In the afternoon Malcolm was off seeing Steven & Simon round the studio awaiting a plumber. I was sat in the office thinking about the books. Al rang up to talk about T shirts but there was the most beautiful rainbow going on over Centre Point – intense enough to produce a double. Amazing. It made conversation a

I don't know why he did it. I think he's really insecure in some ways. It's just that he feels he has a lot to prove. I don't know why. You know, people say it's because of his background, and he's really hard done by. Maybe he was materially. But with his parents and all that he's like his mum's golden boy really. She's like all feather dusters all round him, you know: 'Isn't he lovely?' and all that. So he's really been a bit kind of mollycoddled. He's a very childish kind of bloke. He always wants his own way, very selfish, and if he can't have it . . . You know, if I can't get my own way I say: 'Well, fair enough, there's always two sides to every argument.' But he's got to win every time and he gets really pissed off, you know, goes off in a huff.

Q: I want to ask you – I know that you and Glen didn't get on too well, cos he told me about that, and since he's told me what he thinks about you to some extent, I'd like you to tell me really why you didn't agree. Cos it seems he didn't kind of fit in with the band as a whole . . .
JOHNNY ROTTEN: He never did fit in, right from the start. Cos like Paul and Steve are very quiet people who don't opinion themselves. They just go along usually. But like if they don't like something, then they'll stop. Er, Glen was an ego tripper, very bad one. He always wanted to be in charge. Plus like Malcolm used to really like Glen a hell of a lot. Like whenever there was an argument Malcolm would always say: 'Oh no. It's only his way. You must understand.' Er (*pause*), Glen really didn't like me *at all*. Because the songs I wrote and the way I felt . . . like his idea of the band was to be a nice pop band, like innocent songs which was like everything else before. I just like wanted to do something different. Something I really felt. And something that Paul and Steve felt as well. And he didn't like it. And like 'Anarchy' for instance he despised. Hated the words. He said they were terrible. Wouldn't have anything to do with it. 'God Save the Queen' he would never play live.
FRIEND: Same as on that Bill Grundy interview. He was sitting there, weren't he, in the Bill Grundy interview, like disgusted with everything that was going on around him: he was shaking his head . . .
JR: With Glen there was a class thing. Very definitely. Cos of his mum. Used to keep ringing me up, saying I was perverting her dear little boy. I mean, my God, that's real middle-class for you. Everything we ever done he used to like have moans about because – couldn't walk down the street cos he was embarrassing to the neighbours, you know . . .
Q: But those kind of tensions, haven't they affected your mother, for example?
JR: No way at all. She doesn't give a shit about any of the neighbours.

Q: Why did you leave the Pistols?

GLEN MATLOCK: Well, I'd worked for Malcolm since I was 16 and I was still working for him, and there wasn't any more than that. I couldn't get on with John at all. And Steve and Paul were just a couple of blokes doing it – they had become labourers really. It was just time for a change. I felt it had all been set up and the idea was complete. There was no more to do with it. It was just going out and doing it, but that wasn't where the interest was for me. The interest was like setting it up and making it complete. I'm more interested in ideas than just selling them. Because I think that's what it is now. It's just selling. It's a purely commercial kind of thing now.
Q: What were the events which led up to your leaving the group?
GM: I don't know. It had just been going on. I mean John had left the group twice. I'd left the group. Paul had left the group. And this was like once every three months. And it was just one too many times. We was in Holland and I weren't getting on with John. It was just like being stuck in a hotel room in a foreign country, and where the only people you've got to get on with are the people in the band. If you're not getting on with them you're having a bit of a miserable time. Yeah, that was it really. Just thought enough was enough. I just wasn't interested no more.

It was getting out of our hands a bit. Malcolm had taken even more control. The press had taken it to such an extent where it couldn't be really controlled any more. The idea was set up and no matter what you said it still didn't affect it. I mean, after all that Bill Grundy show thing, no matter what you said to the paper the next day, it still come out that you was like a swearing lout who belched and all that kind of stuff. And it didn't matter whether you said something interesting to them or not, it just wouldn't come out cos they had that set idea of it. There wasn't much you could do to change it. But, I mean, that didn't matter cos that was partly the idea anyway that it was kind of wild. But the idea's there now, so why bother to do that. Do something different.
Q: Do you think Sid was a good choice for the band?
GM: Yeah. I don't see why not. It doesn't really matter who's in the band other than John. It could have been anybody as long as they weren't an idiot. I mean Sid's not an idiot. He's all right. But, you know, it's just a face. But it really doesn't matter who it is. That was another reason I split because it was set up that it was John. You know, I've always been into the idea of a group with like four guys working together.

Q: Something I wanted to ask you, because you came into the band quite late on, is whether you think you being there changed anything?
SID VICIOUS: What, in the band?
Q: Yeah.
SV: Yes, it changed it enormously.

Q: In what way?
SV: Um. For a start the line-up is much more handsome now.
Q: [*Laughs*]
SV: This is a fact. And we play songs much faster now. Also I write differently from the way Glen used to. I haven't written very much lately, I mean, since I've been in the group, but I'm starting to now more. And just the fact that I'm there instead of Glen means that the others do everything differently. Cos they have to adapt it to like fit in with me, do you know what I mean? So yeah, I think it – whenever there's a change in something it – a change is a change, right, so if something changes it is different, it has to be, obviously. It can't be the same or otherwise . . . [*pause*] And the next question.

7 Feb 77
. . . Malcolm is in a bit of a weird mood. Thinking too much about record companies. I continued slugging through the petty cash while he sat & made desultory phone calls – one useful one to Peter Cook [the comedian and script-writer], several to Steven [Pistols' solicitor]. It seems between A & M and CBS. A & M distribute through CBS here & will be in Europe come June so it looks like CBS . . . Malcolm tells me about the different companies. Kissinger President of CBS, very kosher firm, & big. A & M a tight family concern based in L.A. West Coast smoothies v. New York Jews. A weird choice. I just want to go home but have to wait in case of calls from L.A.

8 Feb 77
Sunday night – beautiful dream, kept me going all day – California, I had a big motorbike I was learning to ride, nightime but bright. Slowly going up hill to an open space to ride round & round – too many people, another enclosed space – trees round. I get in there & find most of it is a pool, beautiful but not suitable for learning to ride motorbikes in. Back home – to collect pushbike (I wonder why I had both?) . . .

Barbara rang suggesting we go for lunch. Nice one. We went to the Ship & talked about punk, women musicians, families, relationships, futures, then we moved on to the Star & talked politics till Barbara thought it was a bad idea to be saying so much so loud. It was really nice. I didn't get back to the office till 4.30 not caring anyhow. Feeling very happy. Malcolm still trying to decide over record companies – it's going to be CBS – at least that's what I was thinking when I started that sentence – now it looks more like A & M. Hung about waiting for John. We have to decide about Sid before anything can go ahead. They went off for a meal & to meet Sid. I went home.

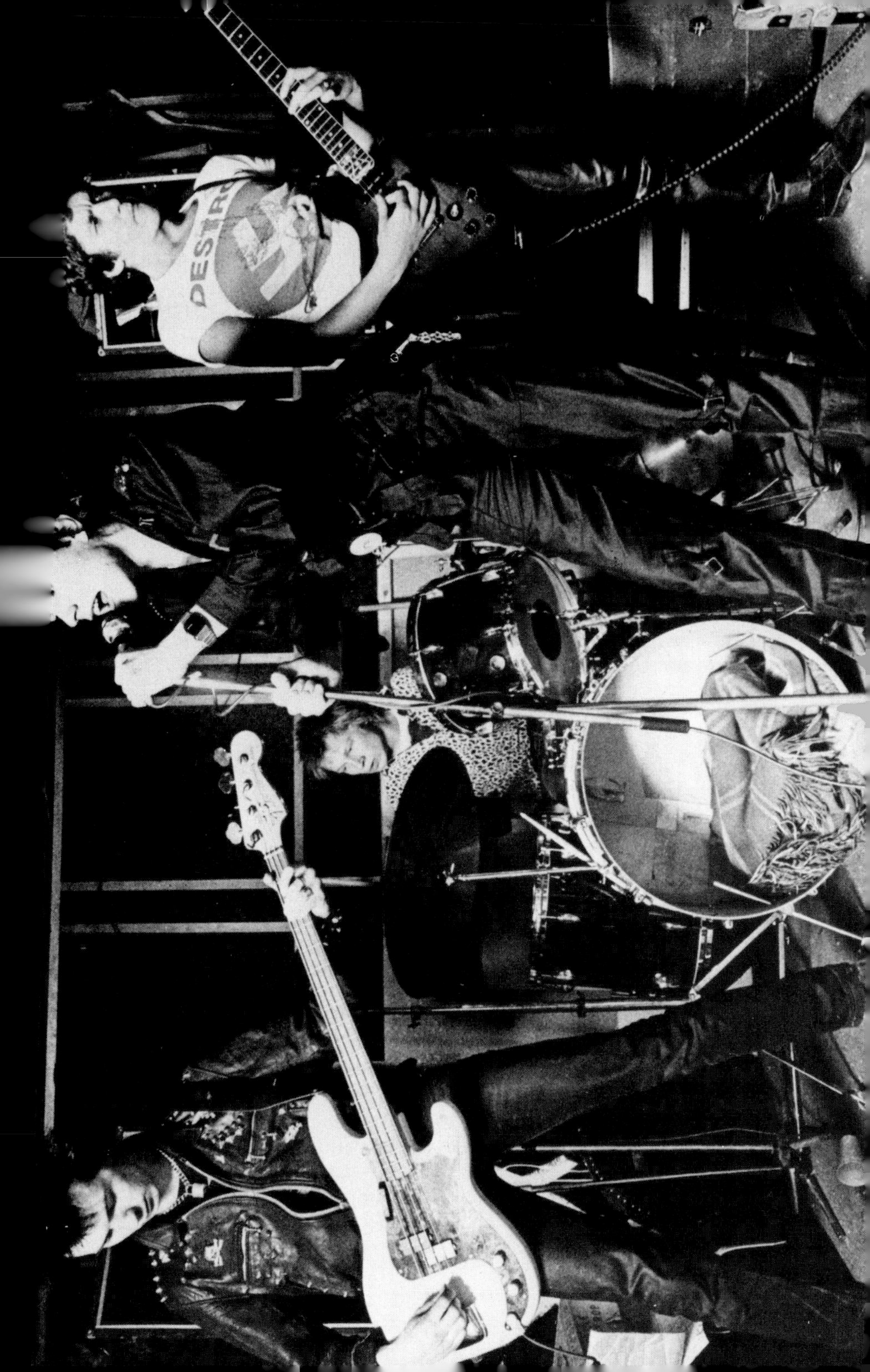

10 Feb 77

. . . The record deal now depends on Mobbs, I think. John is in favour of CBS if they go there. It turns out A & M's distribution deal in Europe is with EMI. The tension grows. John & Malcolm go off to meet Peter Cook – good luck to them!

11 Feb 77

. . . Malcolm arrives still not sure whether to go to L.A. I get the money & do the bookings anyhow. Simon sits around laughing at us.

13 Feb 77

Tear myself out of bed to find out what's happening with M. Not going. Back to bed. 10 minutes later, he is going & I have to go up to Denmark St to get Paul to ring him.

15 Feb 77

. . . Glen comes in & goes off with Boogie. John comes in for his money then Nora arrives & burbles till Boogie & Glen come back & everyone splits, embarrassed? Uneasy certainly. Nothing is clear. I think we've blown it. Completely. Feel like leaving & doing something else. What? I'm not learning anything. I feel isolated, useless, meaningless. Got home & didn't know what to do with myself. Can't write, don't feel, going nowhere. 25 & no ambitions fulfilled. Depression it must be called. Jamie comes in with streaming cold. Can't speak. Hate this flat, hate everyone. Can't decide what to do about moving. Can't face coupledom. Isolation again. Can't face bedsit-land. Can't move out of London again. Don't want kids. No future.

16 Feb 77

. . . Simon came back with all the music papers. Boring. Everyone left. I didn't know what to do with myself. Read a lot of James Joyce. It's easier in large chunks. The text is so fragmented anyhow that if you just read it at bus stops & stuff you lose the threads . . .

Wondering how to possibly face the future. Feel I've been really cosseted & protected till now, even when things were really bad, there was always someone to go to, some possibilities that were vaguely attractive. Now nothing except myself to rely on, my own future to make & I'm scared and lonely. I'd forgotten that feeling of weight in your stomach, there every time you wake up in the night to remind you how awful everything is. Towards morning I relaxed a bit & had good dreams – a plush house, Jamie & me in the kitchen, Elaine upstairs somewhere. Multi-coloured little birds – J & I trying to decide if they should be in their cage, cats around. We keep putting them in & they keep flying out. Eventually, all at once, they fly into my face

& poof! disappear. Lovely sensation.

17 Feb 77

. . . Read *Private Eye* from cover to cover. Simon came & went. Rang Bernie to ask for the £1,000. He gave me a lecture instead which I mainly agree with though Malcolm won't – about how scrappy & nasty things have become, about not becoming obsessed with business wheelings and dealings, all record companies ultimately being a bunch of cunts, about Malcolm's schizophrenia between being an anarchist (?) seditious anyhow, & being successful businesswise, about the loss of energy & enthusiasm, about the rumour-mongering. And I agree but Malcolm won't.

20 Feb 77

Up late. Simon got in the office soon after me. So no time to read the papers. John rang to say Malcolm is back. The music press have got hold of the Sid rumour. I deny it.

23 Feb 77

. . . Viv showed up demanding the money we owe her, I had to go to the bank so she just stormed off again. Drag. I felt really depressed, everything falling apart, bored crazy sitting in the office, depressed by the way the whole Glen thing is being handled. Derek Green [Man. Dir. A & M] & another bloke from A & M were here when I got back – didn't like them much. Green is a smoothy with a beard, seemed a real nit, giggling over the various outrageous things we could do. The promo guy was a hard little chubby businessman. I hated the way they talked, so sat there stony faced.

Tues 1–Tues 8 March 77

A long week it seemed, with little happening. Sid still rehearsing – except by Tues no one had seen him for four days so there was a bit of a panic. It turned out he had flu . . .

Thursday & Friday, band in the studio chaotic apparently, everyone hating Chris Thomas [producer]. Steve doing bass, guitar overdubs, back up vocals, the lot! Bad days in the office – deal with A & M might be off but they compromised I know now . . .

Saturday Malcolm had arranged a photo session but no photographer. Eventually he & Jamie went off with a borrowed Pentax – bad apparently. Sid & John showing off & pissing everyone else off.

A & M

Pistols sign with A & M – 9 March 77

15 March 77
. . . Trouble with graphics – our Queen photo one of Cecil Beaton's? Had to go home to check its source. Dragsville. Jamie in complete panic.

A & M's managing director, Derek Green, said this week: 'The Sex Pistols becoming available presented us with a unique business opportunity to be linked with a new force in rock music which is spearheaded by this group.

'The notoriety which they have already received was not a dissuading factor and would not be to anyone who has been around during the last 15 years of rock music and its fashions.

'I believe the Sex Pistols will effect some major changes in rock music and we at A & M are excited by them, their music and to have entered into a world-wide recording agreement.'

Sounds, 19 March 77

A & M fire Pistols – 16 March 77

There is no longer any association between A & M Records and the Sex Pistols. Production of their single 'God Save the Queen', which had been tentatively scheduled for release later this month, has been halted.

A & M press release

HARLEX LONDON 22233
ATTENTION STEVEN FISHER
AS WE INFORMED YOU AND YOUR CLIENTS THIS AFTERNOON AT APPROXIMATELY 3.00 PM A AND M RECORDS LIMITED RESCIND THE AGREEMENT BETWEEN THEMSELVES AND THE SEX PISTOLS DATED 9 MARCH 1977. THIS ACTION HAS BEEN TAKEN FOR THE REASONS EXPLAINED TO YOU AT THE MEETING AND WE CONFIRM THAT DISCUSSION OVER THE FORM OF A PRESS RELEASE TO THIS EFFECT HAS TAKEN PLACE BUT THAT YOUR CLIENTS HAVE NOT PUT OUR CLIENT IN A POSITION WHERE A STATEMENT FAVOURABLE TO YOUR CLIENTS IS AVAILABLE.
ROBERT LEE
16.3.77 LP
SENT 17.53
23836 PRITEN G
HARLEX LONDON 222339

Pistols sign outside Buckingham Palace, March '77.

Paul Cook

John Lydon, p/k/a "Johnny Rotten

Steve Jones

John Beverly, p/k/a "Sid Vicious

16 March 77
A short morning down the press then up to the office. Malcolm off to an important meeting with A & M in the afternoon. Tony came over again & finished the VAT returns. Jamie sat there for a while till I sent him off with Steven Lavers [freelance journalist] to discuss the mag. So, only Tony there when Malcolm rang up to say the A & M deal was terminated. Shellshock. I didn't tell anyone for a while, made sure the band were all available to hear the news. They say it's because of the public behaviour of the band. Crazy. Pressure inside the industry more like, & Freakedness at the words of the single . . . So what next?

PUNK rockers the Sex Pistols have been sacked again – only seven days after signing with a new record company.

Manager Malcolm McLaren walked out of the Chelsea offices of A & M records early today with a terminated contract in one hand and a pay-off cheque for £25,000 in the other. He was paid £50,000 when the group signed up last week . . .

A & M signed the notorious group up a week ago and planned to issue a new record 'God Save the Queen' next month. Twenty thousand copies have been produced and the group will now try to get them and perhaps arrange alternative distribution.

When the Sex Pistols were dropped by EMI in January because of their public behaviour, the cancelled contract earned them £50,000.

Today McLaren said: 'I'm shellshocked. Four weeks ago I flew to Los Angeles to meet Herb Alpert and Gerry Moss, who head A & M, and a week ago we signed up.

'They knew what they were getting and managing director Derek Green even said that he wasn't offended by the group's behaviour and that he thought they were fresh and exciting.

'Then at 11.30 last night I got a telex from them saying it was all over.

'The Sex Pistols are like some contagious disease – untouchable.

'I keep walking in and out of offices being given cheques. When I'm older and people ask me what I used to do for a living I shall have to say: "I went in and out of doors getting paid for it." It's crazy.'

Evening Standard, 17 March 1977

Interview with Derek Green, Man. Dir. of A & M, on Friday, 23 September 1977 – His first public explanation of the Pistols affair.

Q: Whose decision was it initially to sign the Pistols?
DEREK GREEN: Mine.

Q: How did you hear about them?
DG: Malcolm McLaren approached me.
Q: And when you took the decision to sign them, was that your sole decision?
DG: Yes.
Q: OK. Then whose decision was it, in fact, to revoke the contract?
DG: Mine.
Q: And can you tell me on what grounds that was?
DG: Um. [*Pause*] Well, clearly I changed my mind. I think taking it as an . . . having . . . being in a position to be lucky enough to be able to run my business according to my own means and wants, and, er, in this particular instance, rather than just put the company first, I changed my own mind, and let that carry the day.
Q: It all happened very quickly, didn't it?
DG: The signing of them didn't happen quickly. The signing of them took – it's one of the longest periods of negotiation I'd ever really got into. Which was extremely difficult from the off.
Q: And the period between signing them and losing them at the end . . .
DG: That was short.
Q: Yes, that was short.
DG: Four days, I think.
Q: Four days. That seems like a very short space of time.
DG: Well, I guess that's the hardest point to try and get across to anybody. And that's probably the – in fact, that's almost impossible because I think anybody who's standing off at a distance would expect a lot of intrigue, a lot of, er, [*pause*] sort of Machiavellian plots to have gone on in the background, and none of that's true. And people can either accept that or not. Um, I think in order to try and persuade people to accept that (if we took the trouble) they'd have to first understand the nature of A & M Records and who A & M Records is and why it has the right to behave differently to, er, other record companies and therefore why its chief executive in England, Derek Green, can behave differently.

And it's probably the background to A & M that would be the reason why I would expect any reasonable-minded person to at all accept our point of view. A & M's a very different company. It's a record company first, which is important to why a decision like this could be reached in such a [*pause*], a straightforward way, really, and be so human. You know, it was a very human decision. It was about an individual's change of mind and attitude, you know.
Q: Was it primarily their behaviour then that you were worried about?
DG: No, not . . . [*Long pause*] Was it primarily their behaviour? It wasn't primarily their behaviour, it was what their behaviour created. The reaction to their behaviour. That's what concerned me, yeah. Cos it was other

people's reaction to their behaviour concerned me much more than their own behaviour, certainly their behaviour towards me. It was never particularly bothersome.

Q: Did those other people include other artists who are signed with A & M?

DG: No.

Q: Because Malcolm McLaren does tell a story that . . .

DG: [*Laughing*] Which is totally wrong.

Q: You've heard it, no doubt.

DG: I've read about it.

Q: He claims to have seen a telex from one of your artists on a desk saying that . . .

DG: Well, it's the only, um . . . one of the reasons why I never spoke to the press at the time was clearly it would be very difficult in that environment to have been fairly reported. What did appear was one-sided and it was presented from, obviously from the Sex Pistols' point of view and the mouthpiece was obviously Malcolm McLaren. I never ever intended to deny anything Malcolm McLaren said because every day it was different.

The one that some journalists seem to have picked on as being at least maybe plausible was this notion of Malcolm's that the other artists on A & M put pressure on us. Er, I therefore absolutely deny that as complete poppycock. [*Laughs*] It's rubbish.

The telex that Malcolm McLaren refers to – the fact that he produced it is one of the reasons why I'm quite glad that I'm out of the whole situation – he was in my office one day when I received a telex, having just announced the signing of the Sex Pistols, and we had numerous meetings as one can imagine, and there was a telex on my desk from Rick Wakeman who is one of my dear friends. And the Sex Pistols provoked a lot of humour from other artists, in the nicest possible sense. I don't think any of the other artists really knew what they were. They'd never heard their music, and they're certainly all too professional to really comment as to whether they're good or bad till they've either heard them or seen them. They really don't care that much. They're making too many millions of their own to be bothered about putting up or down the Sex Pistols. And Wakeman in his funny way, being one of the very humorous characters of this business, sent me what was a very funny telex from Montreux, which was just – it was personal to me – and it was very funny; I think showing it to anybody would prove that, anybody would smile. And, er, I think he finished his telex by saying something to the order of: 'Well I guess we'll all have to wear safety pins,' or something, which is clearly humorous, and that's all it was.

The nature of Malcolm, it seems, is to read a telex upside-down on my table. Interestingly enough, he managed to remember the telex almost verbatim – which was very interesting. Course, you take the sense of humour out of it [*laughs*], it can be misinterpreted. I was actually very impressed with him that he managed, one, to read it upside-down and, two, to remember it with such accuracy.

Q: So who were you worried about, that the behaviour of the Sex Pistols would upset? Or the behaviour that they in fact inspired in people. Or . . . ?

DG: I just didn't realize when I signed them how much I wouldn't like it, personally. You know, I don't want to see, I don't like street fights, seeing street fights . . .

Q: I think what seems strange to people is that the example of EMI was already there. That their kind of ability to shock had already been proven. And it seems very strange to . . .

DG: It's not strange. It's a clear error of judgement on my part. You know, I thought what shocked EMI wouldn't shock me [*slight laugh*], being an independent and more a younger person, if you like, being a street person, coming from the East End originally and being a real suburbanite myself, being a football fan, still playing football locally – I still play football in South London, I play in the Surrey combination league and I get into fights on the football pitch. You know, I mean I live a very ordinary life and I hang around with toolmakers and out-of-works, you know, so I thought what shocked EMI I could imagine in a way. I thought it was the old – as George Harrison used to call them – the old grey buggers of Manchester Square, performing as old grey buggers, you know. And I thought that wouldn't apply to Derek Green and his street sense. Wrong.

Q: Another thing that the press brought up was the incident of the carpet on the day of the signing. Um, there was supposed to be vomiting and the staff at A & M were supposed to have been upset by the Pistols. Is that right?

DG: What carpet? And no vomiting. [*Laughs*] There was no vomiting involved.

Q: Oh. That's a story that was put around.

DG: There was no vomiting.

They came in very drunk, but then we've had drunk artists before. They behaved in a loutish way, but we've had that before. That's not new to anybody who worked here. Er, they behaved maybe more loutish.

You know, one of the girls, the secretaries, in the promotion department, was saying how sorry she felt for Sid Vicious cos his foot was bleeding from not having worn a sock for a certain period of time, and she was bandaging his foot up, you know, and she felt sorry for him.

Our sales girl didn't feel sorry for him because she found him washing it in the toilet afterwards. So I was getting a mixture of things . . .

Q: Whose idea was it to sign in front of Buckingham Palace?

DG: That was Malcolm McLaren's idea.

Q: What were your feelings about that?

DG: Oh, I thought it was a very shrewd piece of media playing, you know what I mean? Great way to get press. And that's the whole point. That's what I like about him, that he knew how to manipulate the press, you know. And I'm in that business too. And I thought it was very smart. I agreed. Of course we agreed to do it. The only restriction put on them at all was the fact that I wouldn't be there. And the reason for that is that I can't allow my office to be used as if it were a puppet to a publicity stunt.
Q: I've spoken with Johnny Rotten, and he thinks that it's wrong that record companies should in a sense censor or try and control the behaviour of pop groups. He says it's the business of record companies to put out records. So how would you answer that?
DG: Well, I agree with him. Mm.
Q: Don't you think that you acted as a censor?
DG: I'm not censoring him. No, not at all, not at all. I released him to make a record with anybody he wanted to make a record with.
Q: So really it's going back to saying that it was purely your own personal feeling . . .
DG: Yes.
Q: . . . of whether it was right or wrong?
DG: That's right. Whether it made me feel good or bad, you know. I mean only you know when you go home at night and you've got to sit down and deal with it. It's one thing trying to come up with fancy words and fancy excuses. You know whether something makes you feel good in your gut or bad.

And I was sitting there with my wife and two kids and I said to her I think . . . [*sighs*] Maybe when I was 21 I felt angry enough to be part of the movement. No way now, at 32, am I going to want to be part of the damn movement again. I've come to terms with certain things. I'm not angry any more, you know, and I can't be involved first hand. You know what I mean? I don't want to street parade with them. I've never to this day seen a punk gig. I purposely never met the Sex Pistols individually before signing them, and that was a purposeful stance because I had to treat it as a business – because I had a feeling if I met them, that I wouldn't sign them.
Q: What about yourself, personally. Were you very upset at the time about it? Were you, was it something that was very difficult for you to do?
DG: Oh yeah. I was very, I was very – I was troubled. I was very troubled personally because I was concerned whether I was behaving [*pause*] professionally and doing the right thing for A & M, which is the company I represent. That's what I was concerned with.
Q: Do you then, in any sense, regret your decision?
DG: No, but I guess you know . . . I can't, er, I can't regret it because I feel satisfied that it was right for *me*. It was a totally selfish thing, you know, very

selfish. Things that people in my position shouldn't do. But, every now and again, like anybody else, you say: 'Well, why not?' You know, not 'why not' but you say: 'Well, I've got to think about myself for once,' you know. I mean I spend 365 days a year or whatever else, thinking about it from another person's point of view, thinking in the third person, thinking it's best for *us*, meaning best for A & M. For *once* in my career with A & M Records, I determined to think about, well, what does it mean to me, and my life? [*Laughs*]

Q: Some people might describe that as a, as a loss of nerve. Is that . . . ?

DG: I think some people could describe that . . . I'm not really the best person to answer that. If someone aimed that particular criticism at me I guess I'd have to give some thought and think, yeah, that's pretty possible. No, I wouldn't deny that that's not possible. I don't know. I can't really tell that, can I?

Fri 18 March
It begins to sink in. Bernie yesterday phoned thinking it was a publicity stunt to detract from Clash whose single is released today. Quel paranoia.

Mon 21 March
Notre Dame. Hassles & running around all day. Paranoia at night. Nice drink in the pub after with assorted punks . . .

Fri 25 March
. . . Spent the afternoon reorganizing. Meal with Malcolm & Jamie in the evening discussing possibilities.

Tues 29 March–Fri 1 April
. . . Much wheeling & dealing this week. Polydor came in late. CBS dropped out on Thursday, a relief really. If Polydor are good enough it will be them. Complete coincidence, we only rang them as a favour to some American friend of Malcolm, who has tapes from a Cleveland band.

Mon 4 April
. . . had a quick pint before shooting off to the Cambridge – Boogie, Grey, Jamie, then Elaine & Malcolm. Hysterical conversations. Pissed again. Apparently Malcolm got refused by 5 record companies today. Meal at the Centrale.

Tues 5 April
. . . Misguidedly gave Paul & Steve a load of money for strings/skins. No receipts showed.

Wed 6–Thur 7 April
[Sid falls ill.]
. . . Sid got worse till we had to drag him out of Linda's flat & bring him up to the office where M asked him if he was shooting up & stuff. It was a drag because Boogie, Jamie & I sat around, completely silent . . .

A long painful session deciding what to do with Sid – hotels etc discussed, eventually he went home to mum. I went off to John's to drop his money off – nice estate & a gas to see him dressing up in his tiny bedroom he shares with his brother.

Tues 12 April
. . . In the afternoon Mike Flood Page interviews the band. Steve & Paul arrive first. Then Sid looking yellow. Finally John+Nora raging about Steve having stolen her car over the weekend. Steve very upset. Pat looking for flats – finds something for Paul & Steve in Bell St. After the interview I take Sid off to the Doctor in Fitzroy Sq. Talking about this & that. He moans a lot about the band & Malcolm. Very insecure & young. The doctor confirms hepatitis & asks for blood tests. Back to the office to face the question of where he is to stay . . . After persuasion Pat & Jerry agree to have him.

Thur 14 April
. . . In the morning, photo session for *Bravo* [German magazine]. Chaos. I ring Steve & Paul at Helen's then go off to wake up Sid & John at Pat's – it all takes a while. John looking 40 with his hair Bill Haley-wise. Sid still really ill. Get them down the shop at last. Instant chaos. Will English [film-maker] hanging round, Michael & Sharon. Crazy scenes. Worse when Steve & Paul

arrive – everyone trying on clothes & throwing them off. Over at last. Much gratitude from *Bravo*. Sid gets shoved in a taxi. I take the others back to the office. I really enjoy riding around with them. Reflected glory or just the oddity of the situation? Malcolm not there of course. Busy with the movie people.

Fri 15 April
Ringing round for script writers. Land on Johnny Speight. Good one? Maybe too old?

Sat 16 April
Up early & over to Fulham to pick up Sid . . . Away to the doctor. Hepatitis. Infectious, or was it contagious? Hospital anyhow. St Anne's Tottenham. The nurses are nice & the Doctor great, a tiny young looking guy from Singapore or somewhere who lectured Sid about needles & drugs.

Mon 18 April
. . . Malcolm hangs around waiting to go & meet Speight . . . The meeting with Speight goes on all afternoon – eventually I have to leave to see Sid, having been rung up by the ward sister, desperate . . . Home really late. Found Elaine & Jamie in the pub! Malcolm turned up – freaked, a bag of nerves after the Speight experience. Apparently he'd wanted £25,000 – got knocked down. Will do it though. Not quite the worker we'd expected. Rolls-Royce, swimming pool etc.

Wed 20 April
John has to be organized to get to the dentist. Mucho hassle but he gets there, an hour late. Oberstein [Man. Dir. CBS] rings. Apparently CBS USA are very interested. No call from Polydor – trouble at head office obviously. We start ringing round the smaller national companies. John came up the office after the dentist . . .

Otherwise the various sagas continue – office, short film, long film, rehearsals, flats for the band etcetera. Paul & Steve visit Sid so I don't have to go.

Fri 22 April
. . . Polydor say no today. As do Ariba [German record co.] Depressing. Still, there's always the film. We're going to be penniless if the band buys flats, I realise. Tough.

Tues 26 April
. . . M & I have a small row about paying Dave Goodman – I win & go to the

bank but it's shut. Rain. As I get back, Anthony, a student making a film to whom Boogie has promised bits we don't need is getting turned away. Malcolm is furious, with me, since Boogie isn't there, in front of Gerry & Pat. Ridiculous. Too overcome to answer back. John saves the situation by telephoning me to ask me to come up the studio & control the dreaded Japs from a mag called *Kodansha* so I leave, furious. Pick up John on the way. Good to see him anyway. Roll up to Wessex – the Japanese aren't half so terrifying as Steve had made out on the phone. Quite sweet in fact. I leave them to it in the end & get back to the office. No further explosions. Off to see Sid.

Tues 3 May
. . . Things are coming together, film, record, tour. One big worry is Sid. M is persuaded that the band should see him & we get them down . . . We all go for a drink after – John, Paul, Steve, Gerry, Pat, Boogie, Temple, M & J & me. Good to see everyone. John takes the piss heavily out of Paul when he's there but defends him once he's left. All's well with those 3 anyhow which is great. We all get pissed J & I leave at closing time – Elaine already asleep. Tunafish salad & TV.

Fri 6 May
. . . go up the studio – good as always to see the band. Watch Steve doing overdubs on New York & Bill Price [sound engineer] getting the best bits out of 4. Amazing. Got a bit pissed & leave in a dream rather, out of the real world completely. It must be great to be 20–21 & able to be creative like that.

Wed 11 May
. . . Many letters to write to foreign companies, photos to be sent. Telegrams to Australia etc. The foreign companies are interested but it becomes increasingly apparent that it's going to be an enormous hassle doing it territory by territory.

Thur 12 May
Malcolm came in – lots of cheques to sign. The band still haven't signed to Virgin. Things are hotting up. Virgin getting a little dismayed. Chrysalis put in an offer for the world ex UK, France, USA – we wonder whether to sign with Virgin but Malcolm does in the end on Steven's advice, we've gone too far with the marketing campaign to get out of it easily.

VIRGIN

Pistols sign with Virgin

Fri 13 May
. . . The band have now signed excluding Sid, who is out of hospital today, sounding OK.

Mon 16 May
. . . Malcolm arrived quite early: Crisis – A & M won't let us use their metalwork, [For 'God Save the Queen'/'No Feelings'] that cut much better than the more recent one . . . Sid came up looking good & got sent off to sign the Virgin contract. Then the NF [National Front] issue – apparently we were mentioned on last night's London Programme which was about the NF. Lots of letters dissociating ourselves . . .

Tues 17 May
. . . Gerry arrived, then Malcolm & the fun started – CBS factory refusing to press the record – threatening strike. Oberstein & Stollman [second in command, CBS] both unavailable. Mr Pickle [Branson, Man. Dir. Virgin] in a panic. We sat around all day on edge, wondering if we'd have to get out of the Virgin contract. Would Chrysalis take us for the UK? Mucho panic. Malcolm rang the factory & stuff, spoke to John Blake on the *Evening News*. Eventually it all came through all right. Much relief.

Thur 19 May
. . . I'm sick of keeping a diary. Mainly because very little ever happens in the office, my job seems to consist of nagging people into doing things they don't want to do, the books & other unglamorous occupations. The shitwork.

Mon 23 May
Boogie expected me at the office early but I couldn't be fucked to hurry. All flurry over his idea of filming a little promo thing of 'God Save the Queen' today, combining with the Virgin photo session. Madness as far as I was concerned. Nevertheless I spent all morning running around getting money for it etc. I'm jealous that he has those opportunities to push himself & does so without hesitation. I particularly dislike being walked all over on the way. Not to worry. The thing got done, so did everything else apparently.

Everyone goes to Paris for the showing of the film *Sex Pistols No. 1*

Thur 26 May
. . . over to the cinema – chaos, bunch of hippies putting on appalling plays upstairs. The downstairs where we are to be a total mess & we, unable to make any noise . . . hippies traipsing to & fro . . .

. . . went off for a drink through a mob of posing Paris punks loving the photographers. Met Malcolm et al on the way back. The place already packed. People tripping over the electric wires. We sensible English get irritated. The film gets stopped over & over by riotous French, ripping the plugs out, tearing the screen, some particularly objectionable ones try to knock over the projector.

[Sophie returns to London on Friday]

Sat 28 May–Mon 30 May
Up very early & drove to Durham – hard to stay awake but I made it OK. Lovely sunny day. Dad was mending the desk. We sat in the garden, very quiet day, talking, reading, playing the piano. Sunday was cold & grey but we went for an expedition anyway, up on the moor – lovely though cold. We found a good pub in Barnard Castle. Then home. So nice to see them both. Monday I didn't get up early, lay in bed thinking why should I kill myself getting back to the busy office. So I left at 7.30 or so. The journey seemed very long.

Thur 2–Fri 3 June
. . . John seems very uptight with Malcolm these days – long phone calls trying to argue but embarrassed because I'm pissed off with him too. Friday evening we all manage to meet – John & Sid, Malcolm, Boogie, Howard from Manchester & me in Hyde Park. Very odd it was. I pissed off as rapidly as I could, with Howard. The town was full of Scottish football fans, drunk & barbaric.

Glitterbest and Virgin organize a Sex Pistols boat party to coincide with the Queen's Jubilee week celebrations.

Wed 8 June
. . . Very peaceful sailing down river with reggae. Slightly cold but the free booze dealt with that & the sun came out for a while. Everyone got quite calm & relaxed. Band played a few numbers & got the river police going. Wobble attacked a French cameraman – I managed to break it up but I think it was

probably then that the captain decided to take the boat in. Hordes of police on the pier. Roger, already upset at getting pushed around on the boat got pushed around getting off – Barbara rolled up & told me Jamie had been arrested. I gave Sid & John a fiver each to split with & was wondering what to do when I saw Malcolm getting roughed up. Next thing I knew I was in a police van too. The entire management except for Boogie was there – Jamie, Malcolm, me, Viv, Debbie, Tracy & girlfriend & an American. Took ages to get booked & put away . . . A night in the cells, a girl from Liverpool yelling all night because she didn't have any blankets. They woke us at 5 for fingerprints. Slept till 10.30 when they took us over to the court. Offenbach appeared & advised us to plead not guilty – wrongly in my case I think. Not to worry. We all were out in time for lunch. Back to the office. Congratulatory calls from music press & band. Suddenly Malcolm is a nice guy because he got arrested. Difficult to work. Home to find Claudia so out for a drink, naturally. Didn't intend to stay for more than a pint but somehow got involved & the pub was open till midnight. Aaaagh. Jamie really got pissed – freaked by his charge, assault. Drag.

Thur 9 June
. . . It seems we're to sign with Virgin for Europe. The single is number 2. Good news but it should've been 1. Rod Stewart did for us there.

Q: First of all, I just wanted to ask you about how the signing of the Sex Pistols came about, who was interested in them and why basically.
AL CLARK (Virgin Records' Press Officer): Well, we'd passed on them once before. I don't know why we passed on them then especially, partly I suppose because they didn't conform at all to the way the label was at the time and partly because I think we had a slight resistance to too opportunistic a move at the time. I mean I think we were still in our heart of hearts living in the Arts Council days when everything we did had to have an aura of worthiness about it.

But then the opportunity arose again after A & M and I think it was taken up partly because 'God Save the Queen' was such a good record and partly because it seemed like an exciting thing to do. I mean we figured we could get it right. We just thought we could walk the tightrope – and it was a tightrope . . .
Q: I'm interested in you saying that there was a kind of Arts Council feel to you because I also get the impression that there was more than that: a kind of an art and a progressive rock feel and very much not going for the singles market.
AC: Well, one of the reasons we didn't specifically go out for singles was that we weren't very good at making them successful and people didn't come to us

with them. I mean one of the unfortunate aspects of having a reputation as Virgin did very emphatically from the start is that people come to you with the things they think are going to please you rather than the things that are going to overhaul you. So from the start, because Virgin began with 'Tubular Bells', what we'd get would be processions of people in Afghan coats coming up and down the Yard with concept albums complete with artwork ready. I mean they'd just come with their dream and we were supposed to put it into effect. And what we really wanted, which of course nobody realized at the time because we would have had to have advertised to get it, was a few sort of rowdy records. Um, I mean as far back as 1974 which was when I joined I remember Simon Draper telling me that he would really like a group like Slade on the label.

Q: Was there any particular person in Virgin who set out to get the Sex Pistols?

AC: No, the prompting for signing them was just because, because it seemed like fun. And I mean it had become evident to us a couple of months earlier that we would have to change gear, I mean that we'd have to pursue success rather more aggressively and that we were wasting a lot of potentially bright people here by just giving them routine things to do. And the Sex Pistols provided a break from that routine as well as a change of gear for everybody insofar as I can't think of anybody here whose life wouldn't have changed for at least three months in terms of what was expected of them every day and the pace at which they were expected to work and the sense of improvisation that they would need to bring to their work.

Vivienne Westwood and Malcolm McLaren.

'GOD SAVE THE QUEEN'

PUNK ROCK JUBILEE SHOCKER
by Colin Wills

What's burning up the kids? A disturbing report on the amazing new cult.

Punk Rock – the spitting, swearing, savage pop music of rebellious youth – is sweeping teenage Britain.

Today, after a Silver Jubilee week in which the Queen's popularity has never been higher, she is the subject of attack by a punk group.

The Sex Pistols have burst into the Top Ten with a record which calls the Queen a 'moron'.

Some charts already put the song God Save The Queen at number two. And it is forecast to go to the top next week.

Yet it has reached this position in spite of the BBC refusing to play it. The song is also banned by many commercial stations.

Top chain stores are refusing to stock the record. Concert promoters have cancelled Sex Pistols appearances.

But such is the new-found and disturbing power of punk that nothing can stop the disc's runaway success.

The record may even become the fastest-seller in pop music history. No pop song has ever contained verses like these before:

God save the Queen,
A fascist regime
Made you a moron,
A potential H-bomb

God save the Queen,
She ain't no human being
There ain't no future in
England's dream.

Front page lead, *Sunday Mirror*, 12 June 77

VIVIENNE WESTWOOD: Little boys come running into my shop and say: 'Do you really think the Queen is a moron?'

If someone came to you with a piece of paper and if you signed it another person got executed and you did, wouldn't you have to be some sort of zombie. It's not the act of a human being. Lady Macbeth could never wash the blood off *her* hands . . .

You can talk about her having killed many people too by smiling on hypocrisy. Like entertaining the Brazilian ambassador on a business level, while his country is daily torturing people to death.

If you took away the Queen the army and all those people wouldn't have this figurehead to look up to that smiles at them and pretends everything's all right.

Maybe though, she doesn't know what's going on, the old burke. In that case, let's be very kind for a minute, I feel sorry for her. I'd compare her to those people in the Polynesian Islands who are taken away at a very early age, kept in a dark room and stuffed with food. Then they bring them out once a year so everyone can revel and marvel at these very pale, fat people who can't walk but have to be helped along a sort of catwalk.

I'd compare her to them because she is a symbol of the total wastage of potential. She's prevented from being some kind of wild, crazy, intelligent, creative human being and has to be some kind of a zombie instead. She's an A-1 example of what this country is all about.

Interview in *No Future*, June/July 77

Q: Do the Sex Pistols represent some kind of cultural threat?
LAURIE HALL (EMI): No, you're thinking of all this anarchy and revolution and all this sort of thing. Not really.
Q: But, for example, the BBC banned the playing of 'God Save the Queen'.
LH: Um [*pause*] I think the BBC is always likely to ban that type of record because it has to reflect public opinion, if you want to use the word. And public opinion, as I said, was that which was being expressed in the press. And what the Sex Pistols were doing was allegedly against public opinion and against good taste, as many people like to understand it.
Q: It must have reflected public opinion to some extent else 'God Save the Queen' wouldn't have got to number two, would it?
LH: How do you mean? In terms of record sales?
Q: Yes. I mean, to say that the BBC reflects public opinion maybe in this case isn't true because it didn't allow anyone to voice any anti-monarchist feelings.
LH: Um . . .
Q: It certainly didn't allow the Sex Pistols to, anyway.
LH: I think the fact that the Sex Pistols' 'God Save the Queen' got to number two does not mean that public opinion was behind them. It only meant a lot of people went out and bought their record.

Q: I think the whole issue of 'God Save the Queen' is a very interesting one because I think there is a paranoia in the Establishment about attacks against the Queen; that, for example, the BBC and the ITV as well, in all their coverage of the Jubilee, just assumed that everybody was quite happy to watch all the adulation and didn't allow any kind of criticism. Particularly not of this emotional kind. And therefore I think people have come to wonder whether there has been any political, with a small 'p', pressures exerted or made felt to the Sex Pistols about this record.

DEREK GREEN (Man. Dir. A & M): Oh, I don't know. I think that's a – I think if you try to overthink it all – I don't think the cast of characters involved warrant that amount of thought. I don't think so, whether you're talking about EMI Records, A & M Records, the Sex Pistols, Malcolm McLaren. I don't think any of it's significant enough to warrant that kind of deep thought, raise such deep issues, you know. It's much more innocent than that.

Q: I don't think it's innocent, though, that it provokes strong feelings, and I think the fact that it provokes such strong reaction makes it worthy of deep thought.

DG: Well, then it's the wrong people provoking it cos they can't really articulate their true thoughts. The deepest thought, you know, is a really articulate one. It's a very – I mean the record itself is a very naive, innocent attack at the Establishment, isn't it? It's not really a well thought-out written work on what the Establishment means in a young person's life, you know.

Q: But it does express a strong emotion and that emotion tends to be censored.

DG: Does it? I don't think it's censored.

Q: It tends to be ignored or reacted against so that . . .

DG: We're getting into a discussion between you and I. [*Laughs*]

Q: I wanted to ask you about 'God Save the Queen', a long point really about it. It's to do with the kind of reaction that there was to it. I think that's caused probably the most reaction hasn't it, of the songs?

JOHNNY ROTTEN: Don't know. 'Anarchy' got the worst, being banned, and that was banned for no reason. It was stopped, it was stopped being made. When it got to 28, EMI immediately stopped the pressing. That got the worst treatment. That record had *no* kind of publicity of any kind. If they'd have left it, it would have been a definite number one, easily. This they were very frightened of, cos at the time like there was *nothing* like it. Nothing like it at all. If 'Anarchy' was number one then how would someone like Tony Blackburn say [*imitates him*]: 'And now, Anarchy in the UK.' That's what they were frightened of. It makes them look fucking stupid.

Q: Why do you think it is that people and institutions like the BBC feel so threatened by those words.

JR: Because it's probably what they feel themselves. All those people are like – it's their education i'n'it? They've been repressed. They've been made to feel that they shouldn't have an opinion. So like when someone comes along with like something so fucking blatant, it frightens them. You know, like the tools they used against us was: Aah, the lyrics are naive. Why the hell shouldn't they be? What do they expect? Some kind of like poetry? Cover it up, you know? Evade the point? I mean the first lesson I learnt in English was like if you can say something in one word, say it. Don't use two. That was good English. Say what you mean.

Q: I think that's true. What you say applies to 'God Save the Queen'. I think that probably the people who got most angry were maybe people who were repressing that feeling of resentment against the Queen. Because I think it's a very interesting thing, in this country you're allowed to be anti-monarchy if . . .

JR: You're not allowed to express it.

Q: You are if you're Willie Hamilton and you're saying sort of political things, but if it's an emotional point you're trying to get across, you're not allowed to do it.

JR: Yeah. I mean the bloody record isn't about the Queen. It's about what you *feel* about the fucking woman. She's probably just like everybody else but like watching her on telly, as far as I'm concerned, she ain't no human being. She's a piece of cardboard that they drag around on a trolley. Like, go here, Queen, go there. And she does it, blindly, cos she's in a rut. She does get in a rut, but there's always a way out.

Alas! poor Queen!

Keats, 'Faery Song'

Johnny Rotten was recognized in the pub.

'The gang cut his face and his arm, but didn't manage to do any serious damage.

'Chris also had his face cut and I got a deep cut in my arm.

'It was obvious Johnny was not too popular because of the record about the Queen.'

A spokesman for Virgin Records, who issued the controversial 'Queen' disc, said: 'It looks as though punk rockers are in for a hard time.

'The attackers were not teenage thugs, but men in their thirties.

'It seems they were aiming for Johnny's face to try to disfigure him. We are worried that this could be the start of a wave of attacks on the group and other punk rockers.

'A lot of people were upset at the record about the Queen, and that could be part of the problem.

'Johnny is a target because he is the king of the punk rockers – the figurehead.

'We're going to have to take special care to protect him.'

A Scotland Yard spokesman said last night: 'We are investigating this apparently unprovoked attack.'

Lead story, *Daily Mirror*, 21 June 1977

The surprise at first was far worse than the pain (a nettle could sting as badly). 'You fools,' he said, 'it's not me, it's him you want,' and turned and saw the faces ringing him all round. They grinned back at him: every man had his razor out: and he remembered for the first time Colleoni laughing up the telephone wire. The crowd had scattered at the first sign of trouble; he heard Spicer call out, 'Pinkie. For Christ's sake'; an obscure struggle reached its climax out of his sight. He had other things to watch: the long cut-throat razors which the sun caught slanting low down over the downs from Shoreham. He put his hand to his pocket to get his blade, and the man immediately facing him leant across and slashed his knuckles. Pain happened to him, and he was filled with horror and astonishment . . .

Graham Greene, *Brighton Rock*

Mon 20 June

Sitting in the office all morning denying rumours that John got beat up over the weekend. Paul rings from a phone box to say he got hit over the head with an iron bar. 15 stitches. It turns out John's attack is true – razors etc. Nasty. Totally tied up with the press till Weds. when the *Sun* asks 'was it all a publicity stunt'. Sick. After nagging me for a story . . . We all lose our cool a little.

ANOTHER SEX PISTOL IS KNIFED
by John Blake

A second member of the Sex Pistols punk rock group has been knifed, it was disclosed today.

Paul Cook, 20-year-old drummer with the controversial group, was attacked by five men outside Shepherd's Bush Underground station.

He received knife wounds and was clubbed with an iron bar on the back of his head. His wounds needed 10 stitches.

It is the third attack in a week on the band, whose anti-royal record 'God Save the Queen' was banned by the BBC and independent radio stations – but still became a best seller.

Police fear that the anti-Queen record may have triggered off a war among London youngsters.

Teds, who model themselves on the Teddy Boys of the 1950s, with drape jackets and slicked back hair regard themselves as a rival youth cult to the punks, who wear deliberately torn clothes and put streaks in their crudely cut hair.

Punks have been the targets of numerous gang attacks in London over the past few weeks and one East End police officer said: 'The whole thing is rapidly getting out of hand.

'If it carries on at the present rate I would not be surprised to see pitched battles like those at Hastings and Brighton in the sixties.'

Front page, *Evening News*, 21 June 1977

MRS COOK: . . . when Paul came home that night, we nearly had a fit, didn't we? Oh God, he was smothered in blood in his hair. And he had only gone out previous like in the evening. They had been here for tea, him and Kay, and it, you know, it all happened. I thought I must be getting my nerves steadier now to take it, but I can't stand blood and when I see that I called them everything – whoever done it, you know. I even went round Shepherd's Bush Green and tried to find out. But Paul don't appreciate this. He'll say: Oh, don't get doing this, and don't, you know, keep your mouth quiet about this, and keep your mouth quiet about that. But I mean I'm not that kind of a person. If anyone has done anything like that to my son, well they deserve it back. Off of me if possible. [*Laughs*] You know what I mean?

Q: Yes, I think that's natural.

MRS C: Yes, oh my God, that night, poor devil. And I thought to myself, very often I've said:'Oh, you only come here when you've got trouble.' But I don't mean it, I don't honestly. I am glad – I mean he could have been killed that night, couldn't he? . . .

Some of his old school mates looked for them and that, and they found them and run off, these blooming Teddy boys. There was a lot of that going on round Shepherd's Bush at that time – with anybody. They were knocking old people down. I think it is terrible. I think they should be shot, I do really. Never mind about the punk rockers. I think they should be shot. They've always been flash them rock 'n' roll, they've always been like that.

But we got so that I was frightened of people knocking here.

Q: You got beaten up, didn't you? And John and Jamie. All around the same time, wasn't it?
PAUL COOK: It all happened in about a week.
Q: And the press really blew that up as well, didn't they?
PC: I couldn't believe that. When John got done like, front page of the *Mirror*, wasn't it? [*Pause*] The thing was no one believed that either. They thought it was another publicity stunt. People coming up and saying: 'Oh, you never got beat up really, did you? Just another publicity stunt.' You know, I can't believe the way people could think we'd even do that, to sink that low, you know. They really did believe we didn't get beat up. Even the press like, they wanted to see the scars. We was in Virgin and they said: 'Can we take a picture of their scars to show everyone?'

ANTI-PUNKS, BEHAVE!
PUBLIC OPINION

It is all very well for the *Mirror* to say that Johnny Rotten is 'not too popular because of the records about the Queen!' It seems however that 'patriots' can attack innocent people with razors because they don't like their opinions.

The fact is that the media must bear some responsibility for Johnny being slashed since nobody 'in their thirties' would have heard of the record had it not been for such a hysterical outburst – Ardelia Jones, Bristol.

Daily Mirror, 27 June 1977

Thurs 23–Fri 24 June

. . . Thursday I'm supposed to be working with Tony but get diverted into standing bail for Nancy who has been picked up on offensive weapon (Sid's) & overstaying her visa. So stupid. Friday? I had to drop money off for John at Chelsea Cloisters. Nice to see him. He'd got done over again though at Dingwalls the previous night.

Week of Mon 27 June

. . . THE CRISIS breaks – the band all over the place. Sunday/Monday? night I get a call from Sid at midnight saying they've got to get out of this country. Apparently he rang M at 4 am & babbled on about how he & John just had to get out of the country immediately, total paranoia etc. etc. Monday morning therefore Malcolm rings Cowley [Cowbell Agency] & gets

WINE SHOP

up a tour of Scandinavia – meanwhile back at the office I was receiving phone calls from John moaning on about how everybody has forgotten about him, about Steve & Paul not turning up etc. etc. – a lot of sense really but all very self centered. So. Whenever Malcolm phoned me I told him to drop everything to go over & see John but of course he didn't go till late morning having fixed everything up. Chaos ensued as far as I can gather, everyone yelling at everyone else – Steve & Paul were there & Boogie in the end.

The rest of the week dissolved into flaming rows & endless discussions of who was doing precisely what to whom & why. At the time I had a lot of sympathy for John, not Sid because he just seems to be farting around with Nancy. Also feeling considerable sympathy for Steve who just seems to have had enough of John's jibes & sneers. Malcolm did the wrong thing (I thought) by jumping in so strongly on Steve & Paul's side. Endless telephone calls & persuasions. Boogie did rather well I thought. I had to find them a flat & was fortunate to come up with one in Sutherland Avenue almost immediately – a short let. Spent a fair amount of time getting John to the dentist too. By the end of the week everyone was emotionally drained. The band were at a point where they had to decide whether to patch it up & keep going or split & then what? I think that then what? is what pushed them back . . . The impetus seems lost. My prophecies of doom last December ring back through my mind, but then it seemed easy, a small thing to give it up, I had other options going, felt attachments elsewhere, other directions pulling. Now, I'm hooked & dependent on other people. Dragsville. Wake up.

Anyhow, by the end of the week things were sorting out. John went to the dentist Thur & Fri . . .

Johnny Rotten, the young Sex Pistol who isn't nearly as horrible as he punkly pretends, is, in the view of his dentist, thoroughly aptly named. In the office of the Pistols' manager Malcolm McLaren there is pinned to the wall for all to see a letter from the courageous dentist, pleading with his patient to come in for treatment. A secretary in the office said casually that Johnny didn't seem to care about his teeth falling out.

Londoner's Diary, *Evening Standard*, 27 June 1977

. . . got called over by John panic stricken, penniless. (It must've been Thurs.) Find him & Wobble sitting in Sid's room, coming off speed – moaning. John moans, Wobble backs him up. Still, John's paranoia is understandable, even/especially his paranoia about Malcolm. I don't know if I want to go on standing between those two.

Sun 3 July

Malcolm left for L.A. [to see the film director Russ Meyer] – I had to go up the office with him & Viv to pick up T shirts etc. He would've missed the plane except it was late. M & V quarrelled violently in the office over some arrogance of Malcolm's – quel drag . . . I was glad he left – at least he thought the band was still running, or maybe thought if it was splitting L.A. was a better place to be. That left me to deal with the Swedish tour that John didn't want to do – at all.

Mon 4 July

. . . Took John down the Goldsmiths [pub] & had a strange sort of evening. A couple of girls from the block stared at him a little – he refused to go up to the bar to buy drinks which pissed me off. I was far more pissed off after (at home), when he slagged virtually everything we played. I got bored & irritated & went to bed.

Tuesday – I woke him up to go off to do the Vacant promo film [later shown on Top of the Pops] & then picked up Sid – the driver lost the way & we were forced out to Hammersmith by the flyover. Eventually we got there though. Steve & Paul had just arrived.

Thurs 7 July

. . . the day of Nancy's case. I crawled out of bed somehow, in the middle of heavy period pains, got over to court, no one there except one worried solicitor. Leapt in a cab, over to Sutherland Ave, no reply, so back to court & there they were, Nancy demure in black dress & tights, Sid with his hair slicked down, comforting her . . . Much hanging around. The case before us was a black woman accusing the guy she lived with of ripping her off – he said he took the money for his electricity bill. She got hysterical. The dopy magistrate obviously couldn't cope with the emotion of it all & dismissed the case. He proved even dopier with Nancy, believing her appearance & lies & crying. I was really pissed off, refused to pay her fine, told her she would have to leave Sutherland Ave when the band left then shot off back to work.

TOP OF THE POPS

Mon 11 July
. . . The great debate of Top of the Pops starts – Branson starts his nagging campaign & eventually succeeds. I pass everything on to Boogie who is magnificent, persuades John to do this that & the other, things that turn out badly as it happens but through no fault of his – Top of the Pops & the Tommy Vance interview for Capital (the Punk & his music).

TOMMY VANCE: Something that turned me on to you, [*earnestly*] as a *person*, was watching you do an interview . . . with Janet Street-Porter on London Weekend Television.
JOHNNY ROTTEN: [*Laughs derisively*] Yeah!
TV: I don't know *why*, but I just got the impression watching it, and I watched it again and again and again [*pause*] cos I had it on video, right?
JR: Mm.
TV: And I got the impression that you really *really* know what you're talking about. And that's [*pause*] a strange question, but it is a question. I mean do you *really* know what you're talking about?
JR: Well I fink so, I'*ope* so. [*Laughs*] If I don't then I'm in a right bad state. Yeah, I think I do, *yeah, yeah*!
TV: [*Mocking*] Yeah.
JR: All right, what can I say to that? I dunno. Can't swear or spit.

Capital Radio, 16 July 1977

Wed 13 July
Up early & over to Sutherland Ave. Find Wobble & John have cleared up beautifully. Boogie is there. John on the phone to Malcolm – decision to definitely not do Top of the Pops & reasons why – great. Sid sleepy & being a drag. I spend ages trying to get the keys . . . Wobble comes to the airport with us. Arrive to find Paul, Steve & Rodent [roadie for Clash] waiting but Sid has left his passport behind – aaargh . . .

Branson says he can't get the film [back] off Top of the Pops. Oh yeah?

TOP OF THE PUNKS!
By Mirror Reporter
BBC raise TV ban on the Sex Pistols

The outrageous Sex Pistols shoot back into Britain's homes tonight . . . on BBC TV.

The punk rockers will appear on Top of the Pops, the favourite show of millions of teenyboppers.

SEX PISTOLS
pretty vacant

They will sing their new disc, 'Pretty Vacant', in a filmed recording – which is described by its director as 'pretty eccentric'.

The BBC decision to put the punk rockers on TV is certain to enrage thousands of parents and other viewers.

Yesterday, the Sex Pistols celebrated the announcement of the BBC TV appearance in typical style . . . by firing off a barrage of four-letter words.

Obscene

Reporters found them at Heathrow Airport – and before long the four-man group was hurling seats around in a departure room.

Almost every question received an obscene reply . . . and in one of the politest moments, Johnny Rotten said: 'I ain't interested in talking to fabricated people.'

The group threatened to smash the camera of one newsman with the words 'Have you ever heard the sound of smashing glass – like a camera lens.'

The new record, 'Pretty Vacant', jumped forty places this week to No. 7 in the BBC charts, compiled by the British Market Research Bureau.

It contains no four-letter words.

Front page lead, *Daily Mirror*, 14 July 1977

Thurs 14 July
. . . Over to Virgin. I was *not* impressed. Bad place to meet people but why do they work there? Eh? . . . I watched the prospective Top of the Pops video with Debbie & Derek & hated it . . .

Well that's it then. All my sympathy to the Sex Pistols at the end of their short and contrivedly disgusting career. Now the BBC has agreed to play the punksters' latest record I fear the end is nigh. After all Bill Grundy did for the boys. Young Rotten might as well change his name to Johnny Perfect.

Londoner's Diary, *Evening Standard*, 14 July 1977

Q: Did Virgin put any pressure on you to go on Top of the Pops?
PAUL COOK: Yeah, of course they did. They said: 'Oh, come on – the single's going to sell, it's going to sell so many thousand copies if you go on there.' And we said: 'Oh, we don't care.' We was at number 7 already. 'What's the big deal?' But I didn't mind it going on. I thought it was all right. But I didn't really like the film what we'd done. I don't like Top of the Pops. But there's nothing else, is there?

chorus: we're so pretty oh so pretty vacant
we're so pretty oh so pretty vacant
and we don't care.

A dim desire for annihilation stretched in him: the vast superiority of vacancy.

Graham Greene, *Brighton Rock*

Fri 22 July

. . . Jamie rings to warn me Barclay [French record co.] are importing 'Anarchy' like crazy. Branson rings etc. General panic gives way to amusement. 'Anarchy in the UK' – yeah. And a way to get back at Branson for his dealings with us.

Mon 25 July

. . . Monday dissolved into rainstorms & a trip to the airport to fetch Sid who was looking really healthy & cheerful for a change. It sounds like John is the only one who hasn't been enjoying the tour – it must be peculiar, singing his songs to a bunch of uncomprehending, clean hippies. Sid says the grass is very good over there.

Sun 7 August

Went to see Fred & Judith Vermorel. I was hostile at first but quite enjoyed it in the end. It doesn't sound like a very good book but their motives are very clear.

WHO KILLED RUSS MEYER?

Thurs 11 August
. . . went round with John to his flat . . . Talked to him quite seriously about keeping the flat together & not letting people know where it is. Dropped him at Finsbury Park & came back to the studio – mainly dreadful, but great when Steve & Sid really went loony – unfortunately they didn't make it all the way through . . . Malcolm came up with RM [Russ Meyer] – just as Em [Emma – assistant secretary] had described him – a fat American uncle with a scrubbing brush moustache. We went for a drink together – the band were shy of him & giggly rather. I went off home, they went off to see *Valley of the Dolls* [Russ Meyer's film].

Q: What do you think about the film?
PAUL COOK: What, doing it?
Q: Yeah.
PC: I'm looking forward to it. I think it'll be pretty good.

Q: I wanted to ask you what you felt about the Russ Meyer film.
SID VICIOUS: The Russ Meyer film. I don't really know anything about it. All I can say about it is that is has a very weak script as far as I'm concerned. It doesn't seem to be very interesting at all.
Q: In what way is the script weak?
SV: In every way. There's no story to it at all, whatsoever.
Q: It seems to me that in a way it's trying to embalm the Pistols.
SV: Embalm them? How do you mean?
Q: Well, instead of trying to push them further it seems like it's trying to almost bury them, you know . . .
SV: Really? Oh I didn't get that impression at all. What I feel is that it's a cheap attempt to make money, do you know what I mean? And I don't like it for that reason. Because like, I mean, I suppose we'll make money off our album and our singles and stuff, but like they were made as we wanted them, exactly, with what we had to say and done exactly how we wanted them, right? And like we didn't put them out to make money. We put them out because we wanted to do them, do you know what I mean? And like if we make money from them, who gives a fuck? If we don't, who gives a fuck? I couldn't care less, I don't give two shits.

But the film, the thing I'm unhappy about in the film is that Russ Meyer said to me that he wanted to make a film that would be good for the box office and that people would be interested in and would want to come and see and would make a lot of money. And like I said to him: 'Well, like

what about making something that you're genuinely interested in, that really like means something to you?' And he seemed a little puzzled by that.

Q: What sort of films do you yourself like?

SV: I don't like any sort of film. I hate films.

Q: What is it about them that you hate?

SV: Because people have to act parts in them. Play people who they're *not*, do you know what I mean? And it's pretence, it's lies, it's just shit. It builds things up to be not what they are.

Like if you filmed a day in the life of me, for instance – like a day in the life of a pop star, right – and you had him going round in a flash car and whacking up smack and doing this and that and the other; and like a day in my life is getting up at three o'clock, going to the office and hustling ten quid out of Sophie or something and fucking going somewhere and waiting hours to fucking cop some dope, you know what I mean? And like that is the most boring thing on earth. It's as boring as sitting at home and drinking beer or fucking any other shit thing to do, you know what I mean?

And like films are about lies. They're about making things look glamorous. Everything's a load of bullshit. And it makes me sick to think that people will act out parts and, you know, like make it all seem larger than life, just so that some crud out there can get off on some fantasy: that life is wonderful really and one day . . .

You know, when I was like ten years old and when I used to – I used to think Marc Bolan was great, and I used to think to myself what a wonderful life Marc Bolan must have, just think. And if only I could be like him, gosh, just think of the things he must do. And like I do the things that he done (before that stupid bitch crashed his fucking mini for him, or something) and like he probably did exactly the same thing as what I do now: sit in my mummy's front room cos I don't have anywhere to live, you know what I mean? It's fucking full of shit and I hate it all.

But there's nothing else to do. It's better than doing nothing at all and it's certainly better than doing something I don't want to do.

Q: Do you like the idea of the film?

STEVE JONES: Yes, I love it. Lots of birds in it.

Q: Does it worry you, the idea that you've got to act out a part?

SJ: Well, not really, because like I mean you've got written down a script and what you've got to do, but you like ad lib. You ain't got to – it ain't as if you're an actor and you're told to play the part of Steve Jones of the Sex Pistols. You are him. It's mainly you just act how you want to act, you know. So acting – you are acting in a little sense you know.

Q: What do you think of Russ Meyer as a person?
SJ: I think he's quite a genuine bloke. He's honest, he tells you what he thinks of you. I like him, I quite like him.
Q: What was your very first impression of him, do you remember?
SJ: Suspicious. Seen him in the pub and he was like really suspicious looking at us, like sort of working us out. But that's what he had to find out, I suppose. I think he's all right. Quite funny.
Q: Do you think he's imposing his idea of you on the film or do you think that he's actually learnt about you, that you've taught him something?
SJ: I think he's learnt a little bit about us but see, he's a director, he's directed films before. He's got to put his bit of directing in, his dab, his trademark if you like, you know, birds with big knockers and what have you. But no way it's going to be his sort of film because like we're acting in it and we're going to act the way we want to act, not how he wants us to act.

Q: How do you feel about the film?
JOHNNY ROTTEN: I feel absolutely nothing about it.
Q: I've read the script because initially when the script was written . . .
JR: Well, like there's been several scripts and I've like thrown most of them out because they were just ridiculous. I've cut myself right out of it. I'm just in like the playing bits. That's all I want to know about. The rest can go to hell. I'm not interested in being a movie star. But it could be fun, if it's done in the right way. If it flops, you know, that's just too bad. Worth trying. Anything's worth trying once. [*Northern accent*] Give it a go.
Q: It's the kind of fictional element about it that I don't really like. I mean I think the truth is much more interesting than . . .
JR: Yeah, well we tried that but like it just gets to be like a fucking documentary. And it gets really boring. Truth is funny enough as it is. Leave it alone. Don't need to do a film on that.
Q: What do you think of Russ Meyer's films? Fred, he calls Russ Meyer 'Walt Disney with tits'.
JR: Yeah, he is. But he's got a piss-take about him. And like so has the band. He's also got a fucking sharpness in his films that I like. I like detail. Every scene is like absolutely loaded with detail. It might be based on tits and arses, but this one won't be – [*Irish accent*] cos we don't have those objects.
Q: [*Laughs*] Really? When you were introduced to Russ Meyer, what did you think of him as a person?
JR: Bit pig-headed and stubborn. Um, he had some weird ideas about what I was about and he found out I was just as stubborn as him. I mean like he gave me rubbish like, er – I went through his script and it was a load of crap – [*putting on American accent*] 'Don't talk to me about films.' [*Normal voice*]

Giving me all that bollocks about he's been in the industry long enough, bla, bla. And that's when I lost respect slightly. Cos like ever since the first day we started that's all we heard from people: 'I've been in the music business years; you'll never get anywhere.' I mean like if you listen to those people you never will.

Fri 12 & Sat 13 August

. . . hassles with the flat [John's] – the landlord came round in the morning, 4 windows broken last night – I went round furious – Jimmy Lydon asleep on the couch upstairs, John & Nora downstairs – I burbled on angrily, John went out then Nora explained it was her, arriving late, pissed off at not getting in . . . Things eased. I sat around chatting a while, took John up to see the landlord & smoothed things over . . .

. . . Several phone calls, from Rory & people to deal with, the USA situation is hotting up, Artists & Warner Brothers in the lead with Branson fucking everything up – It's hard enough keeping Malcolm interested without Richard disappearing every time I try to make an appointment. Not to worry.

Mon 15 August

. . . M asked me to arrange a meeting with the band in the evening. Impossible. John unwilling. Steve & Sid unavailable – as usual. Only Paul turned up . . .

. . . shot off to see the Slits at Vortex, via the flat for a gobbled but beautiful meal. Jamie is totally into cooking since I bought The Pauper's Cookbook.

THE SECRET GIGS

Tues 16 August
. . . Boogie running around like a madman over these secret gigs. Virgin know, the rumours are strong.

Wed 17 August
What? MM [Melody Maker] carried our secret gigs on its front page. Minor freakout really, no dates or accurate places.

Q: Can you tell me how you feel about the recent tours and what the thinking is behind your secret appearances?
PAUL COOK: Yeah. Well, we decided to do these gigs like, just for one, cos we wanted to play anyway, and we hadn't played in England for such a long time. And we couldn't publicize them cos if we did some councillor might just come and say: 'Right, you're not playing here,' which they have done and they can do, for any stupid reason. So we decided to go to each individual promoter ourselves, who owned their private clubs and who could put us on without having to ask someone else, and told them to keep it secret.

But we knew enough word would get out so that people would know we were playing – which they did. So it weren't totally unfair on the fans anyway, cos most of them who wanted to see us come to see us. And all the places were packed out, so enough word got round for people to know we were playing.

Which was good, you know, cos there'd been a lot of complaining about not being able to see us at all. Cos when we done that other tour and when we used to play up North, it hadn't really taken off then. And we just used to get hostile audiences slinging things at us. But now there's thousands of kids who get into it and want to see us, and they haven't seen us at all.

your

FALLING APART

BOOGIE: Some of the places we have been gigging in are very small places, very small, where there have been only about 200 people. Some of the clubs in England have been shit holes where nobody would really like to play, no matter who you are. And when you are in those kind of places, um, you have to stay overnight in some small hotel. Obviously the band become pissed off, and they start getting restless and they start talking to themselves, you know.

Fri 19 August
Another dreadful day. All week cold & grey since the rain. RM & John so bad that M thinks the film impossible. Accounts & getting the band off to Wolverhampton. M in conference with Steven all afternoon. J & I wonder if he's discussing getting out of things completely. Who could blame him? The band must learn to hold themselves together by themselves instead of draining Malcolm, Jamie & I & Boogie. Jamie is really good with Malcolm – the only person who talks sense to him I think. I got too nervous to work (accounts still). Organized lifts to Wolverhampton . . .

. . . There was a bit of trouble – 2 fights . . . The Prefects got left out because of the aggro. SPs first 3 numbers were dreadful, then they were amazing . . . everyone pogoed & sang along. There had to be a line of heavies along the front of the stage. John loved it & really got off, as did the others. It was great. I got soaked & exhausted dancing.

Sat 20 August
. . . We watched the Crazy Gang on TV then I wandered off intending to get Sid & John off to see RM & Ebert [Hollywood scriptwriter] – called at Boogie's to get Sid's address. He lost his jacket (leather) keys & address book last night. Definitely nothing to do with me though I sympathize. No luck finding Sid.

Sun 21 August
. . . Laundry in the morning. Home for a drink at lunchtime. Off to the Other Cinema at 5 to see the Sex Pistols films, a band called ?? can't remember & the Slits. Boogie arrived with Kate. Good to see her. Boogie called me & Jamie a couple of cynical old failures – that's been rankling all night. I didn't even have the presence of mind to call him one too. Ray Stevenson was there – I should've smashed him up. Horrible, as usual. I don't enjoy seeing those films – it's slightly necrophiliac. Makes me feel it's time to move on. Tonight I feel like bedsit land & some crummy job where I don't have to think. As Jamie says, I'm lazy. The Slits were great – they have

some good songs, especially New Town which starts just with bass & Ari swinging up on the microphone. I left almost straight after. John was there with his entourage. I need a bottle of whiskey. What's up? Cynical old failures lurking in the back of my mind. Yes Boogie, & no you bigheaded cunt . . . Home. And here I am, alone, feeling down & dreadful. How to drag yourself out of this one? Drastic measures needed. Time to stop lying, get off & do what I want without compromise. But I still don't know what I want. I want all the highs of revolution & rock groups without the boredom of begging or hanging around starving. I've had it too easy, never had to work for anything. Time to organise, be disciplined, actually keep my mythical bottle of vodka for times like this. Boogie has got to be right for it to hurt so bad.

Mon 22 August
. . . find a message – urgent Jamie sees me . . . over to the pub:– M considering ways of selling off the band. Good idea probably? Maybe. The rest of the office furniture arrived. Now instead of looking so bare it looks like a fucking junk shop. Jamie & I went on talking till late. Malcolm (& Steve & Paul) are pissed off at the way Boogie & me & Jamie are so sycophantic toward John. True – we're partly responsible for his super-starness & feed his self importance & paranoia.

Wed 24 August
Up late. Pouring with rain. Cab up town. Sid fucked every one over by failing to turn up till 3.30 – they were supposed to leave at 12. No alarm clock he said. The final script is done . . . Emma found Sid a flat in Maida Vale, unfurnished, 7 year lease – (1984 it ends up). When I phoned Malcolm to OK it he said that's fine, he'll be dead by then. True enough . . .

As from the darkening gloom a silver dove
Upsoars, and darts into the Eastern light,
On pinions that naught moves but pure delight,
So fled thy soul into the realms above,
Regions of peace and everlasting love;
Where happy spirits, crowned with circlets bright
Of starry beam, and gloriously bedight,
Taste the high joy none but the blest can prove.
Keats, 'As from the darkening gloom a silver dove'

. . . Walked home – beautiful. Found lots of good spray painting sites round the National Theatre, good 'cos all the LWT people will see them, apart from the bourgeois shites who frequent the NT. Sky dark & grey as the buildings, down the short cut – makes the buildings feel natural – like trees. Patches of light blue over the river against black. Wanted a quiet evening – went for a drink with Elaine intending to come straight back but Jamie came, then Debbie & Tracie – blind drunk so it turned into a rowdy evening.

Thur 25 August
. . . really angry at *Time Out* Don Letts article that mug is so fucking snide. A year ago they wouldn't write about us. Now they side swipe at the New Wave elite while cashing in with their front cover.

Fri 26 August
. . . Fred, Malcolm & Gerry came in late & discussed the film. Julien, Emma, Jamie & me went for a drink leaving them to it – there's trouble with getting the money. Apparently the American moguls were freaked by the politics of the script. That sounds good to me.

Tues 30 August
. . . [Malcolm] rang the studio to persuade Sid about Pretty Vacant and GSQ on the album. Sid agreed. M: 'Tell John.' Rings John an hour later, Sid told him nothing as Jamie and I predicted. Long phone call, OK, but mad. Chatted about John & his mates – closed cases says Malcolm. And I think how about you? No bother. I really like him when he's tired. About the only time I can speak to him.

Sat 3 September
. . . Bought some patent leather boots – total change of personality. Now I feel arrogant & like kicking things. Can't do that with plimps. Dropped in on Boogie, Julien was there + 2 upper class friends of Boogie's. Didn't stay long but it was moderately constructive. Or am I just arse licking?

Here Sophie's diary ends, just as the band begins to disintegrate. And where the first edition of this book ended. In November '77, 'Holidays in the Sun' was released followed by the 'Never Mind the Bollocks' album. At this point also the band, who had up till then been more rumoured about than interviewed, began to fill the music and national press with their views – Sex Pistols press files explode around Autumn '77. As for McLaren's viewpoint, this is adequately represented in *The Great Rock 'n Roll Swindle*. Given all this, and our brief to document the story *behind* the headlines, we turned to Julien Temple for an account of the Pistols' last days – balanced by Al Clark, who was closest in the Virgin camp to the Pistols' day-to-day extinction and cannibalization ('Some Product', 'Carry on Sex Pistols', etc). Julien, who directed *The Swindle*, was a crucial presence and closer even than McLaren to the Pistols' demise (McLaren was frequently elsewhere, doing other things). As the hype and hysteria reached unprecedented heights, as the band scattered over the globe, as McLaren lost, one by one, the band's loyalty and eventually control of Glitterbest, Julien was not only there, he was (in our opinion) the only person to keep above the bitter personality, artistic and legal feuds.

24th Weds. up late. Pouring with rain. Cabs up town. Sid fucked every one over by failing to turn up till 3.30 – they were supposed to leave at 12. No alarm clock he said. The final script is done. RM has given me my typewriter back. Emma found Sid a flat in Maida Vale, unfurnished, 7 year lease – (1984 it ends up). When I phoned Malcolm to OK it he said that's fine, he'll be dead by then. True enough.

NEVER MIND THE BOLLOCKS

HERE'S THE SEX PISTOLS

NEVER MIND THE BOLLOCKS

AL CLARK: I think it was clear when we signed the Sex Pistols that their flame was going to burn brightly but briefly.
Q: Really?
AC: Yeah. I don't know if anybody voiced that but I think everybody felt it, subconsciously. It couldn't possibly survive because as soon as they made their first LP that was pretty much the end of it, because the whole idea of making an LP was counter-revolutionary.

I mean everybody was going on about, you know, singles are the thing, albums are part of the then-generation – and then they made an album.

Whenever you set yourself those targets, I mean those notions by which to live and then start failing to do so, then the paradoxes eat you up because having the attitude to begin with doesn't allow for paradoxes.

SEX PISTOLS RECORD "NOT INDECENT"
THREE MAGISTRATES, TWO OF THEM WOMEN, RULED TODAY THAT THE RECORD SLEEVE OF THE SEX PISTOLS' CHART-TOPPING ALBUM, WITH THE WORD "BOLLOCKS" IN THE TITLE, IS NOT INDECENT.
ADVERTISEMENTS FOR THE PUNK ROCK BAND'S RECORD — "NEVER MIND THE BOLLOCKS — HERE'S THE PISTOLS" — HAVE BEEN BANNED BY RADIO AND TV COMPANIES, ALTHOUGH IT IS NOW NUMBER ONE IN THE CHARTS AND HAS SOLD MORE THAN 200,000 COPIES.
TODAY, 25-YEARS-OLD RECORD SHOP MANAGER CHRISTOPHER SEALE, IN A TEST CASE BEFORE NOTTINGHAM MAGISTRATES, WAS ACQUITTED ON FOUR CHARGES UNDER THE 88—YEARS-OLD INDECENT ADVERTISEMENTS ACT.

Q: When you signed them was there any resistance from employees here?
AC: No. I think there was a certain amount of suspicion because by then the Sex Pistols had acquired their massive and menacing reputation and the folklore was deeply rooted. I mean some people were keener than others, let's put it that way.
Q: In the early days were relationships easy between you and the Sex Pistols and their management?
AC: Well, I think they were pretty good with Malcolm McLaren because his

DESTROYING THE GROUP

'Stop him,' Dallow cried: it wasn't any good: he was at the edge, he was over: they couldn't even hear a splash. It was as if he'd been withdrawn suddenly by a hand out of any existence – past or present, whipped away into zero – nothing.

Graham Greene, *Brighton Rock*

JULIEN TEMPLE: [During the autumn of '77] Rotten was increasingly annoyed with Malcolm not treating them as a band. And with Malcolm's obsession with the film which really didn't come from the band at all.

There was this really bad breakdown between John and Malcolm. Malcolm was definitely lying a lot to John. I remember being in a taxi where John was moving house and stuff and Malcolm said he'd been round knocking on the door and trying to get in touch with John all the time and John was saying it wasn't true, and we got in a taxi and went to John's house and John said: 'If you've been waiting outside my door, where do I live? Tell the taxi driver to go where I live.' And Malcolm didn't know at all where John lived.

I think what Malcolm was doing was very interesting at that point, but I think he was silly not to be aware that John and all the others needed a lot more support at that stage to go with what he was doing. He had to support them more, you know, just emotionally and intellectually, because they had been deluged with publicity and the tension of what was happening at the time, and they needed support from him, to go *with* him.

And I think John would have been much more amenable to doing what Malcolm was doing at that stage and the whole kind of idea of breaking the group up and not wanting to be just the same as the other rock and roll groups around at the time. Malcolm's idea was always that John was just becoming a star and stabbing everyone, the ideas, in the back by becoming, you know, too precious and inflated in himself. Which was true to an extent but it was largely true because he was allowed to drift away and that was his reaction to not being involved in decisions and things.

Q: What, in fact, was Malcolm trying to do at the time?

JT: He was basically trying to make a film which I think was his long-standing ambition. But he did, I think, even at that stage or increasingly towards the end of the Autumn, he did want to break the group up and finish with it. He was getting more and more bored with it. And certainly he told me before they went to America that they'd break up in America – you know, it wasn't a kind of spontaneous thing completely. I think Malcolm probably engineered a lot of that situation in America where it became impossible for Rotten to want to carry on or need to carry on.

But I think what was going on then was quite good in one way. I think it was right to destroy that group and the Clash are the living proof that it was stupid for those groups to go on to become pop stars in a real sense. I still think at that stage it was a total assault on the structure of how, not just in financial terms but in cultural and media terms, people received pop music, you know. And I think with varying degrees within the group people understood that. I think Sid understood it very well. They wouldn't obviously articulate it in any way. I think Rotten understood it very well too but was alienated increasingly from it purely because of the personal thing between him and Malcolm. I don't know whether Steve and Paul thought that much about it. I don't think they did.

Q: In spite of maybe wanting to destroy the group, he did continue to use them, didn't he, for certain aims and purposes?

JT: Well, he was very much using them to make a film and I think he could have made that film if he'd made sure the group, ie Rotten, were totally committed to it and were involved in it.

And I think that is the beginning of the period where Malcolm saw the group very much as his own construct – you know, he was beginning to see the group far too much as his own creation whereas, in fact, the time and a lot of other factors created that group as well as Malcolm, including the factor of Rotten and Sid, which were crucial I think.

Julien Temple

INVESTORS REVIEW

1977 REVISITED

and FINANCIAL WORLD

21st DECEMBER 1977 — 5th JANUARY 1978

ANARCHY IN THE USA . . . EXPLOSION

The Pistols successfully appeal after having been denied entry to the USA because of their criminal records.

SEX PISTOLS FANS IN RIOT

From JOHN BLAKE in Memphis, Tennessee

RIOTING crowds fought with police and smashed glass doors as trouble hit the Sex Pistols' tour of America today.

In another incident before the battle began, band member Sid Vicious went berserk and stabbed himself with a knife during rehearsals.

A police officer said after the concert that followed: 'I have never seen anything like this shower.

'They seem to be like a bunch of dangerous escaped lunatics. God knows what the kids see in them.'

The fighting began after 300 fans who had been sold £2 tickets for the show were told there was not enough room for them in the 600-seat Memphis ballroom where the Pistols were performing.

As they hammered on doors and windows, frightened staff called police.

By the time a convoy of squad cars arrived, the furious crowd had smashed two large doors.

Details of the Vicious incident were more mysterious.

But his stabbing was seen by Cincinnati disc jockey Spike Riley.

Bottle

He said: 'Sid arrived for a rehearsal at the hall with a bottle of booze in his hand and he seemed to find it hard to stay upright.

'Then he suddenly went completely berserk and started to throw chairs around. Next thing I knew he had stabbed himself in the arm with a knife.

'The wound was deep and there was a lot of blood.

'Some people who were with the Sex Pistols quickly tied a big bandage on to his arm.'

Though Vicious's wound appeared to be deep, he refused hospital treatment.

Vicious, who has previously admitted smashing bottles and grinding them into his chest and arms, refused to talk about today's stabbing.

But during the concert at the hall he stripped off his leather jacket to reveal

a large lint pad plastered to his arm. Suddenly he ripped off the dressing to reveal the gaping wound below.

Front page lead, *Evening News*, 7 January, 1978

ATLANTA – Alex Cooley's Great Southeast Music Hall
The doors open at 7. The show starts at 10 with 'God Save the Queen'. About half the audience is enthusiastic and do an American version of the pogo, the others hurl insults at the Pistols.
MEMPHIS – Talyesin Ballroom
The hall only holds about 700. Outside 200 people riot and smash windows trying to get in. The Pistols get on stage to a barrage of beer cans. The band launches into 'No Feelings'.
SAN ANTONIO – Randy's Rodeo
2,200 seats are sold out well in advance. During the proceedings a cowboy annoys Sid who attacks him with his bass guitar. Taken away by police, the cowboy is interviewed on TV where he denounces the Pistols as 'sewer rats with guitars'.
BATON ROUGE – Kingfish Club
The group is on top form. The crowd is enthusiastic joining in with 'EMI'. The Pistols finish the set with 'Anarchy in the UK'. Bizarrely, the audience showers the stage with money. Johnny and Sid pick it up after the show.
DALLAS – Longhorn Club
All through the concert Sid howls over the PA: 'All cowboys are queers!' This earns him several showers of beer cans. Punched on the nose by a girl, Sid lets himself bleed freely on stage for 20 minutes. Johnny Rotten has the flu.
TULSA – Caine's Ballroom
The Pistols' coach arrives during a blizzard which has practically shut down the town. In front of the hall religious fanatics try to stop punters going in. The show ends with 'Pretty Vacant'.
SAN FRANCISCO – Winterland
About 5,000 people turn up. The Pistols give a brilliant concert and earn an encore. They then give a memorable backstage party. It is their last concert together.

The date is 14 January 1978.

AL CLARK: When they went to America it was obvious they were going to have a hard time. They were signed to Warner Brothers who were used to a particular kind of, um, excess in their musicians. They don't mind musicians who drive motorcycles along corridors, um, cadillacs into swimming pools and beat groupies around the buttocks with live sharks – that's all within the accepted code of conduct for [*American accent*] 'rock and roll madness', as I believe the term goes.

The Sex Pistols were obviously going to unsettle them because their kind of, um, defiance was going to be different from that. Americans are very polite by and large – although the rude ones are correspondingly more rude as a result. They would find the Sex Pistols rude. They did. However excessive you are or however given to drugs and debauchery, they expect you to shake hands with them when you walk into a room. They expect just elementary courtesy which they wouldn't get from the group, partly because of the mood of the group and partly because obviously the whole tour was intended to offend as many people as possible.

And, as you know, the tour omitted the music centres like New York and Los Angeles and Chicago and so on. It was the South and then San Francisco and that was pretty much it. So it was, from all accounts, it was an absolute nightmarish tour: for the group because of the climate, for Warner Brothers because they'd never encountered anyone like them before, um, and for Malcolm, I suppose, because he could see it falling apart. And it did.

ROTTEN DAY FOR PUNKS

By NICHOLAS DE JONGH, Arts Reporter

In an outbreak of mystifying sensationalism the Sex Pistols succeeded in breaking the bounds of most things believable yesterday.

Johnny Rotten was reported from New York as saying that the group had broken up. And Sid Vicious was taken to hospital in the city after what was described by doctors as a 'drug overdose', having taken pills and alcohol during a flight from Los Angeles . . .

The Sex Pistols' wildest day, began with a report from Johnny Rotten that the group had split up. Malcolm McLaren, the Pistols' manager, could not be located . . .

Later Mr McLaren issued a statement on behalf of his company, Glitterbest. It said: 'The management is bored with managing the successful rock and roll band. The group is bored with being a successful rock and roll band. Burning venues and destroying record companies is more creative than making it.'

Guardian, 20 January 1978

Final scene from the unmade Meyer/Sex Pistols movie.

The story: Mick Jagger has been impersonating Johnny Rotten to rejuvenate himself. Jagger and his agent, Proby, hold a party to inaugurate Jagger's 'reincarnation' as Johnny Rotten. The Sex Pistols gate crash the party just as Mick is shot dead by a young girl – in revenge for Jagger's slaying of her pet deer, Bambi.

M.J. is mortally wounded. He begins to slip from Proby's arm. Already dead on his feet and now knowing it, he raises his hands to his face and tries to wipe off the blood there. The blood comes off, and so does his makeup, revealing his own death mask underneath.

Still total silence. M.J. topples forward off the stage and onto the floor, bouncing. The spotlight inanely follows him.

109 AN OVERHEAD SHOT
Shows his prone body on the floor in the spotlight.

The first and only person to move is Johnny Rotten. He walks slowly forward to the dead body. Looks down at it. Turns it over with the toe of his boot, so that the dead face gazes sightlessly skyward. Speaks so softly not everyone can hear.

JOHNNY ROTTEN
(down at the body)
Will success spoil Johnny? (pause)
No. He will waste, spoil, smash, blow up and destroy success! (freaking out and kicking the lifeless body of M.J.!)

Another pause. The room is hushed. Johnny Rotten looks slowly up, chest heaving from the exertion, and directly into the camera.

JOHNNY ROTTEN
(quiet again)
Did yer ever have the feeling yer being watched?

FADE OUT.

SUNTANS

AL CLARK: Steve and Paul stayed in Rio for a while, then came back with suntans which was when the whole thing started to get really comical because you can't adopt those stances and then not fail to be amused afterwards when some of the notions don't materialize. I remember around the time of 'Holidays in the Sun' I took a holiday, um, in the sun, and I thought: Christ, should I really be doing this? And it took me about two days to realize that I was just as entitled to my holiday in the sun as anybody else and bugger them. But when Steve and Paul came back from Rio looking so expansive and suntanned and you could see that they had really fallen for the Latin life and all the sort of excesses that go with it, then it all just seemed a bit joky.

The next few months they were just marking time. John went off to Jamaica with Richard Branson and a guy who worked here at the time called Rudi van Egmond – he was the promotion guy we had and he had become quite friendly with the Sex Pistols. And they went off to Jamaica to sign groups and I think John was unofficial advisor in the wings as he was the only one of the trio who knew anything about reggae. And they stayed in America, and Malcolm had by then decided to make this film, *The Great Rock 'n' Roll Swindle*, and John seemingly kept finding these cameras poking out from bushes as he sat around the swimming pool. And I suppose what Malcolm wanted really was film evidence of John seen sitting by a swimming pool. But I don't think he was ever filmed [*laughs*]. I think he spotted the camera just in time every time.

THE SWINDLE

JULIEN TEMPLE: Malcolm was still very keen to do a film and so we kind of decided that we should try and come up with a framework to use the documentary footage that we had collected. And that was the time of the Brazil thing where Steve and Paul had gone when Sid became ill and John had split the group. And Malcolm came back to England and we decided to go and film Ronnie Biggs with Steve and Paul and maybe Sid would come down there if he recovered.

And we went to Brazil with this camera crew. And we got drunk on the plane and thought up a kind of vague thing to do with Biggs there. Cos the idea was we were going to try to do something with each of the group in different corners of the world and different crazy situations on how to, to spend the money, how to waste the money . . .

But it was very difficult to film in Brazil really – just because of the Carnival and the fact that there were no cameras and things around – and the whole thing was very chaotic. And Biggs was a big let-down because he was, um, you know, very [*pause*] repentant. He wasn't like a bandit figure that I think Malcolm had expected really. And he was OK as a media figure, but as a dashing element in the film he was a bit of a let-down, although he was a nice guy and, you know, it was pretty good to have him singing with the Sex Pistols purely because of his media image, which is all we were really worried about.

Q: And was it hard to persuade him to do that?

JT: No. He'd do anything for money. And he genuinely got on with Steve and Paul. I mean they shared a very similar background and really very much got on with each other, which made it very easy.

Q: How much did he get paid?

JT: Er, I think he was supposed to be paid £2,000 as a fee for doing it plus a royalty of the record. But I don't know whether he did get paid that much. I hope he did – but probably he didn't.

Q: Really?

JT: I think he was really annoyed about that. He may have subsequently got paid but there was a certain phone call from him where he was most insistent that he hadn't been paid.

Q: Was there a problem in Malcolm getting hold of money at that point?

JT: Yes, there was an increasing problem with money. Very much so. In fact, yeah, it was a great worry. I don't know how much the Brazil thing was – it was very cheap, it was about £20,000 I think – but that was a lot of money to have spent then.

Q: How did he actually organize things money-wise? I mean was he running

on like a big overdraft or did he have any assets of his own that he could ever put up? How did he operate?
JT: Well, this was still money, I think, from the record deals – there was still money in the bank from those. But I think it must have been getting lower at that stage because I remember when we went to Paris – the next idea was to take Sid to Paris – and I remember there was a huge hassle to get £10,000 from Barclay Records and that seemed very important at the time. So there can't have been that much money around. Um, and Barclay did pay £10,000 towards that.

Paris was the second thing that we did. In the meantime we had been working on ideas and we'd come up with this idea of the Swindle: ten lessons that Malcolm would give. Cos at this stage Malcolm was beginning to get really bad press. You know, there were a lot of stories about that he had done it just for the money, and he'd taken all the money and he was a Machiavellian figure who'd exploited the innocent Sex Pistols. And so the lessons and the presentation of Malcolm was designed to really exaggerate those elements and make him seem very evil and make unbelievable things seem true by using real facts but exaggerating or lying, distorting them and blowing Malcolm up into a much more prescient figure, you know, having pre-thought everything out and planned it all, really masterminded the whole thing. Whereas, you know, it was really a much more spontaneous reaction to a series of crises each time. I mean there was an overall momentum of ideas that hung the thing together but it certainly wasn't pre-planned.

CRIME PAYS
It's a HIT
THE GREAT
ROCK 'N' ROLL
SWINDLE
45 RPM
STEREO
A
NO ONE IS INNOCENT
(A Punk Prayer by Ronald Biggs
Produced by Steve Jones
SEX PISTOLS
SEX PISTOLS
SWINDLE
Production
From the forthcoming film
THE GREAT ROCK

VIRGIN information

CONFIDENTIAL.   FOR INTERNAL USE ONLY.

SEX PISTOLS RIVER PARTY ... NOTES.

TOTAL BUDGET ... £1500. Virgin contribution £750.

Cost of boat .. £500.

Cost of food £3 per head.

A number of red paint aerosols will be made available to certain lunatics who will proceed to scrawl "Sex Pistols" over any available surface (this is impossible to cost at the moment, but ardent fans will no doubt get to work for a can of lager and a bent safety pin).

The full page Music Press ads. will hopefully consist of the Queen's head and the words "Sex Pistols" and "God Save The Queen' in the usual place, but as this particular ad. and indeed others of the same ilk will probably be banned by the respective journals, then we have another standby ad. which consists of a photograph of the Queen's head accompanied by a teacup. Both the band and myself feel that this is a very strong ad. in its own right. It would be nice to place four different ads. if enough acceptable ads could be found.

The 7-second TV commercial could go out any time at approximately 11.30 p.m. when a suitable preceding programme is found, and this ad. could be held back and placed at the time of release of the single or album. It could of course be repeated at any time thought judicious, and would also make a very good Teaser for the album if repeated at a very cheap rate.

We may also consider the giant Newscaster in Leicester Square for a day, a week, or more. One week would cost approx. £200, giving us 770 exposures and will be visible to approx. 980,000 people.

Film to be shown in disco continuously

No advertising as the boat will be cancelled. IF wrong people

No press release until after the event.

Keith to arrange for projector and screen

Warren Mitchell as disc jockey ?

Malcolm to provide PA

Cooke-Key working on 50 foot flag for boat

Security - Dave and Kevin (+ mates)

Fireworks at each bridge to be provided by rocket man.

Virgin press office and Sex Pistols office to oxchange guest by Friday mid-day. Discretion essential.

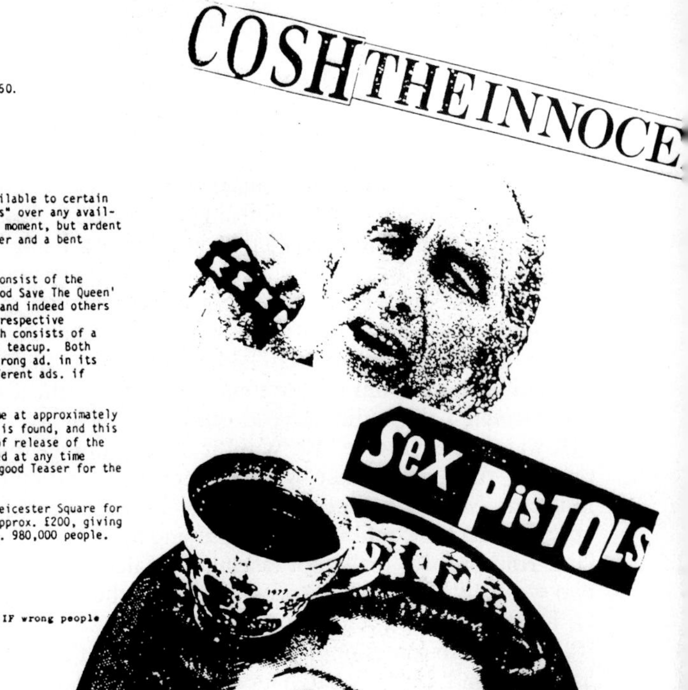

COSH THE INNOCE

Sex Pistols

GOD Save THE QUEEN

Richard Branson, the man who 'outswindled' McLaren, with items from Virgin's Sex Pistols publicity campaign.

SID VICIOUS: FILM STAR

JULIEN TEMPLE: And the next stage we did was take Sid to Paris and basically construct a sequence around him singing to a very, very bourgeois audience – cos at that stage the Sex Pistols were really being lauded as a kind of wonderful thing by a lot of people who they really shouldn't have been accepted by. And *The Swindle* was devised to undercut that and make the popularity that they'd had increasingly amongst people in the music press and so on, to really make them hate them again, which always gave you more flexibility, more room to move and do things with, if they were hated. And *The Swindle* I think did succeed quite well in that.

It wasn't meant to be 'My Way' at the beginning. It was meant to be 'Je ne regrette rien'. And that was an extremely difficult time with Sid and Malcolm. Sid – it's rather sad actually cos Sid insisted on doing this filming only if Malcolm would sign a thing saying he wouldn't manage him any more. Um. And Sid was really not talking to Malcolm at that stage. And we spent two weeks in Paris trying to get Sid to do the song and do the film.

Q: Did Malcolm sign anything like that?

JT: He did sign something, yeah, actually. I don't know what happened to it. I really don't know what happened. I'm sure it wouldn't have stood up either, but Sid, I think, may have believed that [it would]. I don't know. But Sid was really very, very difficult to work with, largely because of the heroin. But also he did have a great hatred of Rotten at that stage which was initially a thing that brought him together with Malcolm.

Q: What was that based on?

JT: Well, based on what Sid saw as Rotten completely copping out in America. Cos if you look at the material of America, Sid was really the one who was keeping the craziness going, you know, and making it more than just a rock and roll group. Um, and I think Rotten regarded him as an embarrassment. And Sid, certainly by that stage, knew he'd inherited Rotten's place really, you know, his importance. And he didn't like Rotten at all. Well, I mean he always liked him underneath but he was very let down, I think, by Rotten at that stage.

But this was mixed in with a complete drift away from any understanding of what the fuck was going on anyway because he was so out of it with drugs. And, um, Nancy really had control over the guy.

I remember we tried again and again to get him to sing 'My Way', for example, and even to start filming, and it was impossible. We spent two nights at a studio getting him to open his mouth – he wouldn't open his mouth. And, er, Steve Jones was flown over to try and help him do it and stuff. And I remember coming back to the hotel one morning, one morning

MY WAY

SEX PISTOLS

SID VICIOUS

From the forthcoming film

THE GREAT ROCK'N'ROLL SWINDLE

Production

after failing to get him to do it, and telling Malcolm – cos Malcolm didn't come to these things – Boogie and me and Steve were spending all the time with Sid. And Malcolm was in bed and we told him and Malcolm got very annoyed and rang down to Sid's room and started telling him, you know, that he was completely finished and that he was just a fucked-up junkie and he had no future of any kind and couldn't even get this together.

And while he was talking, Sid gave the phone to Nancy and Malcolm kept going on to Nancy and suddenly the door of the hotel, this kind of 18th century room in the Hotel Brighton on the rue de Rivoli, was kicked open and Sid appeared in his motorbike boots and swastika underpants and just jumped on Malcolm and started kicking Malcolm – who ran out of the room and along the corridor with all the laundry women saying, 'Oh, Monsieur! Monsieur!' and trying to stop him. And Sid was running down this corridor after him and Malcolm just got into the lift and Sid got into the lift and really started hitting him.

And Malcolm went home after that, just said: 'That's it. I'm going.' And left us with a French film crew to try and do it.

Q: And was he badly beaten up by Sid?

JT: Well, not physically badly injured. But, you know, I think mentally the force of the blows was very sharp and the guy's hatred was very clear, you know, through it.

So Malcolm went home then. And we hadn't even started filming. And what we had to do to make him do 'My Way' was change the words for him which Nancy helped to do a lot. And once he could understand that 'My Way' was going to be changed for him, he was fine with it. Cos the original idea, which wouldn't have been so good, was to have him sing it like Sinatra all the way through. And Sid was saying: 'I want to do it like the Ramones'. And the compromise was one verse, the opening part, in a traditional way and then we did it in a Ramones way.

Q: Why did Sid hate Malcolm so much? Did he talk about it?

JT: Yeah, he talked. His reason was – and I don't think it was a very good reason – his reason was that he was totally infested with a kind of rock and roll tradition by then, through Nancy and through the Heartbreakers, and his big gripe was that Malcolm would never let them play and never let them be a rock and roll group, which Sid really wanted to be, I think.

And he was also pissed off with the film with Russ Meyer, because it meant ignoring the group. Although he was very pleased, in the end, about the filming in Paris, because he knew he would be the star of the film and he was very concerned to try and perform as well as he could although he was quite ill and we used to have to really literally hide him away at times, to get the camera set up, drag him out, have him do the piece of acting and take him away again. Cos he was sometimes in a state where he would hit anybody on the street and with the knife that he had he would attack people.

We did a lot of filming in a Jewish quarter there where he was wearing the swastika T-shirt and that really freaked out the local people anyway, really caused a lot of antagonism. I mean I remember him doing terrible things.

Like he'd be lying around in his room and we couldn't get him out – we'd have the film crew there in the morning at nine o'clock or whenever and he would get up at twelve and lie around ordering drinks and things, and if the waiters brought him vodka and tonic instead of vodka and orange juice they'd be beaten up. And mirrors were smashed and he was banned from the hotel. We were all banned from the hotel.

And I remember when we were shooting, I remember coming back one day – and it was a lot to do with Nancy, because I remember coming back one day and she'd cut her wrists, there was blood all over the bed and she'd faked up a suicide attempt to really make Sid feel that he shouldn't leave her, even for a few hours, to do any filming. Um, she was really in a strange state as well. So that was really difficult. It was made slightly easier when Malcolm went but it was still very difficult.

Q: What was your feeling about working with Sid in that state?

JT: Er [*pause*]. Well, I mean just [*pause*] – I had bad feelings about it at times because he was so ill that it was actually physically difficult for the guy to do it. Um, but he did want to do it. And, you know, he was very . . . he'd always say if it wasn't right he'd do it again and stuff, you know, and he wanted to be as good as possible in it and he'd always ask: 'How was it? Did you think I was good?' and all this kind of stuff.

But it was just a bit sick, the whole situation, because we seemed to attract lots of junkies. I remember the first day before we shot we'd arranged a French film crew and we had a French production manager, all from French TV. And I went round to this production manager the next day and I knocked on the door and there was this incredible rummaging around and clinking and clattering and the guy shouted from behind the door: 'Who is it? Who is it?' and, 'Is it the police?' and all this kind of stuff. And I said, no, it was me, and he let me in and he sort of hurriedly cleaned up the place. But there was a guy lying on a mattress with a streak of vomit coming out of his mouth, a junkie who'd nearly died then, and this was the French TV production manager. And so I just had a feeling we were surrounded by this junk everywhere. And Sid was scoring all over Paris and they'd come for the money to the hotel and, um, it was all a bit sick, you know.

But the reason I was interested still in doing it was because I believed that Sid as a performer had a unique possibility to present things that no one else could present, in which, you know, I think he was tremendous. I think that in 'My Way' his performance was great.

SID VICIOUS: MEDIA STAR

VICIOUS IN A TRANCE
SEX PISTOL IS NEAR COLLAPSE AFTER 'I DIDN'T STAB HER' CLAIM

From LESLIE HINTON in New York

Sex Pistol Sid Vicious almost collapsed in court yesterday when he was accused of murdering his blonde girlfriend Nancy Spungen.

The 21-year-old spiky-haired punk star seemed to be in a trance as he was led into the New York court by a detective.

Before his appearance, Vicious denied killing Nancy, a 20-year-old American go-go dancer.

His lawyer, Joseph Epstein, contradicted a police claim that the punk rocker had confessed, saying: 'There is no basis for that report.'

Staggered

In court, Vicious was helped to a chair as he staggered and buckled at the knees.

His body shuddered periodically as he spent the rest of the 10-minute hearing with his head resting on a table.

Throughout, he seemed oblivious to the proceedings as he was formally charged with murder under his real name, John Simon Ritchie.

If convicted, he faces a prison sentence of 20 years to life.

Punk rock friends of Vicious sat in court during the hearing.

Singer Jerry Nolan wore earrings made of animal's teeth, a silver skull ring, and brass-studded bracelets.

A toy silver six shooter hung from his studded belt.

Half a dozen other friends with him were dressed similarly.

Front page lead, *Sun*, 14 October 1978

I WANT JUSTICE FOR MY SID!
SUN EXCLUSIVE

From LESLIE HINTON in New York

The mother of punk star Sid Vicious, who is accused of murdering his girlfriend, said last night: 'I want him to get justice.'

Chain-smoking Mrs Ann Beverley, from London, was talking to me exclusively after visiting 21-year-old Vicious in New York's tough Riker's Island Prison.

She said: 'He told me, "I didn't do it, mum." '

Sun, 16 October 1978

VICIOUS T-SHIRT ANGER

Sex Pistols manager Malcolm McLaren has been accused of cashing in on the stabbing death of Sid Vicious's girlfriend, Nancy Spungen.

McLaren faces criticism of some T-shirts which went on sale today at his King's Road boutique.

The T-shirts, at £6.50 each, show Vicious surrounded by a bunch of dead roses. Across the front are the words: 'I'M ALIVE. SHE'S DEAD. I'M YOURS.'

Evening Standard, 27 October 1978

Malcolm McLaren hurriedly flies to New York to arrange bail of 30,000 dollars. He also begins negotiations for the Sid Vicious story . . . the book, the film . . . you name it. Sid's bail is revoked after he is involved in a nightclub brawl. He is once again released . . . into the arms of his mother.

SID VICIOUS DIES IN DRUGS DRAMA
MUM FINDS HIM IN HIS GIRL'S ARMS

By CHRIS BUCKLAND and STUART GREIG

Sid Vicious, the tormented star of punk rock, died of an overdose of heroin yesterday.

He was found naked in the arms of his latest girlfriend in her New York flat less than twenty-four hours after he was released from jail on bail.

His mother, Mrs. Ann Beverley, took the couple a cup of tea in bed and frantically tried to wake Vicious.

The girlfriend, Michele Robinson, was completely unaware that he had died while they slept.

Front page lead, *Daily Mirror*, 3 February, 1979

DRUGS KILL PUNK STAR SID VICIOUS

From NIGEL NELSON in New York

Punk rock star Sid Vicious, the inadequate youth who turned a tasteless pop gimmick into pathetic real life, died of a heroin overdose yesterday.

His body was found after a party in his new girl friend's apartment in Greenwich Village, New York, held to celebrate his release from jail on bail – he had been accused of murdering his previous girl friend 'Nauseous Nancy' Spungen, with a knife.

Front page lead, *Daily Mail*, 3 February, 1979

I HELD SID'S HEROIN
ANOTHER EXPRESS EXCLUSIVE
PAUL DACRE in New York

The mother of Sid Vicious revealed yesterday that she looked after his heroin supply on the night he died.

Londoner Ann Beverly, who discovered her son's body in his Greenwich Village apartment, spoke of the fix that led to his death.

But she added: 'I know he didn't have any more that night, because I had the packet in my pocket.

'Besides, there wasn't any works (slang for a heroin syringe). The works they used earlier had been taken away.

'There is no way Sid could have slipped the smack (heroin) from my pocket. He wasn't like that. He would have waited until next day and said, "Can I have some more?" '

Daily Express, 5 February 1979

AN AMAZING MESSAGE FROM SID VICIOUS – I DIDN'T KILL NANCY
DAY ONE OF A REVEALING SERIES
By JEAN RITCHIE

SHE WAS BLEEDING AND I WAS SCARED!

In a candlelit, incense-filled room, a plump, dark-haired woman scrawls obscenities on a pad.

She frowns, groans in pain, and the pen leaps across the page. The words she writes are violent and blasphemous.

Sid Vicious, dead for fifteen months, is telling the world his own story.

Telling how he died, at a squalid heroin party to celebrate his release on bail from prison.

Kim Tracey, the 41-year-old medium, is contacted by Sid through involuntary scribbling.

She sits with her pen poised above a large empty page, and waits until her hand starts to move, guided by Vicious.

At first she doodles. An arrow symbol keeps appearing throughout the eight pages of writing.

Scrawled

'It could be a knife symbol,' she says, later.

Then the words start to appear, scrawled in an untidy, barely legible way, with no punctuation.

Sid Vicious' mother has no doubts that it IS her son who has been in contact through medium Kim Tracey.

And now Mrs. Anne Beverley wants to arrange a meeting so that she can talk to her dead son again.

Mrs. Beverley, 49, cried as she read the words that had been written by the medium.

Daily Star, June 2, 1980.

Anne Beverley, mother of Sid Vicious, doesn't think of her son as Sid – but Simon, the name she gave him at birth.

He was her little lad, the boy she adored.

When he died last year, she had nothing to remember him by other than the paraphernalia of a punk rocker.

The photographs she had of him as a child, the lock of hair lovingly kept, had all been stolen from a box under her bed. Then at the back of a drawer she discovered some photos she'd long since forgotten about.

Thrilled, she made her own family album. Later, the proud mum showed it to Virgin Records, and now the album has been published for Sid Vicious fans. It goes on sale, price £1.95, in September.

Daily Mirror, 9 August, 1980

OUR FOREIGN CORRESPONDENT WRITES:

Top show biz moguls and TV personalities were convicted last week of eating Viciousburgers at New York's prestigious Studio 54 Disco in court hearings last week, after the latest of a series of Vice Squad raids on the 'playground of the idle rich'.

Virgin Record company boss, Richard Branson, 37, TV personalities Dick Clark, 55, David Frost, 42, and several journalists, including Michael Watts, 38, editor of a music paper, were seen consuming several burgers each in what has been described as 'an orgy of vampirism'. 'It was horrific!' said clubgoer Richard DeNunzio of Brooklyn, 'They had several corpses in their mouths.' More showbiz and media names, including some well-known News Reporters, are expected to be convicted as the hearings continue.

The last few years has seen an increase in this bizarre cult of vampirism, of which the Viciousburger is only the latest example. Vampires are noteworthy for consuming star corpses in the form of burgers in the mistaken belief that some of the star's charisma will rub off on them: sadly, as you can see, these attempts are doomed to failure and these cultists deluded. The cult is said to have begun in the 50's with Deanburgers: these were very rare, and contained bits of Porsche wreckage and sunglasses – those cultists still alive who tasted them say 'They were tough but tasty'. Perhaps the worst outbreak of vampirism in recent years before the Viciousburger scandal was the Presleyburger scandal of 1977. The scandal was discovered when an attempt was made to steal Presley's body from the grave by occultists: the body was already stolen! It now appears that it was minced down and turned into the bizarre cult food, Presleyburgers. These are said to be very expensive ($1000 a throw) and high on fatty content, but it still didn't deter the thrill seeking showbiz crowd: Mick Jagger was said to have eaten several before his recent Wembley Concert. Heavy prison sentences imposed in Canada on Keith Richard, another vampire, stopped the spread of this disgusting cult, but with the present Viciousburger scandals it seems to be flourishing. And even now, there are unconfirmed reports of Curtisburgers, gristly burgers with hints of rope and marble. There is no truth, however, in the rumour that Hitlerburgers are freely available: they were only available post-war and reserved for VIP's.

from the Jamie Reid Collection, Victoria and Albert Museum

MALCOLM McLAREN: FILM STAR

JULIEN TEMPLE: It was a very, very unpleasant experience making the film because Malcolm and Vivienne were really against me making it really.
Q: Why?
JT: Well, I don't know why – I don't know why. I mean I think they wanted to do it themselves and, er [*pause*] . . . I don't really know why. I mean [*pause*] I mean I think Malcolm probably distrusted me in lots of ways. Um [*pause*] . . . But just, you know, it was very difficult. I'd feel his arm – he'd pinch my arm [*demonstrates with finger and thumb round upper arm*] and, er, then tell me that he'd sacked me, you know.

He didn't like the people I had working on it either. I had some people who I'd brought in who I'd known at the film school and stuff and he really didn't like them.

I think really it stemmed from the fact that despite a lot of things I pushed him to keep it going. I was, you know, nowhere near as prestigious a person as Russ Meyer and, er, I was inexperienced. But we were all inexperienced. I mean he was as inexperienced a producer as I was a director.

And we kept changing things on the day so that we went over. It was a very, very disorganised shoot. It was a nightmare shoot. Everything took longer. I remember one day Malcolm didn't arrive until one o'clock when we'd been waiting since nine. And there was one day that was a real fuck-up because it rained and we had a helicopter waiting all day and then when it ' egan to rain we couldn't film because the rain would get knocked into the windscreen. And that was expensive and I was heavily bollocked for not having filmed first thing in the morning. And he can be very unpleasant, you know, that's all I can say.

And he was very unpleasant during the shooting a lot of the time. Even more so during the editing.
Q: Can you give me some more examples of it. I mean when you said he gave you a bollocking, I mean what actually happened?
JT: Well, he'd tell it in front of everybody that he was sacking me, you know, shout at me and say: 'You're going to be fired,' you know, 'Tomorrow I'm going to replace you.' Er, which is not a nice thing in front of a crew you don't know particularly well but you're trying to make a film. [*Laughs*] Er, he'd just interrupt, you know, whenever I was directing he would grab hold of, this funny pressure business, like bony fingers in your arm like that [*demonstrates again pinching of upper arm*] as you were talking to someone else

and he'd expect immediately for you to stop talking to them and talk to him. He'd change things that we'd agreed and he was just very, very negative about everything. It was a constant battle to keep him enthusiastic.

And then he had tremendous problems as an actor. In the bathroom sequence, which was a very short little piece, he couldn't remember the lines at all. And we had little idiot boards all over the ceiling – you know, each one had a couple of words on – literally everywhere.

The first day it was terrible. On Tower Bridge. He just couldn't remember the words again and we were there all afternoon. It was getting worse and worse and he said: 'Look, if I have a bottle of whisky I'll remember the words.' He drank a whole bottle of whisky and got even worse. [*Laughs*] I remember it was [*imitating Malcolm's drawl*]: 'The Sex Pistols choose a current event and exploit it to the hilt.' And he was getting slower and slower – he couldn't remember the words – and getting redder and redder. And that was the first day and that was terrible. We never really recovered from that.

And, er, he was hard to direct because he'd blame *me* for the fact that he couldn't remember his words. But it was very hard to help him and I tried to help him as much as I could.

Also, I think one of the problems was that Malcolm started believing the kind of things that we'd dreamt up to say about him, you know. He really did feel that he was some kind of Situationist genius who had planned the whole thing.

Situationist theory, a kind of intellectual terrorism, was basically a total critique of everyday life in Western Bourgeois society. It achieved its greatest triumph during the revolutionary events in Paris in May 1968 when Situationist philosophy was momentarily put into practice by the masses. Although the Situationists no longer exist as a coherent force their ideas continue to influence thinkers and activists throughout the world.

Dictionary of Modern Art

Q: So why did Malcolm come to see you as traitor?
JT: I was a traitor when I refused to become a slave, basically.
Q: Oh really.
JT: Yes, I think that's, that's the point. I mean he then fired me again on the phone in the most extraordinary invective I've ever heard. I mean, you know, he was calling me a middle-class arsehole and telling me that he'd raised me – which is a contradiction in terms – that he raised me from the gutter and saying that he'd checked out with the film school and they knew I was totally talentless and, you know, absurd things.

I mean, you know, it goes against completely what I thought the guy was about, like he would worry about what people at the film school – I mean apart from lying about the fact, what does it matter what my fucking professor at the film school thought? I hadn't been there for two years.

And I was just holding the telephone up like that and Jamie was in the office then and Sophie and they couldn't believe what was going on, you know, it was quite stunning. It was especially dispiriting because I believed very strongly in our working relationship and in the whole project. And, you know, it just became absurd this stuff about public school fascists. You know, there's not that much difference between an art school fascist and a public school fascist.

And I remember this really horrible cutting room in Berwick Street, a real slum of a cutting room. On the staircase Malcolm was looking down. I'd walked out. Malcolm was looking down on the rim, he was screaming down. 'You work as a slave!' was echoing around. I thought fuck this. You know, that was it.

I mean he was really under a lot of pressure then because this was just around the time Sid died and it was also the background of the court case, and he was doing very odd things at that stage. He was thinking that people were going to shoot him and things like that and, er, he was packing all his clothes, trying to go away. And Vivienne was very worried about him at that stage. I mean he looked extraordinary. He looked terrible. His face was completely bright red all the time.

I did see him once again actually in a preview theatre looking at a roughcut of it some time later, but he didn't talk to me and I didn't talk to him either, but lazer beam eyes, sort of horrible contact of the eyes.

The end was a very sad time, sad time. Cos I don't think anyone there betrayed it in any way. They may have got fed up with Malcolm's increasing belief that he was what he was supposed to be in *The Swindle*, you know, which was becoming patently more and more absurd. Especially, you know, when John was crunching all over him in the courts and things and the whole megalomaniac aspect of it was falling to pieces.

The empire of the Sex Pistols had gone.

It was no dream; or say a dream it was,
Real are the dreams of Gods, and smoothly pass
Their pleasures . . .

Keats, 'Lamia'

PART 2

THE CHARACTERS

JOHNNY ROTTEN

GLEN MATLOCK: We did this gig with Screaming Lord Sutch and we was using the PA and their equipment with their microphones. And John broke about three microphones. Smashed them. And after we'd been off the guy from the Screaming Lord Sutch band come and he said: 'You broke our microphones.' John said: 'I didn't.' And he swore blind that he hadn't broken them. But I'd seen him, like a minute before, really like pummelling them into the ground. And he completely denied it. And he believed it as well. I just couldn't understand it. He'd always do things like that. He was like terrible in a way. He'd like say something, and five minutes later he'd completely forget that he'd said it. And he'd believe it, he'd believe that he hadn't said it. And no matter what you said to him, he wouldn't change his mind. Real crazy.

DAVE GOODMAN: John's unpredictable. He used to go through different sorts of moods. He'd like to sit up all night if he could, talking. He didn't like sleep that much. He liked eating good food. He'd like drinking – Guinness or whatever – and he'd like rapping to people. He liked starting arguments or debates. Some people he'd totally ignore and just take the piss out of and put down, and other people he'd find interesting and go to great lengths to find out more about them.

Q: What did he like discussing?

DG: Religion used to come into it a lot. He used to like talking about his past. It really used to vary – a bit of American politics, just about people in general, about narrow-minded people, about the state of the country, about the state of the education system . . .

Q: What would upset him?

DG: If he couldn't get his own way, that would upset him, stupid people. But when he was in a mood no one used to take any notice.

I remember one time when he wanted to sit in the front of the van. We stopped at a petrol station. We all got out. And he'd been in the back – I suppose he thought it was his turn in the front – but when he came back from the toilet someone else was sitting in the front and he had to climb over the front seat to get into the back of the van. And he just wanted to sit in the front. I think it was Glen who said: 'No, get in the back,' and we said: 'Come on, we've got to get to this gig, stop pissing around, don't be childish, get in.' And he really threw a tantrum. And we just found it so funny that it just wore off after a while.

If John's in one of his moods, it's just John. You know, he can be in a good mood one minute, a bad mood the next minute. It's all part of his style which you just learn to accept.

He can be really annoying sometimes. If he was in a mood where you couldn't have an ordinary, everyday conversation with him, everything you'd say he'd pick up and throw it back at you and make you feel stupid, or ignore you in a way where you're sure you're wasting your time talking to him.

Sometimes he'd get like that, yet other times it would be: 'Ah, are you going to stay up tonight and talk? I don't want to go to bed. Go on.' And we'd sort of read the Bible to one another and just go over certain bits and discuss what we felt. Old Testament.

. . . a face of starved intensity, a kind of hideous and unnatural pride.

Graham Greene, *Brighton Rock*

. . . Even Iggy Pop at his most manic could not compare with J. Rotten for the most chilling, manic, dangerously demented vocalist since even God wouldn't know when.

Rotten tears his throat into a thousand pieces, with his face keeping close time with his eyes which look totally crazed. It scares the shit out of you!

He moves around the stage like some twitching convulsive who seems to be waiting to pounce on the first person who notices his freak condition. Freaky but fascinating and although he doesn't move with the timing of a Jagger or hit the notes of a Plant, Rotten puts more effort into a forty minute set than Led Zeppelin total in a three-and-a-half-hour performance.

His eyes look so glazed, his menace so unbelievably disturbing, that you seriously wonder if there isn't some pathological monster straining inside him to get out.

Ross Stapleton, *Sounds*, 30 July 1977

She said with sad conviction, 'He's damned. He knew what he was about. He was a Catholic too.'

He said gently, '*Corruptio optimi est pessima.*'

'Yes, father?'

'I mean – a Catholic is more capable of evil than anyone. I think perhaps – because we believe in Him – we are more in touch with the devil than other people. But we must hope,' he said mechanically, 'hope and pray.'

Graham Greene, *Brighton Rock*

GLEN MATLOCK: John's pretty serious, but I think he takes it with a pinch of salt. Although he doesn't let on, cos if he did his thing would be like cut in half. If people could see that he was treating it like a joke, then he wouldn't be so strong.

He sat perfectly still with his grey ancient eyes giving nothing away.

Graham Greene, *Brighton Rock*

JOHNNY ROTTEN [with friends]: You know what Malcolm's like. Ace controller. Nobody controls me, dear.
Q: Well, that's, that's really why I want to get your point of view because I think it's a different one from Malcolm's.
FRIEND: Make a change to read a nice truthful book.
JR: It will probably be totally boring.
[*General laughter*]
Q: I don't think so because . . .
JR: How people love lies. [*Puts on Northern accent*] That's fucking trouble. [*Normal voice*] Don't they? People like to read a load of garbage: Oh look, they're junkies and drug takers, orgies every night.
ANOTHER FRIEND: That's not bullshit.
[*General laughter*]
Q: You say that the press have misrepresented you. Can you say a bit about that?
JR: They either over-exaggerate how good we are on certain nights or like completely put it down. Like ulterior motives . . . Certain press people like, cos we won't pay for them to like come and see us abroad, right, will write a slag-off article. They're all hypocrites and bastards, the lot of them. And they drop you just like that if they don't get cash. And, you know, like all the earlier ones who supported us like then suddenly like tried to make names for themselves. They're just parasites. You know, they expected us to like give them free trips up North to see us, free hotel accommodation, food and a wage. What's that about? If you write an article on the band it should be fucking honest – your own opinion. Don't expect to get paid for it.
Q: A lot of people have said to me though that people like Caroline Coon and John Ingham, that they really did you a favour, that they really kind of stuck their necks out in the first place. I mean is your criticism directed against them?
JR: Doing me a favour? Like a hand-out? If anyone done anyone a favour we done them a favour. Else they'd still be the same miserable people. Now they're even worse, I think. John Ingham's all right. Caroline Coon, I don't know about. I don't know nothing about her. She's all right. She gets confused. She gets into social implications which just aren't there. Can't talk nonsense like that.
Q: You've been quite critical about education in general in this country.
JR: Fucking hell, who isn't? Yeah. It's shitty.
Q: In what respect?
JR: They brainwash you. They don't educate you. They don't teach you nothing. Everything you learn you learn yourself. They try and take away your brain. They try to make you like, er, everybody else. Just one great mass that's easily controlled. They don't like individuals. They don't like

John Lydon . . . before and after.

people who stick up for themselves. If you have an opinion at an early age in secondary school they fucking get you for it bad. And they tend to be the ones who turn out the most violent. Most crooks, criminals, fucking tealeafs are all, they've all got suss up there.
FRIEND: That's right.
JR: That was their only way out.
Q: Was your own school particularly guilty, because you were at a Roman Catholic school weren't you . . . ?
JR: Oh, Roman Catholic schools have an even worse way of destroying you. Religion, religion and religion. You're not allowed a point of view and all that. At 12, I just said I wouldn't go to their silly masses every morning. So they tried to get me out of the school. [*Irish accent*] But that's not democratic, is it? [*Normal voice*] And I didn't go along with the way they taught for like exams. It was rubbish. Teach you how to fail. I proved that. I mean I passed like every exam I took with ease and that was without going to school, cos they kicked me out. So I went back and took the exams.
Q: You were doing 'O' levels then?
JR: Yeah. [*Pause*] That really unnerved them. I mean I even saw the school report they had of me. You should have seen what they had written down: Hell's angel, like drug taker.
[*Everyone starts to talk at once*]
Q: Did you do English 'O' level? [*JR nods*] What books were you studying?
JR: I didn't study them. I read them once. I didn't need to read them any more.
Q: What were they?
JR: [*Melodramatically*] *Macbeth*. [*Bored*] Keats' poetry. And, er, what was the other one – [*drawls*] *Brighton Rock*, Graham Greene. Complete rubbish. I mean, look, I just read them once and got half an idea of what the story was about and made the rest up. Used a few clever words which you get out of the dictionary the night before and made it sound like you know what you're talking about. You've just got an English Literature. [*Friends laugh appreciatively*]

You just cheat. History was the same. I remembered about two dates and I managed to like bluff it the rest of the way through: 'Shortly after then' . . . 'a couple of months later' . . .
[*General chuckles*]
Q: Has that kind of affected your attitude towards books and reading, I mean are you able to . . . ?
JR: No, it hasn't affected me at all. I just don't like reading anyway.
Q: You don't?
JR: It's just the way *they* try and do it. They don't get you interested in anything. They make the lessons as boring as possible. There's just no

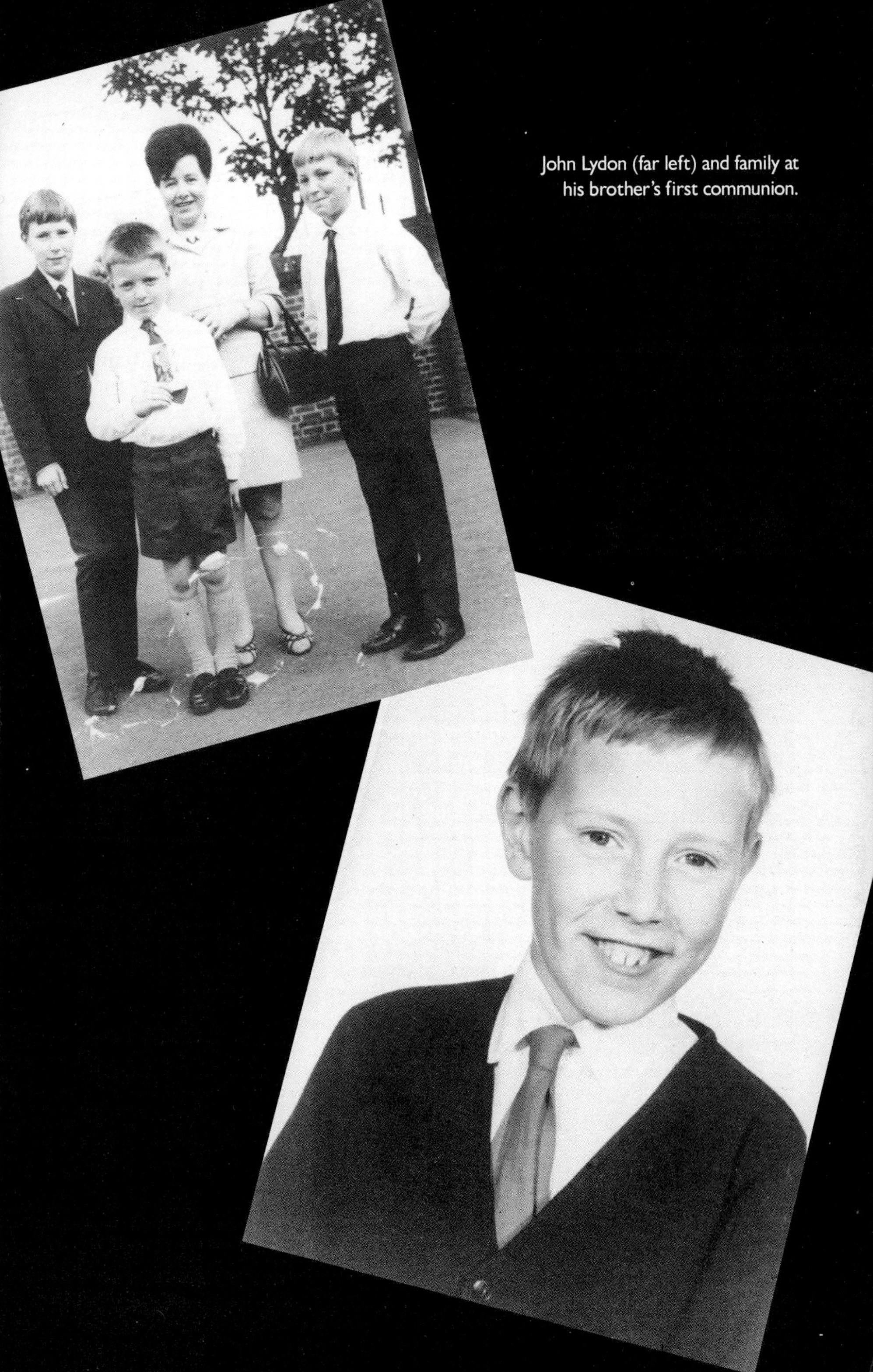

John Lydon (far left) and family at his brother's first communion.

interest. You just don't go. Ridiculous.
FRIEND: When you look at the size of the classes as well, when you think there's about 45 kids in a class . . .
JR: And the teacher's attitude.
FRIEND: In our school . . .
JR: If the teacher's a boring old bugger who hates you anyway cos you're younger than him or something like that – forget it. I think there was only one lesson that I ever like kept awake all the way through, that was maths. That was cos the Irish mad bastard used to whack the living daylights out of us with a cane. [*General laughter*]

[*With Irish accent*] That weren't so funny. [*Laughter subsides*] He died of cancer. Everybody hated him. Like when he died it was all: 'Oh, he was a really good teacher.' He got results all right in exams cos he'd fucking tell you the answer.
FRIEND: Yeah. Or belt it into you.
Q: So afterwards, you went to technical college. Did you stay for a whole year at technical college?
JR: Technical . . . is that what they call it? That's a very polite way of saying it was a shit hole.
FRIEND: It wasn't a technical college, was it?
JR: No.
FRIEND: No, it was a college for further education.
JR: I went to Hackney first . . .
FRIEND: Oh that was a technical college.
JR: . . . they kicked me out of there. That's where I met Sid. Cos we never used to go really. Then we both went to Kingsway [College of Further Education].
Q: And what were you studying there? Or what were you supposed to be studying?
FRIEND: Boozography.
JR: I was studying pints of ale in the [*Irish accent*] local pub. [*Laughter*]
FRIEND: Yeah, that's true. Cos I used to come off the building site every day, *every* day, you know. And he'd be standing in there from 11 till three.
JR: It's easy money, isn't it? Get your grant. I had a load of money then, anyway, from illicit deals. [*Small laugh*]
Q: What course were you doing though?
JR: 'O' levels and English 'A' which I thought was the biggest load of bullshit I ever had to suffer in my life.
Q: What was on the syllabus for that year? Probably more Shakespeare . . .
JR: Shakespeare. All the trendy poets and writers, like all English stuff, all that fucking rubbish, just nonsense. Oh and a new modernist poet called Ted Hughes, ur hur.
FRIEND: Must have been something wrong with it because every person who

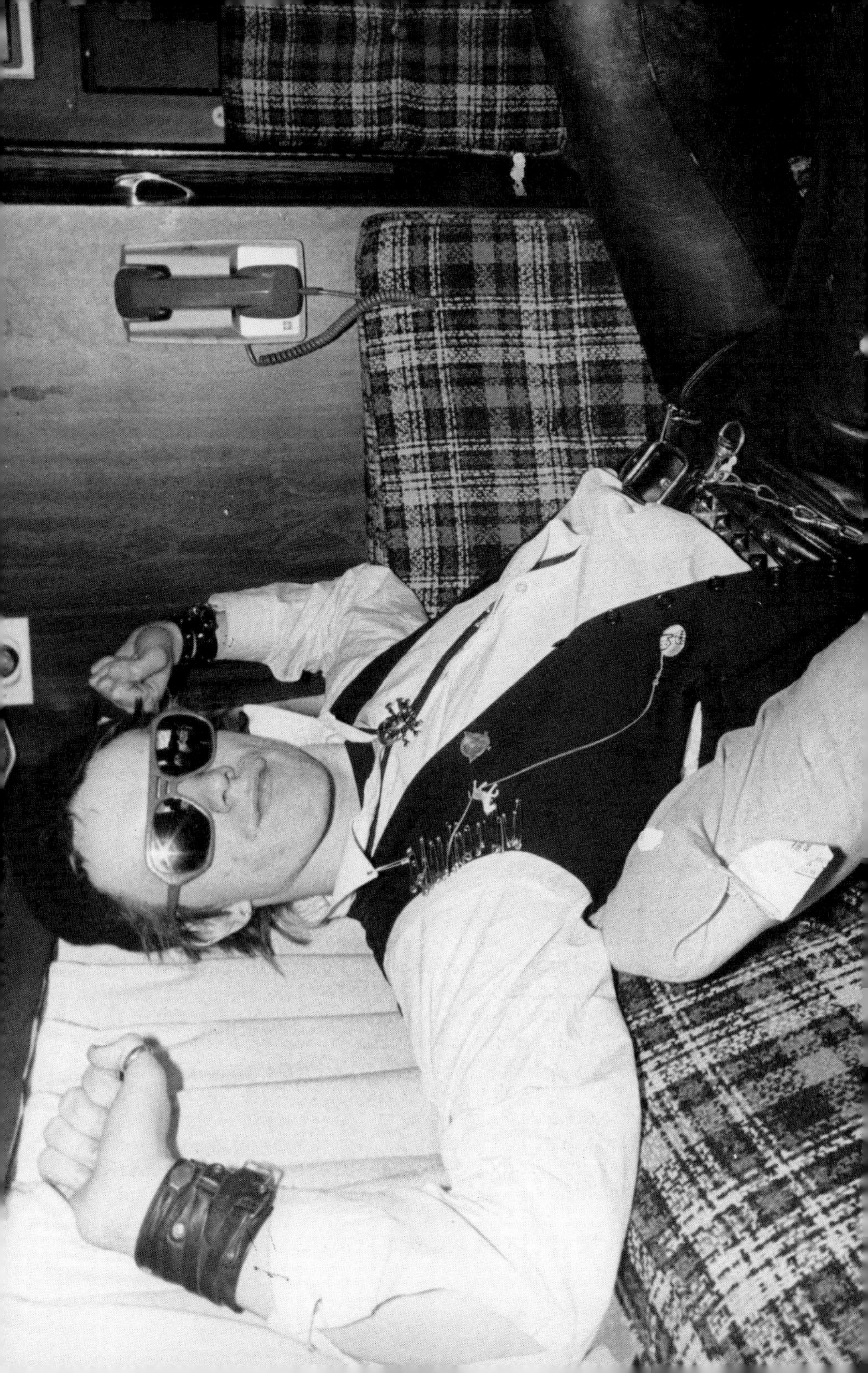

was in that college used to be in the pubs. Didn't they? Every person used to be in the pubs. They were packed solid, Monday to Friday.
JR: Yeah. Ten per cent attendance.
FRIEND: Yeah, and every one of them passed their exams. Didn't they? Remember all the dopes I used to go to school with? Dopey. Like the lowest in the class. All of them. 'O' levels, 'Z' levels, you name them, they got them.
JR: You don't need to be clever to fucking pass an exam, you've just got to have a bit of suss. Either an incredible good memory or you can suss out the bullshit. You can tell what they expect of you by reading the question, say, 'Why is this book so good?' Aaarrr. Learn not to criticize. That's why I don't like 'em you see, exams.
Q: Can you tell me a bit about your first contact with the band? How did that come about?
JR: It was through the shop. They used to watch me going in there. Thought I was a raving lunatic. Cos that's when I used to wear all that safety pin gear. About three years ago, four. Like after about a year they asked me to join. [*Pause*] I get bored with clothes. It's only clothes.
Q: What was it about the shop that attracted you to it? I mean, why did you used to go in there?
JR: Cos it was so fucking different. I thought it was good gear. It says something good about someone who'll wear that kind of gear like and fucking fight back if someone laughs at them. Cos when you look like that and someone takes the piss and fucking . . . you hit back. I mean you can chase off entire mobs cos they think you're mad. But then it became a real middle-class place and I hated that. [*Sniffs*] And now it's got even worse. They just raise their prices. That's why the shop gets kicked in every week.
Q: In what sense is it middle-class?
JR: Cos they're the only people who can afford it.
FRIEND: It's like them trousers Paul's got on in there. What are they, £35, £45?
ANOTHER FRIEND: 150 quid for a bondage suit. Terrible, isn't it?
FRIEND: No it's 65 quid for a bondage suit, i'n'it? Or 75? [*Picture comes up on TV which has just been switched on*] One all, Arsenal. One all.
ANOTHER FRIEND: No them tartan ones are 60 quid for a jacket and . . .
JR: See, when I went years ago it was like real cheap prices. You could get a T-shirt for two quid.
FRIEND: Cos it's trendy now, they've put the prices up.
JR: Now like Malcolm's left the shop, he has nothing to do with it. It's Vivienne. Since Malcolm left the prices went up. Dramatically. Malcolm you know like devotes all his time to the band. He has nothing to do with the shop at all.
Q: One of the things that the band is reputed to be is anti-sex, in the sense

that you don't play on sexual emotions in your performance. Is that true?
JR: No. I think you mean love.
Q: Oh, is that what I mean? [*Laughs*]
JR: Yeah. Definitely not anti-sex. Wouldn't be called Sex Pistols if it was anti-sex. I hate love. There isn't a love song in us. There's piss-takes of them: [*Northern accent*] Luv, true luv, runs deep like the ocean. [*Normal voice*] We *don't like love*. It's bullshit.
Q: Doesn't it exist, or is it something you despise if it does?
JR: Love is a lust. It's as easy as that.
Q: A lust for what though?
JR: It's greed, i'n'it? Selfishness. Marriage. I mean if you're going to live with someone then live with them, but why do you have to have a fucking legal document in between it, so that you can't separate if you want to. That's lusty. That's lustful. That's vile. That's horrible and crude and evil. You're signing your life away. Death sentence. [*To Debbie who appears in doorway*] I'd love a cup of tea, thank you. Can I have a cup of tea, Debbie?
DEBBIE: Er, no.
JR: Oh, go on, make it.
DEBBIE: Oh all right, seeing as you're doing an interview.
JR: Thank you, Debbie. *The* Debbie. Thank you, Debbie, juvenile film star. [*General laughter*]
DEBBIE: [*From the kitchen*] Bollocks!
Q: The other thing, apart from being anti-love, is the anti-star thing.
JR: I despise stars. They're bullshit people. They live in their rich mansions, fucking completely out of touch with reality. They know nothing about real people any more. They're just drugged-out arseholes.
Q: Terry Slater at EMI, you know the bloke who did the publishing deal, thinks that you're all going to become like that, that there's no other way for you to go.
JR: Yeah, exactly. That's their reasoning. It has to be that way because it happened that way before. Well like where we can reverse it – it's only one generation have become stars and that's the sixties bands. Before them like rock 'n' rollers, I mean they weren't out of touch, were they? They kept their roots. Cos they had it in them. It's all the sixties bands have just got bullshitty: I'm out of it, man – cloud nine stuff. It affected their brains, if they had any to start with. And [*funny accent*] we're learning from them.
Q: You as a band, or you and your management as well?
JR: Yeah, well you have to, don't you. I mean they are the management.
Q: Yeah, but somebody like Fisher [Pistols' solicitor], he strikes me as belonging to the world of business and not to . . .
JR: Oh, yeah, he works like in other businesses, but he's part of Glitterbest, the company that works for the Pistols. Malcolm is Glitterbest. The Pistols

are company owners. Glitterbest cannot exist without the Pistols. It's a subsidiary. Like when bills come, they go to Glitterbest, not to the Sex Pistols. It's a devious way of beating your tax man, holding him off, rotten bastards.

Q: So are you a company, the Pistols?

JR: Yeah, you have to put yourself down as a company or else they'll fucking fleece you for every halfpenny you've got. I mean they're fucking doing that right now. [*Pause*] And if we didn't have someone like Fisher I mean we'd just be easy pickings. That's the reality of the situation. The music business is full of cunts. I hate the lot of them. Evil. They try and fuck you up in every way possible.

Q: Deliberately or unconsciously?

JR: Bit of both. Many unconsciously. They don't even know when they're cutting your throat. To them the band is just another piece of fodder for that week. A new item to sell. New article of clothing. Like we have all our own artwork, our own promotion, so they can't interfere with that.

Q: Can you describe a typical day for you?

JR: I don't usually get up during the day. I'm usually in bed all day and I'm up all night. That's a typical day.

DEBBIE: I'll describe John's day for you.

Q: Go on then.

DEBBIE: Very weak. Always pissed. Um . . .

Q: He's not pissed now. And it's not night time now either.

DEBBIE: We won't go into details.

Q: But you get up in the afternoon, don't you? Not at night? I mean you do see the daylight.

JR: Not very much. I hate day. When we gig it always kills me. Cos we travel all day.

Q: Do you rehearse most days?

JR: Yeah. We start rehearsing about six and go on till about ten, catch an hour's booze on, arrive at Willesden Lane, get a crate of lager, come back, sit around, act like general arseholes, go to sleep at about eight in the morning.

Q: You all get paid a kind of wage, don't you? How much is it, 60 quid a week?

JR: 50. Which I spend on the first fucking day. I've got ten left.

Q: The film's cost a hell of a lot as well, hasn't it?

JR: Fucking half a million.

Q: Is that what it's going to be in the end?

JR: That's what it is *now*. It's not the end yet. That's where all the money is going. Like, some of that's ours, about ten of it, and the rest is like from backers.

Q: Do you think any film's worth that amount of money?

McLaren and Lydon conspire

JR: For a film that is excessively cheap. That's dirt cheap, these days. That's dirt. That's nothing.
Q: Well, supposing you didn't have all the unions and so on to deal with, the film union . . .
JR: Well then it would be like very good, wouldn't it?
Q: Well, this is what I never understood, why . . .
JR: It's like you have to have this and that, and that and this, you have to have a fucking camera holder, a camera operator, the man with lights, accessories . . .
Q: But I mean you don't have to do that, unless you're making a feature film . . .
JR: That's what it is.
Q: . . . so I wonder why it isn't more like a documentary or something.
JR: I despise documentaries. I don't want it to be a Whicker's World.
Q: Well, they don't all have to be like that. I really think nowadays that fiction's really boring. I think fact is much more interesting.
JR: Fact? The facts? Everybody knows the facts.
Q: No they don't.
JR: Well, they know some of them. Which is a lot more than I know. [*Laughs*] It gets very confusing.

Q: What was John like when he was young?
MRS LYDON: When he was young he was very quiet, reserved. He was always very sensible as a boy, very sensible, very grown-up. When he was very young, if you told him something, he picked it up straight away. As he was growing up, when he was eight years old, he could even mind the place. You had no worry. He always knew what he was doing, you could trust him.

When he was eight he got meningitis. It frightened me, naturally. I had it when I was 11 and when I seen him with it, I knew what it was. But when I got him to the hospital he was very – I thought he had gone, because they said to me they thought it was much worse than meningitis. He couldn't see and that. It left him with bad eyesight and I don't know if you ever notice John, he stares. Sort of a stare in his eyes. But it hasn't left him with any deformity or anything like that, you know. He was a week in hospital and he was getting better, and I went up one day and he was gone – gone unconscious. Of course I broke down. I thought, my God, one way or the other he'd either come out of it or go. I came out and I broke down. I was back up that evening. He was sitting up in bed. [*Laughs*]

He was fine at school, very interested in art, and that, and he always had good reports from the primary school. When he was going to the primary school he got a lot of prizes for art and he also done some drawings or something for the library. They asked me would I let him do some drawings for 'Blue Peter' on television.

And then when he left his primary he went on to the next school and got on very well with one particular teacher who was there. He got on very well with him for about three years. And he was a very strict teacher as well. He wasn't a teacher that would go running to the headmaster with anything. If he caught you doing anything he'd punish you himself and that was it. But he died – cancer or something I think he got – and after that John didn't seem to get on very well at school at all.

There was one particular teacher there that he never got on with at all, although he done his work and everything for him. But no matter what John done, this particular teacher seemed to have had it in for him all the time. I don't know what it was. And John wrote a poem which I found very funny and the teacher went in and told the headmaster and the headmaster brought me down to the school. There was a big hullabaloo over this poem.

Q: What was the poem about?

MRS L: Oh, it was something about leaving pills on the shelves and a baby getting the pills and he said you'll end up with something – you'll end up with dead babies if somebody leaves pills on the shelves. It was all rhymed in and it was funny to me and I started to laugh and then of course the headmaster said to me: 'It's not funny.' I could see it was funny and I could see where John had seen the funny side of it, but this headmaster, oh, very stern, very priggish, as if he's looking down on you, you know. No matter what he said, no matter what happened, John couldn't do nothing right.

I was working in Woburn studios at the time, up near the school. I looked out of the window and I see John coming up the road. He was always early for school, although he didn't particularly like school then. He never refused to go; he always went and it wouldn't trouble him going there. And he came up and he said: 'The teacher just expelled me.' Of course I couldn't believe it. So then I got on to the education authorities and they said being as it was a Catholic school there was nothing they could do about it, but would I get on to the Bishop, which was the head of the school. So in the meantime Johnny was at home and there was his 'O' Levels coming up in January and all this, and this was December.

In the end I got hold of the Bishop and he said to me he couldn't understand it, because, he said, 'I am the principal of the school. I should have been there,' he said. So he went on and on and the Bishop said John was to go down and take his 'O' Levels in January. He went down in January and he got the 'O' Level, he passed it. And he went down to the school and that teacher had the blooming cheek of turning around and saying to him: 'Hallo, John,' he says, 'how are you going? I hope you do well with your 'O' Level.' Yes. I thought it was a cheek.

But when he was going to secondary school, there was a computer came up. And he was always interested in music and poems and writing poems, you see, and that. He used to be always writing. And this computer said that – he was killing himself laughing – he'd finish up in the music business as a songwriter or a poem writer. And we were laughing when he came in and told me this. He said: 'Never. Can you see me doing that?' He said: 'I'd love to do it, but can you see me getting that chance in life?' he says.

Maybe two years after that, he finished up doing that. I was away on holiday when he rang and told me. I nearly died laughing, I did. I was thinking back to what happened, you see, and of course when he got the chance he took it. So he left college that year.

Everyone says to me: 'Oh, your son is a star, he'll buy you a house.' I said to them: 'I don't want a house.' They can't believe it. They think that I want to move out in the country and have a big cottage with a swimming pool and God knows what. I mean that would deform me. [*Laughs*]

You wouldn't believe how people's minds work. Everything I do to help John, the first thing they asked me: 'Did you get paid for it?' I've done television and things like that and the first thing they said to me: 'How much did you get for that?' You know this is their idea.

PAUL COOK

Q: What sort of jobs have you done?
MRS COOK: Oh, everything: cooking, cleaning, hairdressing, sewing, anything that I can get hold of, apart from when I have been in hospital from time to time and that, and short intervals when I have been away just for a little bit of nerve trouble over domestics. [*Laughs*]
Q: Have you always lived in C— Road?
MRS C: 16 years.
Q: What sort of a baby was Paul when he was very young?
MRS C: Well, a bit miserable, yes, bit miserable. You couldn't leave him in the pram because he cried, you know, if you went shopping. But other than that he was a pretty baby boy, lovely baby actually, little girl's features. He was a blondy, real blondy, like he is now and he was cute. [*Laughs*] Apart from that he was a normal child for playing with boys and getting into trouble and mischief. He was in a day nursery in Fulham, the old Fulham Hospital actually, and he joined in with the other children. I worked there, funny enough, at the time. I was doing the washing for the children in the nursery in Fulham Palace Road.

Always playing with something as a child, always playing with a biscuit tin – which I told the *Daily Mail* [*laughs*] – playing that all the time, or banging something or the other. We've had no end of neighbours complain about the drums. And I didn't ever really believe that they would ever make it. [*Laughs*]

But as regards giving me money, he just do not want to know. I hope you publish that. [*Laughs*] He says to me once, when he was here last and he was going abroad, not so long back, he said – what was it he said to me? – 'Here's 50p.' I said: 'What's that for?' He said: 'Get yourself a packet of fags and get on the Valium.' [*Laughs*] That's just what he said!

When he was supposed to have come in for that money, I said to him: 'What are you doing with it all?' He said: 'It's not to spend.'
Q: No, they seem to be putting it back into the company now.
MRS C: Yes, why's that?
Q: I think it's so they don't have to pay tax.
MRS C: Well, they won't get it in the end, will they? Someone must be getting it. I am the kind of person that worries over anything, definitely, and I say that myself.
Q: Well, you've had quite a lot to worry about.
MRS C: He's a wonderful boy. He's not lazy, he's always worked, and as far as I'm concerned he's the only one out of the group that has worked really good.

But I couldn't believe it when he was born. I said to the doctor – he said it

Top: earliest known picture of Paul Cook.

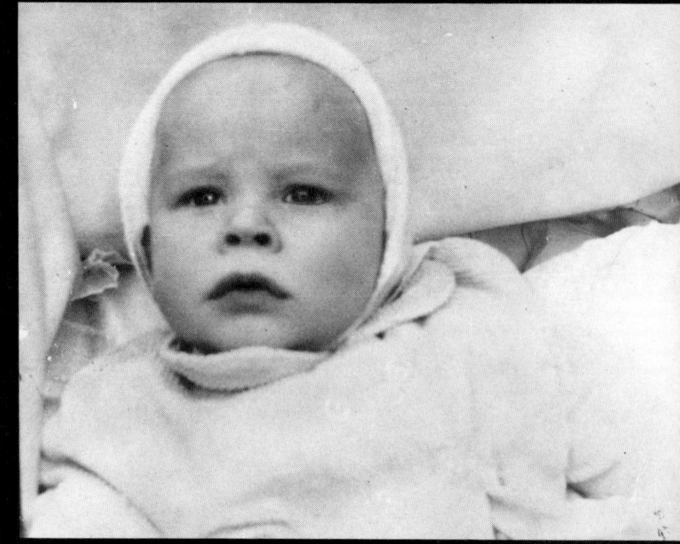

Below: Paul Cook as a boy.

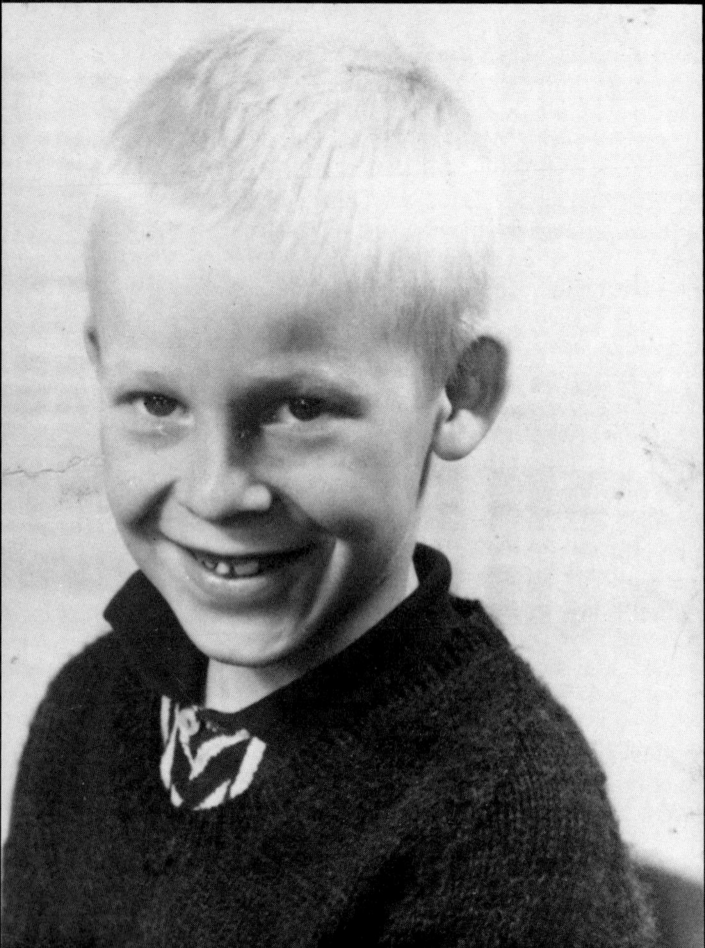

was a boy, and I said: 'No, it ain't,' and he said: 'Yes, it is.' And there he was, his little white nob, his head. [*Laughs*] My Dad always called him Peter Grievous because he said he was always crying. [*Laughs*]

I haven't got any of his records at the moment because I'm so proud I give them all away. But I think it is funny, especially their last one 'Pretty Vacant'. And often I get my little grandson saying: 'I'm pretty vacant!' He once said to me: 'You're pretty vacant, nanny.' But I think it's wonderful. But do you think that it is going to be like the Rolling Stones and just die out, or what's going to happen?

Q: I don't know. I don't think anyone knows. Tell me what happened when Johnny Rotten came round?

MRS C: What happened then? Um, what, when . . . oh yes. When he came round, he sat on the step out the back, and I thought: Whatever have I got here? All his hair standing up and he had a jean suit on, all torn and burnt holes in it, and a safety pin through his – I don't know whether it was through his ear or through his damn nose, but he did, he had some safety pins on him. And I thought to myself: He looks a bit undernourished – and he really did look queer, you know. And I thought: Is he not well, or what is it?

But he sat on my step and I said: 'Hello, Johnny,' and all the kids in the street was waiting to get their autographs and everything. Gavin next door – he was an actor, our next door neighbour, on television – and of course he wanted to see him. And he went all shy and he sat on my back step in the garden and he looked so depressed. So I said: 'Well, we are all depressed, Johnny,' and he started to laugh, and he seemed as though he was a bit embarrassed by what I was saying.

And I said: 'Do you want something to eat or drink?' And he said: 'I'll have a drink.' And I made tea and I'd made a dinner for Paul and Steve, and he said: 'I'm very parched,' and I believe he ended up drinking the bottle of lemonade or half of it. And I'd made an apple tart that Sunday, and I said: 'Are you hungry?' and he said: 'Yes,' and when I looked round he'd eaten half the apple pie. [*Laughs*] And then he came to Paul's bedroom and I was playing some records in his room, and we were sitting here, and he looked so fed up because I was playing something that I liked, and he kept tittering and, well, I think he is a great boy and, as I say (never mind about Bill Grundy), he never swore at me, nor none of them haven't.

I think they are great. I do honestly, I'm not kidding. I know I've said some rotten things about Paul, but I think they're wonderful. I think they are down and out and they've come up to other people's levels. I wish they were all my sons. I'll sum it up, the four of them, and I wish they were all supplying me with money and I'd never have to work again. [*Laughs*]

PAUL COOK – SCHOOL REPORT, 1967–68, FINAL

Subject	*Assessment*	*Remarks*
English Language	B–	Work has reached a steady standard – satisfactory!
Mathematics	A–	He has reached a very high standard of work and now I hope he maintains it.
French	B+	Satisfactory progress.
History	A+	Maintains a high standard.
Geography	C+	Satisfactory progress.
Science	A–	Test work good but there is room for improvement in classwork.
Religious Knowledge	B	Very good work.
Art	B+	Excellent results. Always works hard.
Music	B	Steady work.
Physical Education	A	A very good year's work.
Woodwork	A	V. good result.

Attendance 229/230. Punctuality: V. good. Conduct: Good.
Activities: Form captain.
School rugby, cross country, cricket, athletics team. House rugby team.
Form Master: I am pleased to see that Paul's work has improved and has reached a high standard. I hope this is maintained next year. He has made a quiet, conscientious form captain and also represents the school at athletics.

PAUL COOK – SCHOOL REPORT, 1969–70, FINAL

Subject	*Assessment*	*Remarks*
English Set 2	C+	I should like to see more effort.
Mathematics Set 1	B–	Good progress. Could do better.
Science	B	Has good potential – could be an excellent pupil if he settled down a bit.
French	B	Very disappointing this half year.
History	B–	A very satisfactory year's work. Keep it up!
Geography	A–	Tries hard and produces good results.
Music	C+	A better standard of behaviour is required.
Physical Education	B+	Needs more effort.
Art	B–	Some effort and interest, but he seems to find it difficult to sustain.
Brickwork		A good worker.
Plasterwork	B+	Produced some good work.
Plumbing	B+	Quite a good worker.
Religious Knowledge	A–	Excellent.

Activities and Interests: Form Captain (Summer term)
Football team
Film Club

Attendance: 277/294. Punctuality: Good. Conduct: Satisfactory.
Detentions: 0. Merit Marks: 4.
Form Master: The general opinion appears to be that Paul could do much better work if he put his mind to it. Also his choice of friends occasionally leads him into trouble. I hope he becomes more settled next term.
Year Master: If Paul decides to be his true self he will have an excellent career.
Head: Keep trying.

PAUL COOK – SCHOOL REPORT, 1970–71, Dec, 1970

Subject	*Assessment*	*Remarks*
English Set 2	B	Slightly disappointing. He's not bad at times but I always feel that he could do just that bit better. If he wants to improve (and I think he does) he will have to put himself out even more.
Mathematics Set 1	B–	Occasionally impresses with flashes of work; he is frequently and all too willingly distracted.
Physics Set 1	C	Rather disappointing so far this year. Paul is too easily influenced by others.
Geography	B	Has done some excellent work despite his late start in the set. His map work is up to standard, but he needs to improve his other Geography.
Chemistry Set 1	D	His recent test mark of 32% is not a true reflection of his ability. I am sure that he could do a bit better if only he would really concentrate on his work.
Technical Drawing	B	He produces high quality work.
Craft	B	This term is allocated to 'O' level woodwork.

Attendance: 110/112. Punctuality: Good. Conduct: Good.
Form Master: Paul is very easily led by others who are around him and I believe he is now of an age to decide for himself as to what he wants to do. Whether to begin concentrating on his work and achieving good 'O' level results next year or run the risk of failing in all subjects.
Year Master: Paul is now definitely failing to work independently of unfavourable influences. This year is vital.
Head: Noted!

Q: What did you do when you left school?
PAUL COOK: I just had one job, in a brewery in Mortlake as an electrician for three years.
Q: You took the City & Guilds exam while you were there, didn't you?
PC: Yeah, I got that, so I'm sort of qualified. But I didn't learn fuck all there. They just got drunk all day, all the blokes. You didn't have to do nothing. Most of them just sat around drinking all day and by the end of the day they was really pissed. I was training to be an electrician as an apprentice or something. But I didn't learn fuck all because no one was willing to . . . the blokes were all right, they were a great laugh and that, but they just liked a piss up. I don't blame them either. The only bad thing was getting up in the morning. Cos we used to have to rehearse. I used to have to get up about seven every morning, go to work and straight when I came home from work used to come up the West End and rehearse till late.
Q: How did you get on at school. Did you like it?
PC: Yeah, we had a laugh. Me and Steve was in the same year – we were in a different class though. Used to just fuck about and that. We got expelled once. I lit a fire on my desk. Nearly set the whole fucking place alight. They went mad.
Q: Did you feel that school was repressive?
PC: No, not really. We used to have a good laugh because we had a load of nutters in our year. But it was repressive sometimes. Gets you down school. It's boring. The only things I enjoyed was what I got 'O' levels in: technical drawing and woodwork. No one used to go to any of the other lessons. There was some good teachers there, you know, like sort of modern day teaching, you know, used to sit down and talk to you, get on with you. But a lot of them weren't. The trouble with most of the schools now is that all the teachers leave. New ones coming in every day like and they don't get settled. When the kids see a new teacher they start fucking about.
Q: What about English? Did you enjoy that?
PC: No, not really cos I hate reading. Can't stand it. Get bored after a couple of pages. Except a couple of books. Only read two books, I think: one about the Kray brothers and *Clockwork Orange*.
Q: Now that you're so much the centre of attention and you have in some way become stars, what's that like for you? How has it affected the way you live from day to day?
PC: Not much. It hasn't affected a lot. It's just that [*pause*] when you go out a lot you've got to watch where you go – you know, if you go to the wrong places you'll end up in trouble. Especially in that few weeks, you know, when me and John did get beat up. It was really heavy then. It's cooled down a bit in the last couple of weeks though.

But when you go out to other places and all, like people won't leave you alone. I mean I don't mind talking to them but they don't realize that after they've finished someone else comes up to you and starts talking all about the same things, about ten times the same night. Just different people, you know: 'What are you doing?' 'How's it going?' 'When's your album coming out?' 'What's on it?' It really gets a bit boring. [*Yawn*] And you can't really say, you know, fuck off.

SID VICIOUS

BOOGIE: Sid's a great one for being a personality. I mean like we were in Sweden for three and a half weeks. Towards the end of the three weeks, everybody was getting a bit exhausted, a bit tired of [*pause*] well, not of each other, you know, of what was going on. Because, you know, it was the first time that they had done that ever, that group, it was the first time that they had played that many dates consecutively even with Glen. And, towards the end of these three weeks, Sid was becoming the real kind of nucleus, you know, the guy who sort of kept the spark alive. You know, he's a, he's a very, um, oh what's the blasted term? [*Pause*] He's a great person to work with, you know, in that situation.

JACK LEWIS (*Daily Mirror*): . . . I did do a piece on Sid Vicious. Now the Sid Vicious piece I did was Sid Vicious talking. That's all I had to do was to get Sid into a corner and chat. And once he started to chat I just wrote. Rather like I'm say speaking to you now, he spoke about his opinions, his life, how he was educated, his struggles and problems and this gave a better insight into Sid Vicious that anything that I could have done.

There were people who would have read that and said he's condemned himself out of his own mouth. Perhaps he had for those people. On the other hand there would have been people who said right, now I understand the man better. And there would have been the third kind who just hung onto every word he said because he was Sid and because to them he was something of a hero, if an anti-hero . . .

PUNK AND DISORDERLY

It was education, says Sid Vicious, which made him a punk rocker . . .

. . . 'I'm not a vicious person, really. I consider myself kind-hearted. I love my mum. She understands me and is glad I've found something in life I really enjoy.

'Still, I'll go on being myself, drinking, eating good food, having girls. Not just one steady girlfriend – why should people always want to own each other?

'I'll probably die by the time I reach 25. But I'll have lived the way I wanted to.'

Daily Mirror, 11 June 1977

SID VICIOUS [with Nancy Spungen present]: OK, what did you want to ask?
Q: I was going to ask you about the Jack Lewis article and how that came about and what you felt about the result of it.

SV: Well, that came about because just previous to that there'd been some incident at the Speakeasy where somebody had got injured. John Rotten and I were suspected. Course [*sarcastically*] we had nothing to do with it whatsoever.

He picked me out to interview because my name was Vicious and it was obvious he was trying to find out from the questions he asked – like he asked me if I was violent and things like that and if I did this and that, all very subtle, designed to a person of low intelligence, obviously such as myself.

I would be totally foiled by this, and he would get it all out of me and I would say: 'Yes, I'm big, tough and vicious and I beat up all these people and split people's heads open.'

And this was what he came along to do. And he was so sure he was going to get that. So I told him exactly the opposite of what he wanted to hear. I told him what a nice intellectual boy I was and I wouldn't dream of doing anything like that and I had pet hampsters and things like that, you know what I mean? Made myself seem like butter wouldn't melt in my mouth.

And he fucking fell for it as well. They're just so thick they wouldn't know a string quartet from a string vest. They're just totally dumb. They don't know a fucking thing. They make me sick. They make me physically ill because they're not in touch with what's going on. They've got no idea of what is happening. And they can't, you know, they can't handle it.

That's why, you know, when people read how I love my mummy and she's pleased that I've at last found something that's near to my heart . . .

Like, as far as I'm concerned, anybody with any suss looks at the picture of me standing there and looks at what I said and says the two don't go together. Of course, he lacks the intelligence, like most grown-ups, to do anything of the sort.

Grown-ups have just got no intelligence at all. As soon as somebody stops being a kid, they stop being aware. And it doesn't matter how old you are. You can be 99 and still be a kid. And as long as you're a kid you're aware and you know what's happening. But as soon as you 'grow up' . . .

. . . I've got absolutely no interest in pleasing the general public at all. I don't want to because I think that largely they're scum and they make me physically sick, the general public. They are scum. And I hope you print that. Because that is my opinion of like 99 per cent of the shit you find in the street who don't know a fucking thing.

Q: But is it actually the people who annoy you?

SV: Yes, it is. It's the people and their God-awful attitudes. What I want to do is put something out that I like, and like whoever else likes it will find it, do you know what I mean? And like if nobody else in the whole fucking world likes it, I couldn't give two shits. If it doesn't sell one copy, who gives a fuck? The point is that it's what we want to do. We have fun making it, we have fun

listening to it. I listen to our records a lot because I like them. I think they're good records. Otherwise I wouldn't have had any part in them. I like our music to listen to as much as I like the Ramones to listen to. The Ramones are my favourite group, by the way. But do you know what I mean?

Q: Yes. What do you feel about television?

SV: I hate it and everything to do with it. It's the worst – it's depressing, television, it frightens me. The way they fucking kiss arse, you know what I mean? The way they say: 'And now the wonderful this, that and the other.' They don't mean one fucking word, you know what I mean? So why do it? Do you know what I mean? I hate insincerity. If you do something you should only do it because you like it and you want to do it. Cos anything you gain is just a load of hogwash anyway. What do you do with money, for instance? I can think of *one thing* to do with money. [*He and Nancy laugh.*] One thing. That's what I do with all my money. Every halfpenny of it.

Q: You were at technical college with John. Weren't you? Did you get on all right there or not?

SV: What do you mean, work-wise?

Q: Any-wise. Well work-wise and with . . .

SV: I got on really well with John. I got on there really well with the black kids – they were great, the spades at that college. They were really cool, you know what I mean? And they used to have these reggae discos with massive sound systems and they were really good. But like everything else was shit. I hated work. I never did *anything* at all. I didn't do a *single* thing. I used to be always making excuses. And I couldn't do any of the work anyway, not because I was unintelligent or anything, but simply because I wasn't interested in it. I'm incapable of doing something I don't want to do. I just can't do it. I just can't force myself to do things. I either want to do it or I don't.

Q: Before you went there, did you anticipate that it would be good?

SV: No, I knew it would be shit. But I couldn't think of anything else to do and I was not of an age when I could just hustle, you know what I mean?

Q: How old were you when you left school?

SV: 15.

Q: And what school were you at?

SV: Clissold Park.

Q: That's a comprehensive isn't it?

SV: Uh huh.

Q: Do you read a lot?

SV: No, I never read. I read comics mostly. Cos I hate books. Find them tedious. I only like very entertaining books. I like horror books.

Q: Don't you think that books have anything to offer that other things haven't?

SV: No. I think nothing has anything to offer. Specially television and books.
Q: There's a much bigger range of books though than there is of television programmes.
SV: Well, I find that if I want to know something, I know about it anyway or I find out about it. And the things I don't want to know about just, you know . . . I can't say I like books, but if it's necessary for me to read a book to find out something I want to find out, I will read the book, happily. But as such, I can't generalize about that. I can't generalize over anything. I don't like anything particularly.
[Sid was reluctant to let us speak to his mother.]

NEWS OF THE WORLD

BRITAIN'S FAVOURITE SUNDAY PAPER

No. 7,120 PRICE 18p

JUNE 15, 1980

Shock confession of punk star's mum

EXCLUSIVE:

I GAVE SID THE DRUGS

By DAVID MERTENS

AS PUNK fans flock to see Sid Vicious in his Sex Pistols film, The Great Rock 'n' Roll Swindle, the truth about his fatal overdose can be told for the first time.

His mother bought him the heroin that killed him.

Outrageous Sid, 21, who revelled in spitting, swearing and insulting his audiences, took the overdose at a party 12 hours after being released on bail.

For two months he had been in New York's Riker's Island jail, charged with knifing to death his punk girl friend Nancy Spungen.

Vicious, real name John Ritchie, died in a New York flat in February last year. Lying naked beside him on the bed was his new girl Michele Robinson.

He was found by his mother Mrs Anne Beverley. She said next day:

"I'm very sad but his death is hardly a surprise to me.

"What distresses me so much is that someone gave him enough heroin to kill himself.

"That's as bad as murder. And there were plenty of people watching as he took that fix."

But at her home in Canterbury, Kent, last week Mrs Beverley told me: "I bought the drugs that killed him."

Fate

"I suppose it was fate really. He died because I tried to help him.

"Though he constantly talked of being cured of his drug habit, I knew that while he was on Riker's Island he just thought of that first fix when he got out.

"The day before the court hearing that got him bail I went out myself and bought some for him. I'd just had some money through from London.

"I realised that the first thing he'd do would be to traipse down 32nd Street or wherever it was he got the drugs.

"It would have been stupid because he'd have been recognised and there would have been trouble.

"So I bought them myself.

"What I didn't realise was that I'd bought heroin that was 90 per cent pure. Usually heroin bought on the street is only about ten per cent pure.

"A New York policeman told me afterwards that it was the purest heroin he'd ever seen.

"Sid had a very high tolerance of drugs. He and Nancy were always taking a bit of this and a bit of that and mixing them.

"But he couldn't take this. It was just too good."

On the anniversary of his death, 48-year-old Mrs Beverley, who wears a punk hairstyle and rides a 750 cc motorbike, took an overdose herself. She recovered in hospital.

She blames Sid's addiction on Nancy.

She said: "Before he met her he experimented a little, like every other youngster.

"But it was only after they started living together that he really got hooked.

"It was impossible for him to come off them while living with another addict."

Sid, who always denied murdering Nancy, gave himself the injection of heroin at midnight at a party celebrating his release.

He went into a 45 minute spasm, but appeared to recover so no-one called for help.

He died seven hours later.

War on the dealers of death: Page 5

12 HOURS FROM DEATH: Vicious and his mother after he got bail

An...

THE... STA... REA... OUT

SECRETS ... THE SPIRIT... WRITINGS

End of a cult? Now the extraordinary drugs confession of the mother of pop star Vicious

I HELD SID'S HEROIN

ANOTHER PRESS EXCLUSIVE

Drug addict Sid Vicious with his mother Ann Beverly. She said: "I am just glad that he went out on a happy note"

PAUL DACRE in NEW YORK

THE mother of Sid Vicious revealed yesterday that she looked after his heroin supply on the night he died.

Londoner Ann Beverly, who discovered her son's body in his Greenwich Village apartment, spoke of the fix that led to his death.

But she added: "I know he didn't have any more that night, because I had the packet in my pocket.

"Besides, there wasn't any works (slang for a heroin syringe). The works they used earlier had been taken away.

"There is no way Sid could have slipped the smack (heroin) from my pocket. He wasn't like that. He would have waited until next day and said, 'Can I have some more?'"

The 21 year old former Sex Pistols guitarist died on Friday after a party celebrating ... bail from prison ...

... a bit too much." She said that Sid opened his eyes again 40 minutes later.

"We all had a good laugh," she added.

Soon the party ended and Mrs Beverly went into the bedroom to say goodnight to Sid and his girlfriend Michelle Robinson.

Orange

The following morning she ...

Our last night, by Michelle...

Schoolboy who was SID VICIOUS

SEE PAGES 12 and 13

...azing message from Sid Vicious...

I DIDN'T KILL NANC[Y]

Tracey

● PUNK rocker Sid Vicious, the outrageous star of the Sex Pistols, spat, swore and sneered his way to the top of the pops.

● And, after a short life of drugs and debauchery, he died. He was killed, aged 21, by a heroin overdose, while on bail in America, charged with stabbing to death girlfriend Nancy Spungen.

● But his spirit lives on, claims medium Kim Tracey, who has remarkable evidence that Vicious, along with other dead pop stars Keith Moon of the Who and Rolling Stone Brian Jones, have communicated through her.

● Here, witnessed by two Star reporters, is Vicious's message from beyond Nancy's death — and his own!

Message from the grave?

She was bleeding and I was scared!

IN A candlelit, incense-filled room, a plump dark-haired woman scrawls obscenities on a pad.

[illegible] groans in pain, and the pen leaps across the [illegible]. The words she writes are violent and blasphemous.

[illegible] dead for [illegible] months, is telling the world his own [illegible] told how he died, at a squalid heroin party to celebrate his [illegible] from prison.

DAY ONE OF A REVEALING SERIES By JEAN RITCHIE

[illegible]

Scrawled

[illegible]

Spewed

[illegible]

Party

After writing about [illegible] he started to tell Kim about the party at which he died.

[illegible]

Lovers in the loo: Sid Vicious and Nancy Spungen were outrageous in life—and death!

'It sounds just like my son!'

Mrs Anne Beverley

SID Vicious' mother has no doubts that it IS her son who has been in contact through medium Kim Tracey.

And now Mrs. Anne Beverley wants to arrange a meeting so that she can talk to her dead son again.

Mrs. Beverley [illegible] cried as she read the words that had been written by the medium.

"It's spooky, because I have just started to recover a little bit from Sid's death," she says. "But I feel it really is him. I feel as if I've been talking to Sid again."

About the murder of the former punk star's girlfriend Nancy Spungen Mrs Beverley says:

"He really did love Nancy, and he always referred to her as Nancy.

"He talks about her opening him up to love, and it really was like that."

Mrs. Beverley believes Sid wanted to put the record straight.

"I never talked to him about it. Nobody ever heard Sid's side of the story," she says, "he died before he stood trial, but I'm convinced he didn't do it."

She says that the details about that night are very accurate.

"I cooked him his favourite meal, spaghetti bolognese, and we had a bottle of red wine."

Mrs. Beverley confirms, too, the description of the drugs used at the sordid party.

"I know the stuff was wrapped in paper," she says, "because I insisted on taking the remains of it away at the end."

TOMORROW: KEITH MOON and BRIAN JONES

● SID Vicious was a sick person and will not be missed by me. But I do feel sorry for his mother, Ann Beverly.

She gave him all her love and support to the end.—Mrs. R. Barwell, High Wycombe, Bucks.

STEVE JONES

Q: Can I ask you, first of all, since you've become in a way a pop star and wherever you go people recognize you, has that affected your life?
STEVE JONES: No, not really. Because like I do get recognized like, but not like John. John stands out a mile. I still just go down the pub and nobody bothers me. It's different with John. I'm all right, it don't change me a bit, I'm exactly the same as I was four years ago.
Q: Even in your kind of day-to-day life? I mean obviously that's . . .
SJ: Well, that's different because like you're doing a different thing from what you did four years ago. It's more fun now anyway.
Q: It's more fun?
SJ: Yeah, you know, you seem to have more things to do.
Q: What are the major advantages then of being in a band like the Pistols?
SJ: The changes. Like every day like something goes wrong or something changes, you know what I mean? Like it's never boring. Like one day you could say: 'Well, we've got an LP coming out in three weeks time.' The next day you say: 'Oh sod the LP, bring a single out.' Like that, you know. Nothing's ever definite, which is – it's all right. It's chaotic in a way but it's just better than having a normal job.
Q: Had you done any jobs before?
SJ: Yes – window cleaner for about three weeks. It was all right but I didn't like that because I didn't like the money. I only got 14 quid. And I spent that in a night. Ridiculous.
Q: What was it like? Were you unhappy?
SJ: Not really, because I'd never done anything else. That was a laugh like, you know. [*Pause*] But that was pretty exciting. You used to get some birds asking you in for a cup of tea like and you end up in bed with them – you see it in the films, but it's true. That was a laugh. But the money was no good.
Q: So what were you doing immediately before you joined the band?
SJ: Nothing. Sod all.
Q: You were on the dole, weren't you?
SJ: No, I couldn't be bothered to go to the dole. I was really lazy. I lived at home for about a year I think. I lived at me mate's for about six months when I had this job as a window cleaner. Then I went back home and I was just interested in music and all, you know, like pop stars and that.

I used to go and try to get into the Speakeasy, just to see the pop stars and that. I used to go and see the Faces and I got backstage once at Wembley and I was talking to Ronnie Wood and that. I couldn't be bothered at all about jobs. I didn't think about them.

I used to steal a lot of cars. I got caught for it, got put in an approved school

at Ashford for about three weeks. I've been caught 13 times since I was a kid, different charges – and the only thing I ever got there was approved school. I was lucky I didn't get like Borstal or detention centre.
Q: Is Ashford an approved school?
Q: It's a sort of a remand centre, but like you can do a long time there. But it ain't juveniles. Like older juveniles, but not men, you know what I mean? Young men I suppose.
Q: What do you enjoy about playing?
SJ: The excitement, playing on stage, do you know what I mean? Because the audience, they get into it just as much as what we do, you know. It's good to feel that you've done something which like – you feel like you're doing something worthwhile.
Q: What about all the business of staying in hotels and stuff like that, do you enjoy that?
SJ: Oh, yes, that's OK, except in Sweden it wasn't. Shoved in some silly hotel like made out of cardboard out in the middle of nowhere. Where every room is the same as the one 30 miles away, you know. There's nothing to do, there's nothing on telly, there's nothing on the radio. Anything on telly is like an English programme with sub-titles or something like that. The gigs were really good. But I don't know how anyone could live over there.
Q: Does touring have its compensations, with girls and stuff like that?
SJ: With birds, yes, there's plenty of birds. That's one of the best things. That's what I always look forward to after a gig, is the crumpet. It's easy to pull birds when you're in a group.
Q: How do you feel about the people at the other end of the King's Road, the shops in Knightsbridge and things like that?
SJ: I don't know. I don't think a lot of them really.
Q: Why?
SJ: I don't know. It's so rich, you know what I mean? So dull in there. It makes just you sick. All these old ladies and that. I don't like it at all. They're more stupid than working-class people. Working-class people have got more common sense than a middle-class person, because he doesn't really know what life's about. Working class is what life's really all about, middle class is just like fantasized living. I'm not saying working-class people are clever. I mean I'm stupid. But I've got more savvy than a middle-class person. You know what I mean? They might have gone to a fucking clever school and that but just like silly things, like they wouldn't know what the hell you were talking about.
Q: What differences do you see between the Pistols as a band and the Beatles, for example?
SJ: Er – soap and water. They was too clean and, you know, they used to write lovely little tunes. They was more like a manufactured thing after a while.

They was just told to do this and told to do that. I mean, I don't know. I don't have any interest in them. I was more in favour of the Rolling Stones – although the Beatles were more popular: like it don't matter where you went you couldn't get away from them. I remember that when I was about 12 or 10 – I was only a nipper when the Beatles were going. I don't know – I was just fucking glad when they broke up.
Q: The band don't seem to have written many songs lately or is that a wrong impression?
SJ: Well, you go through phases. I mean earlier this week we got three tunes, just need lyrics to them, which John writes mainly, the lyrics, and like that's three new songs. I mean since we've ever started we've never really writ a lot of songs. It's easy to knock any song out and I mean it could be shit but we'd rather wait till we got a good one and knock that out. Because I'd say on average we knock one out a month.
Q: When you're writing what part do you play? It seems to me that you all work together on them, after John has perhaps done the lyrics. Is that right?
SJ: Yes. You've just got to have a tune like, just write the tune.
Q: So who does that?
SJ: Well, I do mainly the tune like and everyone chips in when we're in there. But you get a tune and write it out and John just puts lyrics to it.
Q: How do you think the band's going to go, in the future?
SJ: How's it going to go? Up the wall, I don't know. That's what I mean like. We could be doing this, the next day we could be doing that. I mean tomorrow we could all say: 'Oh, fuck it, I don't want to do it any more,' you know. I can't say how long or what we're going to do.
Q: Is there any major factor in that? What is it that makes the band like that?
SJ: Personalities really.
Q: In what way?
SJ: Well, if we was all nice boys and all got along fine it would show in the music we do, I suppose, and you wouldn't get the chaos what we've caused or anything. If we was all nice boys we'd still be with EMI making lots of money, being nice pop stars you know, pin-ups and what have you. We're from the streets and that's all there is to it. We don't give a shit. Look, we don't care about our future, you know. Well, I don't anyway. That's why I never bothered getting a job. My old man used to say: 'Get a job. You've got to think of yourself in old age.' I don't give two fucking shits for when I'm older.

Q: Can you tell me a bit about Steve when he was younger, what was he like when he was a boy?
MRS JONES: A lot of trouble. [*Laughs*] Yes, well it was all right, I mean it was till – till he sort of got to a certain age you know, and then he started to get up

Steve Jones as a boy.

to all the tricks. I mean, you know, he was all right until he went to the bigger school. He never used to tell you anything. A dreamer. A dreamer.

Q: What did you think when you heard that he was in a rock band?

MRS J: He's always sort of liked that, and he had – he used to have a guitar when he was about 15, you know. From then on he wasn't interested in going to work.

Q: Can you tell me what you thought when you heard about the Sex Pistols, and they suddenly made a name for themselves?

MRS J: Well, I was glad for him, you know, because that's what he wanted to do. It's awful music.

Q: Don't you like it? [*Mrs Jones shakes her head*] Why not? What is it that . . .

MRS J: Well, it – it's just nothing really, is it? I mean I suppose that's what they go for, because when I was that age it was drapes, like Teddy boys and that, you know, and Teddy girls, I suppose. Another fashion. And – oh, it's OK, some of it's all right.

Q: Do people connect you with Steve Jones?

MRS J: No, only where I work.

Q: What sort of things do they say to you?

MRS J: That I should be getting some money by now. [*Laughs*] A treat. Well, that's up to him. If he doesn't want to, he doesn't, you know. He doesn't come and see us or anything.

Q: Can you remember about when Steve was sort of very little. Are there any incidents, anything that sticks out in your mind?

MRS J: No, not really. I lost a baby and he seemed a bit upset about that. He seemed to go really down from then on, you know.

Q: How old was he when that happened?

MRS J: He was a bit of a wanderer when he was little. Used to wander off. Oh, he was about four then, about four.

Q: You think that upset him?

MRS J: Yeah. I think it did a bit, yes. He sort of changed from then.

Q: I know that Steve is very friendly with Paul Cook. Did you get to know Paul quite well yourself?

MRS J: Yes. He used to come round, you know. He actually was quite friendly right from about 15, 13 or 14. I can't remember if he used to go to school before, the small school, you know.

Q: Did they used to get up to mischief together?

MRS J: Yeah, really. Dunno about Paul so much. He was quiet really. But Steve, he used to go with a crowd that used to get up to things a bit.

Q: How did you get to hear about things like that?

MRS J: Oh, when the police come. They come and tell you and that, you know.

Q: Was it mainly just nicking stuff?

MRS J: Right. Yeah. Motor bikes and things.
Q: What did you used to feel like when they came and knocked on your door?
MRS J: Used to go mad, cos you have to go and collect them. It used to be at Richmond and places like that. You have to go, otherwise they won't let them go, you see. Now he's of age it's up to him. I think he's all right now he's got his group. I mean he seemed all right from when he started it, you know. I don't think he's up to that any more.
Q: What used to happen when you used to go and get hím?
MRS J: I used to have a go at him. Cos it was sometimes three o'clock in the morning see. My husband had to go out. He gets up early. Up at five. Bit much that. Well I mean Steve didn't seem to worry about it, know what I mean? I think they thought it was all a good laugh.
Q: What do you feel like when you see Steve on television?
MRS J: It's exciting, seeing him on that. I like to see him. People keep after me: 'When is he going to be on Top of the Pops?' I was glued to it. I don't know if he'll be on there any more, you know. Quite a laugh really, I suppose.
Q: What do you think would happen if the Sex Pistols fold up? What do you think Steve would do then?
MRS J: Oh, don't know what'll happen then. He'd try and do something else, some other group. Don't know really. I suppose it don't last for ever. Unless they get really good. Perhaps if they changed the music, Johnny Rotten . . .
Q: Don't you like Johnny Rotten?
MRS J: No, I don't. Well, you know, his singing – I don't mean personally. Don't know what he's like. I don't think his singing's really good. Someone with a bit more voice probably be better but I suppose they don't want that. [*Laughs*] I think the music is a bit 'by the way' in some respects.
Q: What sort of music were you listening to when Steve was growing up?
MRS J: Well, I like *music*: the Supremes and that.
Q: Did he have lots of girlfriends?
MRS J: Yes, seems as if he did. There was always someone phoning up. From teenage, you mean? Yes.
Q: What sort of things would upset Steve? When would he get really depressed?
MRS J: Well, I think it was because he was always being moaned at really, that used to get on his nerves. You couldn't tell him anything, couldn't tell him off or anything. Used to get upset if you told him off. But I don't think he used to get that depressed. I mean he didn't start getting depressed until he was a teenager. He used to be all right when he was smaller. No, he didn't get depressed really. I don't think he was depressed. I think he was just bored all the time. As I say, he'd never tell you, never talk to you. If you asked him things I'm sure he thought you was moaning at him all the time. He used to

get fed up in his job. I think probably the group is the only thing he doesn't get fed up with.

Q: What are the happiest times you remember?

MRS J: Oh yes, there was a lot of happy times. We used to go away on holiday. He's quite funny really, you know, makes you laugh, quite a joker, you know. He was always all right until he got older, and they sort of go . . . I don't know, they go funny when they get older, I think.

Q: It's called the generation gap.

MRS J: Probably. [*Laughs*]

MALCOLM McLAREN

RON WATTS: Malcolm McLaren? Great. What a hustler. I think he's very unusual. Bags of energy. Goes off like a firecracker in all directions. Fights for what he believes in, too. I mean everyone was laughing up their sleeves at him one time. But the opposite is true now. By September, October of 1976, they was taking him serious, really serious. It had become business then, become property. He had proved his point. A lot of people would have liked to have seen him down at one point. Probably still would. Because he was a threat to their established little bleeding empires: you know, progressive twaddle, etc, etc.

Q: In the early days what was your relationship to Malcolm?
JOHNNY ROTTEN: To Malcolm? Hardly anything. I've always been like the loner on the outside. I don't hang around any of them. Malcolm gets on with like Paul and Steve, mainly Steve. They hang around together. I keep my distance cos it suits me and I have my own life.
Q: Some people have said that Malcolm is totally responsible for the way the band developed.
JR: This is total bullshit. Absolute. It's a complete lie. We developed because we were ourselves. And that's it. I mean, don't need to say no more. That's a fact.
Q: I get the impression though that, at the beginning, Malcolm was much more a *presence* there, almost like say the fifth member of the band.
JR: I've gone down as saying that. Malcolm *is* the fifth member. At the moment he's not around so much because of the film. Like, trying to raise the money is an incredibly difficult thing. [*Pause*] But he never interferes. I insist upon that. No one interferes except those who are in the band. I won't listen to *anyone* outside it, only those in. I cannot be influenced.

Q: I get the feeling that you've recently become more independent of Malcolm. Is that right?
SID VICIOUS: Independent? What me, personally?
Q: No, the band as a whole.
SV: Oh, the band have never been dependent on Malcolm, that old toss-bag. I hate the geezer. I'm not dependent on him at all. I'd smash his face in quite happily. I depend on him for exactly nothing. He gave me a free T-shirt once. Years ago. And once he gave me a fiver and I stole a tenner off him a little while ago. And that's all. Loathsome creature. Hate him.
Q: Why? Do you think he's mean?
SV: [*Laughing*] I *know* he's mean. I don't think anything.

Q: Well, your feeling like that towards him must alter how the band as a whole . . .
SV: Why? Do they feel differently?
Q: I think that, er – yes, I think they do feel differently from you. All of them.
SV: Why, do they *like* him?
Q: [*Pause*] 'Like' is a funny word. I think he's regarded as slightly separate, although both Paul and John said to me they regarded him as the fifth member of the band.
SV: Err. How *vile*. I certainly don't. Fifth member of the band? He never even turns up to gigs.
Q: Do you feel he ought to? I mean do you feel he . . . ?
SV: Yes. I fucking well do. I feel he ought to turn up to every gig we do if he's got any bloody interest in us. If he's a fifth member of the band he should be at every gig. Boogie's the fifth member of the band . . .
NANCY SPUNGEN: Yeah.
SV: Boogie's a laugh. But Malcolm, no way. Boogie's the fifth member of the group. I wouldn't even call him that, but if anybody is, it's him.
Q: So why do you put up with him as a manager?
SV: Cos he's – he's OK, you know what I mean? I don't dis . . . I don't, how can I put it? I hate his guts, you know what I mean, but I like him just enough, so he's enough like us to be able to be our manager. I can't think of anybody else that I could tolerate. Wouldn't have anybody else as our manager.

MARK P: I think Malcolm's a very clever guy. I don't think he manipulated the media, but he took advantage of every little thing. Down to the finest detail. Like every detail on his T-shirts. Every T-shirt he ever done, not one word was out. Like the Sex Pistols. No matter where you look, straight down the line, everything's perfect. Even their press handouts they used to have. Every detail. And it always used to be a nice colour. Always original. Like just everything. You could go on forever just saying how good they were. Even when they do old songs like 'No Fun' no one puts them down for doing that, they do it so fucking well. They're so clever. Malcolm's so clever. He's a great media person. Knows how to work with things. Knows how to sell a band.

Q: You've said that you act independently of Malcolm, but would the band be the same supposing Malcolm decided he didn't want to be the manager any more? What would happen then?
PAUL COOK: I don't know. I mean I'm not saying he hasn't really helped us, cos he has. He's done a real lot. He's really hassled around for us. He's like the fifth member of the group, if you like. And his contribution's just as big

SEX

as ours, I suppose, because he's prepared to work for us. Because he's more a friend, you know, than a business man. I doubt if we would even still be here if it weren't for him. He's held us together and it was all splitting up and everything, you know, right in the early days.

Q: Were you being consciously directed by Malcolm? I mean how were the ideas passed around between you?

PC: How do you mean? Ideas for what?

Q: Ideas for presentation, ideas for songs, a feeling of working on what you were doing . . .

PC: That was all ours. All the music side of everything and what we've done and what we were. Like people think that Malcolm tells us what to do, dictates to us what to do and what to wear. That's just bullshit, you know. He doesn't tell us anything like that. We do what we want to do and write all the songs off our own bat. And it's got nothing to do with him. He just looks after the business side of the thing.

Q: Some people have said to me that, that he dressed you down to the last detail . . .

PC: Yeah, I know.

Q: . . . that he was careful about details and things like that . . .

PC: That's just bullshit. I don't know why people say things like that really. I think [*pause*] people who are jealous say it maybe, like who want to put us down like. That's one of their excuses for putting us down, you know. They have to say that someone's doing it for us, like they didn't think we could do it off our own bat. Lots of people have said that in the past, you know. Not so much now but . . . it's just rubbish anyway.

Q: What was your relationship with Malcolm?

GLEN MATLOCK: It always just seemed like I was working for him. If you come up with an idea about something like he'd go, 'Ummm,' you know, as though he wasn't really interested and two weeks later you'd find he had it in his shop. I don't know, you just felt kind of cheated a bit because he would never even admit to it that it might even be slightly your idea. He would take things like that.

But he never gives anything – like credibility – back, any credence to the fact that it's your idea. When you're working with somebody you need to feel as though there's some kind of partnership. But it was always just a one-way thing. And in fact that's why I split with him in the end.

DAVE GOODMAN: [Not acknowledging people's full worth], well, this is part of his tactics and part of his style. And at times it can get very frustrating. I don't know, I used to find he was very tight with money which used to annoy me. To get anything out of him you had to like nag him, and he

McLaren as a mustachioed 21-year-old student standing beside one of his enormous constructions (Chelsea Art College).

wouldn't acknowledge you. But as time went on we built a relationship. He puts me on the same level as himself now; or rather he doesn't, but he treats me more as a friend than someone who's working for him. On the 'Anarchy' tour we used to stay in the same hotel room together. Out of all the people there he chose to share it with me. Must mean that he didn't mind my company. And like now he phones me up from time to time and says come on over or let's go out for a meal, or comes round and has a chat. We sit up all night, you know, and he only leaves you when you ask him to: 'I'm going to bed now, Malcolm.'

As long as the Sex Pistols are going I'm sure Malcolm will be involved, whether it's 24 hours a day or whether he sets it up so that it takes up a lot less of his time. This he could do if he had the right people working for him. He could sit back and do something else and just keep control of what they do. I wouldn't blame him for putting all the headaches and problems onto someone else's shoulders. Films he wants to get into. It will be interesting to see where it all ends up. Where his highest point will be. I'm sure it'll be above the Sex Pistols. He's probably established himself more than they will.

He's a megalomaniac, isn't he? I think he must be interested that in the society he's living in he can gain a lot of control. It's not really power, it's just like a form of communication, where you can say or do one thing and it sparks off 10 people or 100 people or a million people just for your thing. Great, if you can do that, say something in the press incites all these ideas in the people reading it. Or if you make a film, give all these people ideas – and it's coming from you! And if you can threaten! . . . Cos I know what he feels about the Establishment. He's even got power over them. Which is great. He can change the course of history, throughout, world-wide, the whole world, everyone on this planet almost. He can influence and change their ideas in some way. Ah, tremendous! But he's into a good time. He just wants people, I *know* he just wants people to have a good time, to see the funny side of life.

Q: How does Malcolm react to physical violence?
JOHNNY ROTTEN: He's frightened beyond belief of it. It terrifies him. I mean like when that punk v. Ted thing was going on, why he even slicked his hair down, didn't he? [*Dick Emery-type laugh*] Ha ha ha.
DEBBIE: Shit himself. Completely.
JR: It absolutely terrifies him. Can't cope.
D: He can't believe it. He can't make it out.
JR: [*Irish accent*] He told me he wasn't going to talk to you either, to do the book.
Q: When did he say that?
JR: Yesterday.
Q: Christ! [*JR laughs*] Why?

JR: I don't know. He's a bit scared, I suppose.
Q: What's he scared of?
JR: [*Laughing*] You might suss out his bullshit way of talking to people. He does bullshit an incredible amount and like everything he'd say would just make a real joke. It would be giggles time. The giggles part. For Malcolm.
Q: What's he frightened of? Me talking to him, or the book in general?
D: He's frightened of the whole world knowing about him.
JR: [*Laughing*] He'd prefer to remain a mystery. That way people might have [*Irish accent*] some kind of respect for him. [*Laughs*] You know what I mean?
Q: But he's not worried about anyone else being interviewed, like you, for example?
JR: Um, I don't know. I never bothered to ask him. It's none of his business.
Q: Tell me what he said to you.
JR: Um, I can't remember. Just: 'No, no, don't want nothing to do with it. Oh, no.'
Q: That's really funny cos Fred knows more about Malcolm probably than anyone so I don't know what he thinks . . .
JR: It's the man's paranoia. I mean he won't say a word to Vivienne for fear of her like drawing her own conclusions . . .
Q: I wonder what he's – I mean what he's frightened of that might come out about him?
JR: Being himself. [*Long pause*] But like no other manager would ever have stayed with us with the amount of trouble we cause. That's where he's good. Very good.
Q: Yeah. Sophie said that he really kind of looked after you and gave you a lot of time.
JR: Well, he put a lot of his own money into this. Hell of a lot. He's not in it for the money. If he was he'd have fucked off before now. I think he's in it like – really he'd like to be in the band but he couldn't. He could never do it himself. So we do it for him I suppose.
Q: And is he from your point of view replaceable as a manager?
JR: No, cos if he leaves it will stop happening. He is 'the manager'. It's as easy as that. He is about as replaceable as Steve is on guitar, which is not at all. They're part of it.
Q: Supposing he got bored with it, what would happen then?
JR: Then he'd go, wouldn't he. That would be just too bad. I don't really care about the future like that.
Q: Would that mean the end of you, or would you just carry on?
JR: I don't know, do I? People around me don't affect me at all. I don't think another manager would be as open as . . . but then we could always manage ourselves without any great difficulty. You should always work with people you know.

BERNIE RHODES: I asked Malcolm for a partnership. I felt that I was just as important as my ideas were good and I was a pretty fast-working person. I thought that together we could come up with something that was truly great. I think that's what we were both thinking about, not just like another thing but almost *the* thing. But I *knew* that Malcolm would never give anyone half share. He'd always want to be in control.
Q: What ideas did you work well on together?
BR: Ideas that weren't flippant, but were constructive ideas. Ideas that were the backbone of the situation. How to make a thing strong. We worked in a kind of circular motion, meaning we went through the same things over and over again. There was a calm period. Then it was like fist fights and shouting. And then it was like great excitement. And then it was a down period. And it went back round the circle again. So it kept going round – not in that order, it was variable – but it kept coming up again: here we go. And we both kind of knew we were going into it.

But I don't want to say that I was an equal part. I wasn't. Malcolm made sure that he was *the* scene. So no one could get in there. Everyone got to a point and then . . . I always felt that I was criticizing Malcolm all the time. That seemed to be my job. And I think that's the job of the Pistols and the Clash, to criticize each other. They criticize us, we criticize them.
Q: On what grounds do you and Malcolm criticize one another?
BR: We have a slight difference. Because Malcolm's working on the premise that anything goes, right? I suppose Situationist theory. And I think if anything goes, the status quo goes. I think you've got to define your limitations and like keep it to a point. Everybody has a different method of working, but like he tended to get an idea, work with an idea for quite a long time and then change it completely, twist it upside-down, and that would be the idea.

I don't think Malcolm's aims and mine were ever the same. We had a particular point where it was necessary to work together quite intensely. Could have been any two people. But if you're talking about our relationship, it's all to do with upbringing, you know, your background. He's got a specific background and I've got a different one. The way we deal with things is very different.

Malcolm, he says it himself, he's a snob. He is. He likes to be of that nature. I'm a kind of snob but not that obvious.

AL CLARK: Malcolm is still quite bitter towards Richard [Branson] and continues to make it very evident in any interview he does. And I think the reason he is bitter towards him is that, um, ultimately I think he feels outswindled which is something I don't think his pride can handle too well. I mean 'swindle' being in inverted commas. But he was so used to having his

McLaren briefs the Pistols in their Denmark Street loft in 1976.

own way in everything and, you know, he was the man who walked out of EMI with the cheque and A & M with the cheque, and then in Richard he came across somebody who was his equal – I mean who was just as astute, just as inventive, just as evasive and certainly just as tenacious. So I suspect some of the bitterness is rooted in the feeling that Richard pulled a few doves from up his sleeve at a time when Malcolm was still doing the juggling.

JULIEN TEMPLE: What I find very funny is this idea that the guy's a genius – you know, it's crazy. And I think he believes that too much, that anything he does, however pedestrian the lyrics or obvious the ideas are, you know, if it comes through Malcolm it's, people have this idea it's genius at work, which I find very funny.

[Written by FV for the first edition in 1977.]
Malcolm's thinking is fundamentally visual: he thinks with colour and shape and tends to see things as 'wholes'. His thinking also tends to be mythical. In other words he is the opposite of the ruling sort of analyzing, critical and literary intelligence – rather than taking things apart or examining structures, Malcolm imagines and brings *together* and *mystifies* structure.

His work has displayed a remarkable continuity in its concern with the themes of blackness and non-appearance; with blackness as anti-colour, negation and 'badness'. His earliest notable work (when he was about 19) was a series of self portrait drawings: heavily cross-hatched into the paper; drawings whose black intensity emerged through shiny graphite layers of incision. This sense of 'black' identity was developed through painting and sculpture, and in fashion.

Malcolm's fascination with 'evil' can be opportunistic and anti-human. For example: his aesthetic use of the 'Cambridge Rapist' motif in T-shirts etc. seems insensitive to the feelings of rape victims.

Malcolm was a 'punk' way back: for instance, he used to characterize hippies as 'hippos': indolent and boring.

He developed his garish surrealism from the mid-sixties. I well remember the outrage of an art school Maoist at Malcolm appearing at a revolutionary meeting in fluorescent green buckled women's shoes – 'counter-revolutionary' was the Chinese verdict.

It should be said that Malcolm has a puritanical disdain for the sexual deviations – narcissism, exhibitionism and fetishism – he exploits through his work.

Malcolm's preoccupation with blackness comes from his need to conceal himself or make himself 'invisible', a need expressed through ultra-exhibitionism and the making of loud and 'definitive' statements, orally and in dress.

Malcolm is an intensely oral person of 'devouring curiosity'. This is interesting in respect of the oral harshness he has cultivated in the Sex Pistols' image.

It is interesting that Malcolm's style of flaunting and carping, a fierce flash and studied resentment – arising from his chosen reaction to social marginality (Jewishness) and psychological rejection (by his family) – has now been taken up as a ready-made social attitude by so many people.

Malcolm has the vision of an artist, the heart of an anarchist, and the imagination of a spiv. There are signs that entrepreneurial success may flush out his receptiveness and creativity. I hope not.

PART 3

FEELINGS

PUNK

PUNK[1] *Obsolete* or *rare archaic* 1596. [Of unknown origin.] A prostitute, strumpet, harlot.

PUNK[2] Chiefly *U.S.* 1707. [Of unknown origin; c. FUNK, SPUNK.] 1. Rotten wood, or a fungus growing on wood, used in a dry state for tinder, touchwood, amadou. 2. A composition that will smoulder when ignited, used to touch off fireworks 1869. 3. Chinese incense 1890. Hence PUNK a., PUNKY a. (chiefly *U.S.*), rotten.

Shorter Oxford English Dictionary

To children in south Somerset a punkie is a home-made mangel-wurzel lantern of more artistic manufacture than those commonly made elsewhere for Hallowe'en. At Hinton St. George, where Punkie Night is the fourth Thursday in October, some sixty children come out into the street with their lanterns, and parade through the village in rival bands, calling at houses and singing:

It's Punkie Night tonight,
It's Punkie Night tonight.
Give us a candle, give us a light,
If you don't you'll get a fright.

It's Punkie Night tonight,
It's Punkie Night tonight,
Adam and Eve wouldn't believe,
It's Punkie Night tonight.

And this, incidentally, is another custom which the police have tried to stop.

Iona and Peter Opie, *The Lore and Language of Schoolchildren*

POLITICS

TOMMY VANCE: Somebody once said to me that Malcolm is a fascist.
JOHNNY ROTTEN: That's absolute rubbish. He couldn't be – he's a Jew for a start. No. Nobody, nobody should be a fascist.

Capital Radio, 16 July 1977

DEBBIE: I sometimes day-dream. Like one day I was day-dreaming and I was dreaming about like if the Pistols took over all the country. I was listening to their record and I was just thinking they could take over all the country. There wasn't a Parliament. It was more run by people like John. Not run by anyone really, but all of us lot, kind of thing, sort of walking around in freedom more or less. Through John. Cos I mean it needs a lot of people to change things and there's just not enough people to change things at the moment. But I mean, you look at this country and it's growing and growing. And there's kids that have come from really well-off families that have actually rebelled against them and torn their clothes up. They live in slums. They don't want to live in this great big rich house with their mother and father who are so snobby. And this music just doesn't appeal to one type of person.

BERNIE RHODES: Politics is when more than three people are in a room. That's politics. You can't live without politics. On the other hand, you don't need to display it every ten minutes. It's there. It's like the pair of shoes that you're wearing, right? They're there. You don't have to keep on touching them to make sure you're wearing them.

LAZY SODS

MIRROR COMMENT
PUNK FUTURE

It's not much fun to be young today. If you think otherwise take a look at yesterday's jobless figures.

Is it any wonder if youngsters feel disillusioned and betrayed?

Is it any wonder if they turn to anarchistic heroes like Johnny Rotten?

In the plight of the young, Britain is now beginning to reap the bitter harvest of inflation.

A brave new generation of talent and purpose is turning sour before our very eyes.

Editorial, *Daily Mirror*, 22 June 1977

Q: What would happen if the band broke up for whatever reason? What would you do?
STEVE JONES: I'd start another group. I wouldn't – I'd never get a fucking working job. I couldn't, not now, get a working job. I just couldn't. It would do me up for good, I think. I'd become a cabbage or something.
Q: Why?
SJ: Well, having all this excitement, you know, and doing exactly what you're really into doing, you can't just carry on and work for a job from nine to five or whatever.
Q: Lots of people do though, don't they?
SJ: Well, there's a lot of silly people as well – people are stupid and do anything you ask them to.
Q: What do you think is so dreadful about work then?
SJ: Getting up early in the morning! It is – really it depresses me.
Q: Does it?
SJ: Yes. And for working at something you don't really want to do, just to get money. I mean I wouldn't, I just wouldn't do a working job.

Q: What do you like best about being in the band?
PAUL COOK: I don't know. I just like being in the band, in *a* band, cos that's what I want to do. And it's not work really – it's work, but you enjoy doing it, so it ain't work. It's a good laugh.

Q: After you left school did you go straight to work – you went to technical college didn't you?
JOHNNY ROTTEN: I was working while I was at school.
Q: Doing what?

JR: Like building sites and things. Being a lazy cunt and being paid for it. It's so easy to dodge on a building site. Then I went to work at a sewerage farm with my old man.
FRIEND: But he left cos the foreman's breath smelt.
JR: Killing rats that was a really fucking good job.
Q: Why's it a good job?
JR: Because it was fun. Something to do, weren't it?
Q: In what way was it fun?
JR: I hate rats. And you chop one in half in mid-air when it fucking lurches towards you. [*Irish accent*] It's kind of exciting.
Q: But there are jobs and jobs, aren't there? And some can be really sort of tedious and make you really miserable and . . .
JR: All jobs are tedious.
Q: Do you think so?
FRIEND: Shops, factories and offices.
JR: The only thing that keeps half the people alive in factories is the fucking radio on all day.

Q: What do you think about the journalists who have taken a more kind of serious approach to you and even the kind of sociological jargon that has got used about you?
SID VICIOUS: Oh, Jesus. Can you give me an example?
Q: Well, I think the most famous example is 'dole queue rock'.
SV: Oh, my God. Dole queue rock. Well, I mean like I'm not on the dole. I was never even on the dole before I joined the band. I think I went down there one week and from then on I couldn't be bothered to go down and collect it there. I could ponce more than like £10 in a week, do you know what I mean? I had no source of income whatsoever, but I never starved. If it's not what you want to do, it's shit. You know what I mean?

LAZY SOD

You're only 29 got a lot to learn
But when your business dies
You will not return
We make noise cos it's our choice
It's what we want to do
We don't care about long hair
We don't wear flairs
See my face not a trace, no reality
I don't work I just speed
That's all I need
Lazy sod

'FOAMING AT THE MOUTH' – AN MP SPEAKS

MARCUS LIPTON (MP): The Sex Pistols is only one of several punk rock groups and they all look the same to me. I mean there don't seem to be much difference between any of them. All I am concerned with is the fact that – I mean I don't mind the music that they provide, but their general behaviour which they think is a part of the act, and which is just calculated to appeal to a low mental group or just to offend people. So it's not just music. I mean I like music, I like hard rock, but I don't like punk. I don't care very much for all the sort of sexual antics, plus the crudity with which they put it over and which the managers are deliberately exploiting so as to get the young kids sexually excited. That, I suppose, probably goes back to Elvis Presley. Probably started by his pelvic manipulations. So he may be considered the father. And out of it all these things have developed. And so you have one aspect of it. The other is the wearing of the very tight trousers is the nearest way they can get to demonstrating the size of their genitals. It's got nothing to do with *music*. But Jones, Tom Jones, he wears these very tight trousers, so I suppose the kids like it. Another fellow actually split his trousers on some occasion. And then you get, carried one stage further, swearing and spitting. I don't say the Sex Pistols are guilty of these things, I don't know them specifically. They're just part of the general kind of attitude or symbolism or whatever you like to call it with which they're putting across their music. Now, you see, the managers of these groups obviously come to the conclusion that the music by itself is not going to stimulate and get the crowds, so they get hold of these fellows who are willing to perform these antics, and their behaviour, because they think it arouses the cheers of the multitude, just gets outrageous. From my point of view it's got nothing to do with music. And you could build up a whole thesis just on that thing. And there's some group which spits at the audience, or spits at each other, or something like that. A commercial exploitation of sex and depravity. And to that extent I don't like it very much. I mean I don't mind people who want to be depraved in private. They can do what the devil they like. But to make a public spectacle or whatever, that's something which doesn't please me very much . . . It's a pure, deliberate commercial exploitation by these managers – I don't know who they are, God knows what sort of people they are – who think they're on a good thing. And so they get the money from the kids. And it's the kids that flock to these things. And so they work the kids up into a state of frenzied excitement, just like witch doctors or whatever it is in Central Africa – you

know, you keep on *banging* the drums and that sort of thing, and they start foaming at the mouth and that sort of thing. Well, this is the Western equivalent of it. And I was told by the manager of the Odeon, Hammersmith, or some place or other, and he said that the smell at the end of one of these concerts was terrible. All these little girls are wetting their pants. The accumulated odour of all this is overpowering. You've got them excited, they're wetting their pants and getting excited – there you are . . . The influence is to excite them and stimulate them sexually. That's the whole object of the exercise. Because in no other way will they get the audience. And the basis of it all is to appeal as far as they can to the sexual instinct of kids at an age when the sexual instinct is highly developed. It slows down a bit, thank God, when they get a bit older, settle down and get married . . . Take another aspect, the way these punk rockers behave in hotels. They smash the place up. The excitement goes to their heads too because they think they're good God Almighty, you know, the world belongs to them. And they've got all these girls running around in their bedrooms, so a good time is being had by all . . . It's the girls – the fellows don't get so excited at these pop concerts. They go, they like the excitement, but the main appeal is to the young girls and their dreams of a life of shall we say a kind of love and luxury and booze and fornication all mixed up together . . .

The gad-fly he hath stung me sore –
O may he ne'er sting you!
But we have many a horrid bore
He may sting black and blue.

Is there a man in Parliament
Dumbfoundered in his speech?
O let his neighbour make a rent
And put one in his breech.

Keats, 'All gentle folks who owe a grudge'

MUSEUM PIECES

Q: I think a lot of people would find it a bit curious to find that the V & A were buying visuals associated with the Sex Pistols, only a couple of years after the Sex Pistols had been in existence. Have you got any comments on that?

DANNY FRIEDMAN OF THE VICTORIA & ALBERT MUSEUM: Yeah. A couple of people are surprized by that but, um, the problem is that if you allow something to slip up for too long, two things happen: one, bits and pieces start vanishing into people's own pockets and just being lost, two, the price goes up.

Q: How did the acquisition of the Sex Pistols material come about?

DF: The contact was made by Robert Fraser [the art dealer]. Robert Fraser had been in touch with us before about some other material to do with the Stones and the Beatles, and when that deal went through I sort of became quite matey with him and he mentioned that he knew Jamie Reid very well and thought that he would be interested in getting rid of this material. So I arranged to go over and see Jamie and I saw him and I saw his stuff.

Q: Do you think of the [Sex Pistols'] visuals as a kind of art form?

DF: Um, art form – that's a funny word. I consider the visuals artwork. Art form – I don't like the word because it's a bit too elitist. I think the importance of the designs that came out of Jamie Reid and the Pistols is that it – just as the Sex Pistols were important in democratizing music, the designs deomcratized art. Because anyone can do it, you know. All you need is a newspaper and some scissors and an airbrush if you get a bit flash later. I mean the whole thing about photo collages, xeroxes, polaroids was really bringing Art with a big 'A' right down to where anyone could do it. And that's what's important about it I think.

Q: Can you see, um, the Sex Pistols' graphics increasing in value and are they going to hold their value?

DF: Sadly, yes, I think they will. And they'll eventually be put on pedestals and, you know, appear in art galleries and museums I suppose. Um, I think they probably will keep their value simply because it was such a one-off thing with the Pistols, you know: they came and they went all in the space of about two years, in terms of their impact on the public. And also the style has changed. The cut-up letter style is no longer acceptable any more. So it was a one off thing. And yes, as it's sort of unique, and as the Pistols were a one band movement, I think they will maintain their value, which is a bit sad.

Most of the opposition to having the Sex Pistols in a museum, in fact, doesn't come from orthodox museum establishments. It comes from the people on the street. You know, they say: 'How can you, how dare you bring

Sex Pistols into museums, this is destroying what they stood for, this is not anarchy, this is organization, this is bureaucracy.

'FIRE UNDER THEIR BUMS' – LETTERS FROM FANS

Dear 'Sex Pistols'!

There are writing to You, two young, nice and rather fine girls from Poland. What do you think about it? We hope this is the first letter You have got from such an egzotic country like Poland. There's a cold and dark night behind us, we are drinking coffee and writing this letter to You. Our names are B—— and C——. In Poland, 'punk rock' isn't known very well, but we know quite a lot about You, though we haven't heard any of Yours compositions (songs), yet; but we have heard a lot of goods of yours. Though You aren't known very much, but we'll believe that you'll be famous very soon as for instance: Jimi Hendrix. We are very sorry that we're dared to ask You, but we would like to know, why You are called 'Sex Pistols'. And now something about our hobbies. C—— likes: babies, long hair, play tennis (have You heard about Fibak – he's her ideal), hippies, and she is able to play drums very well and she is in a platonic love with ex-Deep Purple guitarman – Ritchie Blackmore. I like: cats, dogs, golden fishes, speedy motor-cycles, spaghetti and I'm able to play the guitar quite well and I am in a platonic love with Mahavishnu John McLaughlin.

We are seventeen years old, we are rather poor girls and we still go to school. We like You as the boys, though we have never seen You, but Your faces seem us very nice and though we don't know You, we think that You are very fine boys. We hope You understand our English, we are very sorry for the mistakes, but we've written this letter as best we could. We are really very sorry. Now we are finishing this letter, and we ask You to remember our words or our oracle: we believe we'll be very famous and you'll be able to go to Poland and we'll be able to come to your concert. If you can, please write us, it will be a great pleasure for us.

Shandy Street,
London E 1
5. 4. 77

Dear Glitterbest.

Maybe I'm stupid & don't have the right connections or something but how come nowadays I only get to hear the Sex Pistols playing *after* the actual event? I want to be childish & scream 'It isn't FAIR!' at you – well, after all, you do like to get to see your favourite group once in a while! It's rather ironic after McLaren going on & on about giving 'the kids' what they want – since when has he given a real thought to 'the kids' and not just himself & the Pistols image? I'm sick of being patronized! And you too reading this letter will be smirking away cos it's not Your problem. Maybe I'm self-pitying, maybe I'm misinformed, but I can't help not being as hip as all you lucky people 'in the clique' (& talking of cliques, when is no. 2 of your in-crowd mag *Anarchy* coming out?) So what if you & Malcolm & Johnny couldn't care less about me, I don't mind, all I want to know is, will the Pistols be doing any more 'secret' gigs in the near future? There *are* still people who like to go to see rather than be seen, cos they are the greatest group in the world. Please, isn't it possible to let us know via the press rather than the whispered word, when they are appearing? Are they scared of anyone turning up who isn't 'one of them'?

Anyway, despite all the shit going round, here's my best wishes & all the luck in the world – hope they get signed up again soon & *nice* things start happening.

Yours sincerely & frustratedly,
Molly Gilligan

Shandy Street,
London E 1
18. 8. 77

Dear Fred & Judy V.,

Of course you can quote my letter & I'm not such a shrinking violet as to wish it to be anonymous, as long as you don't put it out of context and make me look an old cunt.

I'm glad you're writing a book about the Pistols. I hope it won't be sanctimonious twaddle like Caroline Coon though & you'd better not make Rotten into the fab far-out messiah. If I can be of any assistance, just drop a line, but actually now I come to think of it I can't see any reason why you should want to. The only out of the ordinary experience I had was going to see them in Leeds on the Anarchy tour, which was a right balls-up, everybody loathed them. Leeds is where I come from originally and I can tell you, it's where the thickest cretins in England are bred (ooh, I don't mean ME!)

Oh yeah, I once got my hand cut up at the 100 Club but that must be fairly common.

I'm right pissed off with not being able to see the Pistols. I was going to Sweden last month but some villain nicked my savings. HUH! I also got sacked once for being a Pistol's fan and ½ throttled by a Ted. What a *wonderful* incident packed life I lead eh?

You must be bored stiff with this letter so I'll pipe down now.
Molly Gilligan

P.S. Make sure you say what cunts McLaren & Westwood are.

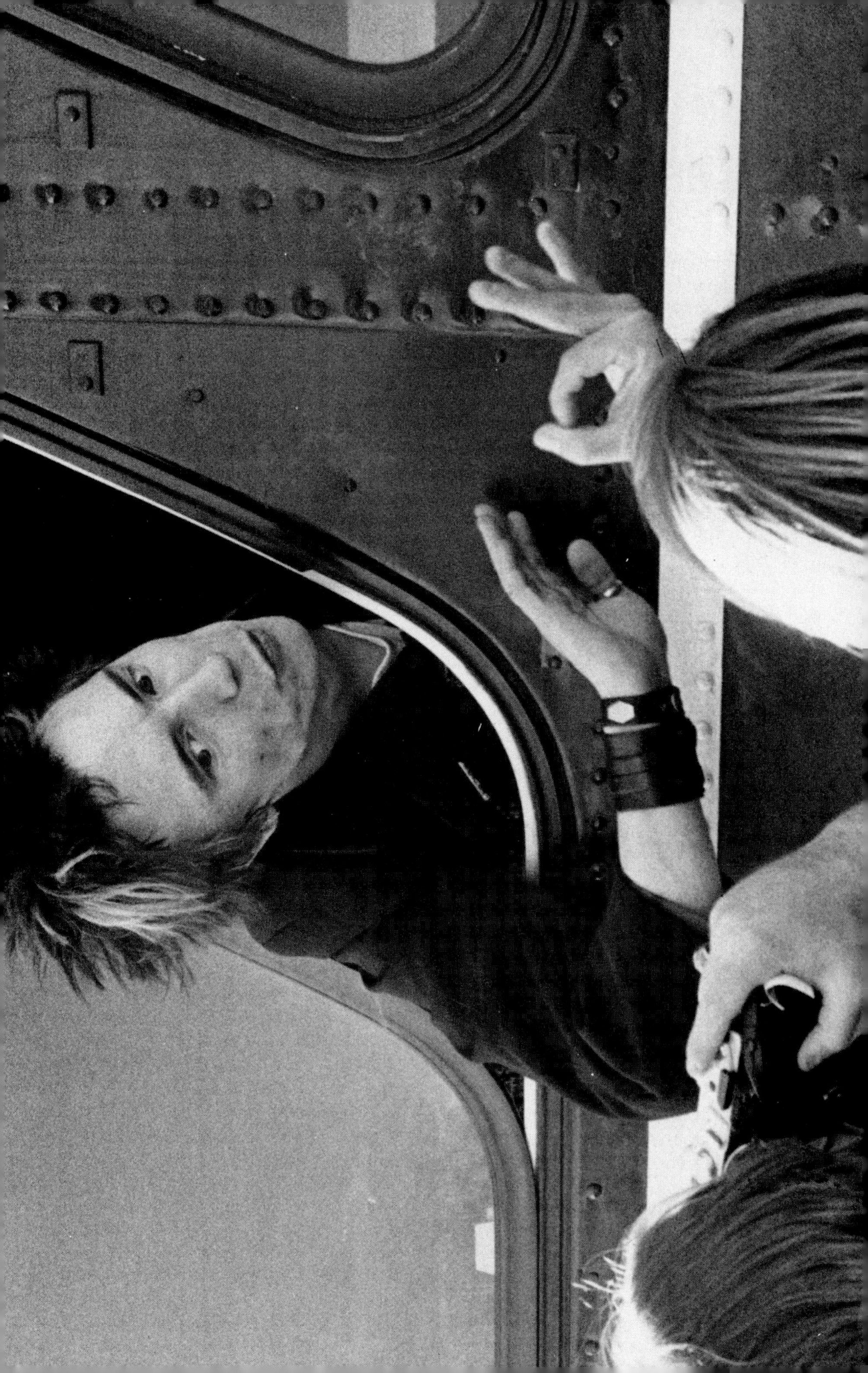

. . . when are the pistols coming to Hull?

If they can't find anywhere to play, they can come and play at our house, it's only a council tenancy but still I'm sure they won't mind.

OK

Keep rocking

S. R. Mc. D

Cubbran
Gwent

Dear Paul,

This letter is from Estel, (remember me from the Caerphilly concert). I don't know if you've read my first letter yet, but I thought I'd write you another one anyway . . . I know you left my phone number in the hotel, so here it is ———, just in case you fancy giving me a ring sometime.

On Wednesday night, I had a phone call from someone who staying at the Park Hotel, he must have seen the piece of paper that I wrote my telephone number on, and he asked me to meet at my house at two o'clock in the morning. I was a bit worried, he must have been a nympho. He said that he knew me but when my sister answered the phone, he did not know which Estel to speak to (as my mums name is the same).

Hope you had a good time in Holland and I hope you get some gigs in Britain soon, because if you do Laura and I would like to go. As soon as you find out, you can either give me a ring or write to me, to tell me. I would appreciate that very much. I wish that I could have made it to the Plymouth concert, but I couldn't make it, which was a pity because Laura was lumbered with Jeff Spanner *all* the time. He keeps hanging around us, which is a bloody nuisance because people think that, either Laura or I go out with him (so when you see Steve Jones, perhaps you could mention that). The next time you have a concert, Laura and I are coming without Jeff Spanner, and that will make things quite a lot easier. Neither Laura or I have ever been out with Jeff Spanner and don't intend to. All the boys around here make us sick as Jeff Spanner and we are only interested in you two (i.e. you and Steve Jones) don't laugh about what I've just told you because it's true, all the boys in Wales sicken us. We hope that we get another chance to stay in your hotel again. Show this letter to Steve, because Laura wants you to.

Laura and I have now both got ten copies each of Anarchy in the U.K., and we play them all the time, we can't wait for you to bring out an album.

So, goodbye for now and don't forget to tell me if you play anywhere.

Lots of love and kisses from

ESTEL XXXXXXXXXXXXX

P.S. Don't forget to give me a ring.

Ampleforth College,
Near York

. . . It's really great to know that some people outside Yorkshire realize 'Public School' boys aren't just young 'farts'. A bloke in my house called R——— sez he knows you and sends his regards.

Hardly anyone else is into New Wave. I've even tried to start a group but no one caught on! However there are the faithful few.

Some monk saw the last issue [of 'Anarchy' mag] and tried to find out your address. He also told me to take off the Pistols badges I was wearing. However don't judge them all on that 'cos he was a nurk of the first degree. Give my thanx to the secretary in the office . . .

Hallo Sex Pistols!

I am a 16 years old German girl. I am 171 cm tall, have grey-green-blue eyes and brown hair. I have read your interview in 'Bravo', and I have thought: Gretel, you must write these boys, which have fire under their bum. I like boys, motor-cycles, cars and riding. I hate tedious people who only look in a newspaper or a book. I like to hear music from: KISS, ELO, SAILOR, RICK Dees + Cast of Idiots and also your music. Are you so sexy as your name? If there is any way to meet you, please write it. I am not such a girl, who say I love you or without you I can't live, but I want to speak with you. I have momentary no boyfriend. I wait for the right boy, and I have time. Have you girl-friends? I am ready with school, and now I work. I make an apprenticeship in an law-court. It's a job like an secretary. My friends say it is not the right job for me, I must become an actress because I have the mouth and talent for that. But now I make an end. Please write back to me. Good-bye.

Gretel

P.S. I wait from now every day for the postman.

Dear Glitterbest,

I am just writing to see if you are still in existence. I am still heartbroken over the Sex pistols choice to break up, I know everyone says they done the right thing but I dont think so. They let the councils win before we all gathered enough people to shout for the pistols. I havent had the chance to see the pistols, now I dont suppose I ever will, it just isnt fair. All my mates are taking it very casually but I cant, I feel as if the bloody world has stopped turning cos you hardly hear anything about the pistols nowadays. I'll love them forever I guess. I really don't know why they're all picking on Sid because it seems to me that he was the only one keeping up the usual Pistols spirit in America. I thought he looked beautiful with his face and chest covered in blood. I honestly think Johnny changed more than anyone else. I mean well this bodyguard business shows he was the one who was turning himself into a rich important star, and I've loved the pistols since he was the cheeky bugger that swore at bill grundy (he doesn't deserve Capital letters) that's the way I liked Johnny. Arrogant with his fixed opinions, but these days he is polite spoken and he talks a load of rubbish, well I think he does cos I collect everything I see with pistols written across it and he can say something one minute and completely change his mind and say the opposite the next. Now what am I, the fan, supposed to believe? I think he's really frightened now and I feel really sorry for him, there will always be a place in my heart for Johnny Rotten. I wasnt lucky enough to be born in London and see the sex pistols in the early days.

Please send me some of those gorgeous glossy pics of the everlasting Sex pistols. I collect them, and I would be very grateful, I've enclosed an SAE. By the way thanx Sue for phoning me back at a telephone booth and talking to me when I needed someone. Anyone who says the pistols are dead are Morons. THE PISTOLS WILL NEVER DIE.

PLEASE PLEASE REPLY – thanks.

Shirley X

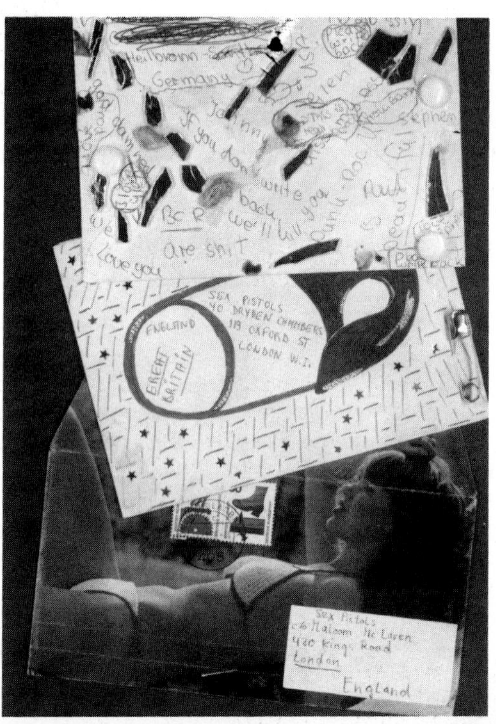

WESTWOOD
REID
DEBORD
BACKGROUND
NOTES
YOUR
NEVER MIND
THE BOLLOCKS
HERE'S THE
EMI
Wanna
Be Me
(Rotten—Jones—Matlock—Cook)
EMI Music Publishing Ltd.
Sex
Pistols
SEX
PISTOLS

THE (EARLY) LIFE AND CRIMES OF MALCOLM McLAREN

Malcolm's Scottish father (surnamed McLaren) left home when Malcolm was an infant. Malcolm's Jewish mother remarried as Edwards and began a successful clothes wholesaling firm with her husband. Malcolm was brought up in middle-class comfort mostly in Edgware with his elder brother and younger step-brother.

Malcolm's relations with his mother and step-father were always strained. Haunted by his missing father, he sought refuge in the confidences of his maternal grandmother and several aunts who raised him as much as his parents. These aunts were ex-Portuguese Jewesses with a rich East London tradition. They would sing Malcolm ribald music-hall ditties and entertain him with saucy anecdotes about Marie Lloyd and readings from Charles Dickens.

After leaving school at 16 minus 'A' levels Malcolm worked as a clerk in a wine wholesalers in Orange Street, WC2. At this time he was a mod and in the summer of '63 spent a suitably mod-ish holiday in the casinos of the South of France where he saw and was captivated by Dionne Warwicke.

The following year, after being turned down for the Royal Academy of Dramatic Art, Malcolm scraped his way into Harrow College of Art (where FV first met him).

In 1964 Harrow Art College was a labyrinthian 19th century building (since demolished) of white stone and twisted iron railings. It was also the centre for miles around for bohemian frenzy, mixing the local gay community with beatniks, drug peddlers, sexual delinquents and mods.

Malcolm's many disputes with his mother culminated in his being booted out of the family home and forced to leave college. For a brief period he dossed in Harrow on the Hill cemetery among the gravestones, where FV would take him refreshments and news of the outside world. FV then found him more comfortable accommodation in a friend's battered old Ford. This friend was Gordon Swire, Vivienne Westwood's brother. Visiting Gordon one day, Vivienne became intrigued with the peculiar looking redhead kipping in Gordon's car. She was introduced to Malcolm over a bowl of Shredded Wheat and immediately fell in love: 'The most extraordinary person I'd ever met.'

Malcolm however was not impressed, having got into a total art trip which left no time at all for women.

The Royal Academy portrait painter Theodore Ramos, then teaching art history part time at Harrow, now befriended and patronized Malcolm. Ramos's perverse suavity shaped Malcolm's own cynical charm. FV remembers Ramos standing in the middle of a particularly appalling end-of-term show by one student and declaring: 'Anyone *this* bad *has* to be good.' 15 years later Malcolm was to say the same of Steve Jones and Paul Cook.

At Ramos's suggestion Malcolm became assistant to a theatrical set designer and was put up in his studio. This arrangement ended when some fluted columns for an Indian temple of love carved by Malcolm out of polystyrene for a New Arts Theatre production proved so bad the producer kicked them off stage.

Malcolm next tried his living as a freelance artist. He hawked oil paintings around the art galleries of Swinging London with little success. Then he discovered environmental art and persuaded the owner of the (now defunct) Kingly Street Gallery to give him his first ever show.

Taking over the gallery for an evening, Malcolm recreated the interior as a series of mazes and false levels with hundreds of empty boxes and rolls of corrugated cardboard. Spectators/participants were obliged to clamber up and down ladders, through cardboard tunnels, and over makeshift floors. Meanwhile, cut-ups of 'found' (actually nicked) 35mm schlock movie footage were beamed and blasted from various vantage points.

Things began to get out of hand when around 10pm Malcolm and other participants, by now fairly well pissed, began extending the show into Kingly Street. A traffic jam ensued and several cars were decorated with cardboard. Audie Murphy war movie footage was projected noisily all over the street. Two constables from Savile Row police station turned up and began taking details from the gallery owner. Just then a piercing scream came from inside the gallery. A blind-drunk soldier on leave had wandered upstairs and crashed through a cardboard floor. He lay moaning, vomiting and bleeding on a pile of shredded cardboard. Malcolm buggered off.

Malcolm's grandmother now found him lodgings with a Mrs Gold. Mrs Gold said: "No women and no mess." Her home smelled of boiled cabbage. Malcolm barricaded himself in and began work. Soon his bedsit was splattered with paint and littered with planks of wood and rolls of fabric. Alerted by the continuous banging and sawing and suspicious because he hardly ever came out (he used to pee in the sink), Mrs Gold sneaked into Malcolm's room one day when he was out buying Nescafé. Instant eviction.

Malcolm now briefly took up residence in a Notting Hill brothel but left soon after one of the girls told FV that some of the forks had been used in a recent abortion. He then took up lodgings in a Greek shoemaker's flat in Berwick Street, Soho, but was ejected after the Greek complained of Malcolm's night-time screaming fits – Malcolm suffered horribly from nightmares around this time (mostly about his mother). Gordon now came to the rescue again and found Malcolm a room in the Chiswick house he rented with several film college cronies.

Vivienne meanwhile had left her husband (who was a freelance pilot and former manager – so he said – of the Who) and followed Malcolm to Chiswick. Malcolm began complaining to FV about Vivienne appearing in his room naked. He affected disdain for her charms for some time, but eventually succumbed. 10 months later, to Malcolm's astonishment, their son Joe was born.

Malcolm now began a seven year career in and out of various colleges on 'A' level and fine art courses – paid for by a succession of dubious grants and borrowings from his ever-doting granny.

At Chiswick Poly, inspired by the idea of 'total art', Malcolm tried to learn piano – with disastrous results.

Even so, his musical interests were rich and eclectic. He was equally at home bopping to Long John Baldry at the Wealdstone Railway Tavern as going to see Verdi at the Royal Opera House in Covent Garden. And when FV once commandeered the record player at a Chiswick party to play non-stop Edith Piaf, Malcolm silenced the opposition by ferociously declaring: 'Piaf and Elvis . . . ARE LIKE THIS!': twining both forefingers.

Now a word about Malcolm's personality.

Malcolm has always suffered (less conspicuously nowadays) from a rare nervous disorder called Gilles de la Tourettes syndrome. This is distinguished by manic bursts of energy, muscular incoordination and the compulsive copying of other people's behaviour.

In fact he was sacked in his student days from two casual jobs because of this disability.

The first, at a Heathrow Airport coffee bar, ended after complaints that he was spilling more coffee over customers than was left in the cups. The second was at the old Lyons Corner House opposite Charing Cross station, when being assigned to refill the sugar bowls Malcolm left a trail of sugar over the floors and tables – to the incredulous fury of the assistant manager.

And Malcolm's later incarnation as a pop star was in doubt when Trevor Horn discovered that Malcolm is physically incapable of keeping time.

Malcolm, however, early developed a persona which turned his disability to advantage. By affecting a larger-than-life, 'who gives a fuck' attitude (whereas being a snob he was frequently deeply embarrassed) he gave the impression his grotesque mannerisms and physical gaffs were deliberate snooks cocked at the world.

In this way he was able to create a legendary aura around himself – fairly easy in the art college/fine arts context where the idea of genius as behaviour (rather than work) has been accepted at least since Marcel Duchamp.

For Malcolm's greatest and most endearing quality is turning disasters to good use. After all, the Sex Pistols' history was one disaster after another, only brilliantly exploited and turned, often against all odds, into wonderful victories against common sense.

But his bizarre behaviour was largely unproductive until channelled and put into practice by Vivienne Westwood's Northern determination to MAKE GOOD. (Just as it was later channelled by a succession of assistants/producers from Jamie Reid to Trevor Horn.)

In fact it was Vivienne as far back as 1966 Chiswick days who began to run up a series of eccentric costumes for Malcolm from his 'crazy' ideas. The first was a bright yellow 'boiler suit' several sizes too large. (Before that Malcolm's main sartorial extravagance had been an omnipresent tartan scarf.) It was Vivienne too who began making jewellery from Malcolm's designs which she sold on a Portobello Road stall to supplement their meagre income – Vivienne's salary as a junior school teacher had to support herself and two kids (Ben from her first marriage and Joe) as well as supplement Malcolm's grant.

Now back to Malcolm's college days.

Following Chiswick Poly, Malcolm spent a brief period at Chelsea Art College where he produced several impressive large-scale constructions (see page 187).

At Chelsea too he was politicized by Stan, a Trotskyite art student who played a mean jazz saxophone. Then, in 1967, Malcolm was arrested with a South African expatriate called Henry Adler for attempting to burn the American flag. They spent the night in police cells and subsequently became friends. Henry (a patient of the radical psychoanalyst David Cooper) further radicalized Malcolm, introducing him to the ideas of R D Laing and generally educating him in international politics.

Henry was into every possible variant of art radicalism. He introduced Malcolm and FV to the first London Arts Lab where they saw Kenneth Anger's movies as well as Lenny Bruce and Alan Ginsberg live, and where they also heard (and were revolted by) the beginnings of psychedelic rock.

Malcolm now enrolled at Croydon Art College where he met and befriended Jamie Reid and Robin ('Pop Muzik') Scott. Malcolm and Vivienne had meanwhile moved into Aigburgh Mansions, Hackford Road, at the Oval. Here they gave several memorable dinner parties. Vivienne cooked, served and washed up and also put the kids to bed, while Malcolm disputed politics and art with combinations of Henry, Robin, Jamie, FV and others. This was before Women's Lib.

The magic year 1968 came and went (see following notes). Malcolm finally passed his 'A' level history and graduated to the prestigious Goldsmiths' Art College. This was noted, as it is now, for a freewheeling style. Malcolm went in for photography and movie making.

He also engaged in a reign of post-'68 intellectual terrorism inspired by Situationism. The highlight of this was the Goldsmiths' Free Festival. The Festival was organized chiefly by Liz Martin (the first feminist Malcolm ever met – the sparks!) and by Nile Martin (no relation to Liz). Malcolm however stamped the affair with his personality and took most of the credit when hardly any of the bands advertised turned up and in the resulting chaos the police were called and a mini-riot developed.

At Goldsmiths' Malcolm also befriended Helen, the dwarf who features in *The Great Rock 'n' Roll Swindle*. Helen was another South African expatriate and made a suitable companion for Malcolm's nocturnal sorties. Malcolm, Helen and FV gate-crashed several elegant parties around this period, Clockwork Orange style. At one, in a Hampstead penthouse, Helen defaced several op art masterpieces while FV redecorated the bathroom with Situationist slogans and Malcolm started a small fire in the living room.

For his Goldsmiths' finals Malcolm tried to make a 16mm short on the history of Oxford Street with his granny doing voice-over. But this proved too ambitious to complete. Instead, Malcolm discovered some 8mm footage of a lecturer's summer holidays: beach scenes, ball games, etc. This he cut up and randomly re-edited with upside-down, back-to-front and mutilated sequences and handed in. The film tutor, who failed to recognize his colleague, pronounced it brilliant. However, before it was officially assessed Malcolm decamped from Goldsmiths' and never did get any diploma.

By this time Malcolm and Vivienne, Joe and Ben had moved into a tiny one-bedroomed flat in Thurleigh Court, off Clapham Common. This flat was found for them by Malcolm's grandmother and was five minutes walking from her own flat. She frequently looked

FREE

GOLDSMITHS' COLLEGE ARTS FESTIVAL

FREE

Goldsmiths' College, New Cross, S.E.14. is being taken over by the students and public on Monday, 30th June at 5 p.m. and going on through till late Friday, 4th July.

FRIDAY		
BACKFIELD	1 p.m.	Pretty Things Deviants Skin Alley Brew Da-Da Lives Groundhogs Pegasus Sour Milk Sea Robin Scott
THEATRE	6 p.m.	"Turquoise Pantomime" mime by Lindsay Kemp Vermillion Dance Troupe Action Theatre
LECTURE THEATRE	11 a.m.	"Modesty Blaise" (film) and cartoons
	2 p.m.	William Burrough's cut-ups Alex Trocchi film
	3 p.m.	Frederic Vermorel "All in a day's work"
BAR	EVENING	Di Soar and Chris Jordan – Folksingers
RECITAL ROOM	3 p.m. and 7 p.m.	"Anan" – group singing their own songs and music
SMALL HALL	7 p.m.	DISCUSSION with R.D. Laing, William Burroughs, Alex Trocchi, Michael X, Jim Dine, Paul Hoch, members of F.S.C., squatters, radical students and workers will discuss the Revolution, Anti-public relations, formation of resistance groups, etc.

after the kids while Vivienne was out selling jewellery. Malcolm also had a bed at his grandmother's flat and spent quite a lot of time there doing unaccustomed stints of reading, including Machiavelli's *The Prince*.

As a student Malcolm was quite fascinating and extremely generous. He unstintingly gave time to whatever crackpot or hairbrained scheme came along. And in a typical burst of enthusiasm he secretly (and as it turned out unwisely) married a foreign (Greek, if I remember rightly) woman in order to give her British citizenship. He got no money for this, just did it for the hell.

But when his college days ended in 1972, Malcolm was suddenly lost. For a time he was like a bird circling for direction. He inexplicably painted the hallway in his and Vivienne's flat completely black. And one afternoon he was arrested for stealing paltry items from a local Woolworths store.

But then Malcolm got organized.

He adopted the surname McLaren and with some money from his grandmother's pension and Vivienne's ex-shopkeeper parents leased the back part of 430 King's Road, then a boutique called Paradise Garage.

In 1972, Malcolm and Vivienne took over the entire premises and Vivienne quit schoolteaching to manage the shop.

Malcolm now discovered and practically reinvented youth culture. Rechristening the shop 'Let It Rock' he turned it into a Mecca for Teddy boys with a variety of clothing, knick-knacks and secondhand rock 'n' roll records. An old juke-box was installed to play suitable classics and the shop became a hangout for lost souls (like Steve Jones and Paul Cook). Malcolm and Vivienne also began creating their own Teddy boy designs.

But as Malcolm grew disillusioned with the political and cultural conservatism of his Ted clientele, his and Vivienne's designs turned into a general fifties' retro style. At this time, Malcolm, inspired by the success of *The Rocky Horror Show* also toyed with the idea of a musical based on the 1958 Notting Hill race riots.

The shop increasingly preoccupied Malcolm and he began seeing less of his grandmother. When her husband died suddenly, she was plunged into dejection and began neglecting herself. But she refused out of loyalty to Malcolm to accept help from his mother. After one long absence Malcolm, suddenly worried, visited her flat. He found her sitting naked and bolt upright in bed. She was dead from starvation.

Malcolm's mother never forgave him or Vivienne. Some years later Malcolm boarded a subway train in full punk regalia and without at first realizing it sat down next to his mother. They spent the entire journey without exchanging a word.

Growing bored with the fifties just as mainstream fashion caught up with his designs, Malcolm happened upon a catalogue for a Walthamstow lingerie shop. This, unusually for the times, openly advertised 'scandalous lingerie and glamourwear'. Changing the name of the shop to 'Sex', Malcolm sprayed its interior in fluorescent paint with slogans from Valerie Solanas' *Scum Manifesto*.

Then, looting Soho porn shops for design ideas, he and Vivienne gradually assembled the range of bizarre, fetishistic clothing which turned into the Punk Rock look.

Malcolm had by now begun a series of business trips to the USA. Teddy boy and sex designs were no go in that more conservative atmosphere. But New York was an ideas' goldmine for Malcolm. He was excited by the conspicuous de-

bauchery of the seedy and gay areas, and inspired with American gusto and know-how. From this point he always wanted to live in the US.

And in New York he first heard and stored the name 'Sex Pistols' – originally that of a New York street gang.

Over the years the shop had established itself as a source of props and costumes for rock and pop stars, being patronized by Iggy Pop as well as the New York Dolls. Malcolm now began moving more and more in rock circles and in 1974 tried his hand at managing the New York Dolls. They however proved unmanageable (Malcolm confiding to FV they were so far gone they could hardly articulate or even respond to speech – Malcolm instead had to grunt and gesticulate and physically push them about). But during this frustrating period Malcolm also saw Richard Hell and was greatly taken by Hell's spiky coloured hair and rags held with safety pins. Now there's an idea . . .

Malcolm's experience of the New York rock scene grew into an ambition for the most notorious rock band ever. Returning to London he started to look around for a suitable band and began visiting his former art college friends to co-opt them into his vision of a rock band seemingly stepped straight out of a porn horror movie onto the world stage . . .

From here the story is taken up by the Sex Pistols themselves, at the beginning of this book. [FV]

INSTITUTE OF CONTEMPORARY ARTS

OUTRAGE ?

The film, HURLEMENTS EN FAVEUR DE SADE, to be shown for the first time in England on 21 May, caused riots when shown in Paris. The Institute is screening this film in the belief that members should be given a chance to make up their own minds about it, though the Institute wishes it to be understood that it cannot be held responsible for the indignation of members who attend.

Saturday 18 May 8-11 pm — **AT HOME**
Dancing to Don Simmons' Group.
Members 3/- Guests 5/-

Tuesday 21 May 6.30 pm — **FILM**
HURLEMENTS EN FAVEUR DE SADE (1952)
First performance in England.
This, the last of Guy Debord's three films, represents his most radical break with 'good cinema'. He claims that the making of this film marked the death of an epoch. The film, a product of the Mouvement Lettriste, caused riots at its two showings in Paris cinema clubs, before it was banned.
(*See Editorial*).
Members 3/- and one guest only 5/-

Thursday 23 May 8.15 pm — **SCIENCE**
Dr. E. C. Zeeman: TOPOLOGY.
Topology is a branch of mathematics. What exactly is it, and what sort of problems does it try to solve? The speaker will attempt to answer these questions, and then describe his own aesthetic appreciation of it.
Members 1/6 Guests 3/-

Saturday 25 May 8-11 pm — **AT HOME**
Dancing to Norman Jackson and his Noveltones.
Members 3/- Guests 5/-

MONDAY - THURSDAY 26th September - 29th September
MONDAY - THURSDAY 3rd October - 6th October
TWICE NIGHTLY AT 6.00pm & 8.30pm
Tickets on sale at the Box Office - 75p (plus 25p membership)

INSTITUTE OF CONTEMPORARY ARTS
NASH HOUSE THE MALL LONDON S.W.1. Telephone 01-930-6393
Cinema entrance on the Mall, by Duke of York steps

FROM SITUATIONISM TO PUNK

Since the look and feel of the Pistols owed so much to Situationism, I tell the story here as I know it.[1]

Situationism grew out of the early fifties' Lettrist movement, a kind of avant-garde *reductio ad absurdum* founded by the Rumanian poet Isidore Isou. The Lettrists declared that since even words had been bankrupted by modern life, they would return to individual letters. The Lettrists also had an elaborate contempt for the whole of post-War consumer society, ridiculing its social absurdities, cultural sterility and mass-produced banality.

In 1952 a group of Lettrists broke up a press conference being given by Charlie Chaplin at the Ritz hotel. 'We believe,' they explained, 'that the most urgent expression of freedom is the destruction of idols, especially when they present themselves in the name of freedom.'

'Culture' was a dirty word for the Lettrists, as was 'work'. So they invented the art-form of 'psychogeography'. This entailed wandering the city for days or even weeks at a time in clothing provocatively painted with slogans – frequently intoxicated or otherwise high. The idea was to map out the city's secret territories and networks, and to search for repressed images of desire: instances of disorder, rebellion, wonder, madness, play.

Lettrism eventually split into warring factions and in 1957 at a conference of radical European artists and architects, Guy Debord with some other former Lettrists inaugurated the Situationist International.

Proudly adopting the title of 'intellectual terrorists' the SI developed a scathing critique of modern life. This fused the insights of Dadaism and Surrealism within the perspective of a libertarian (rabidly anti-Soviet and anti-Maoist) Marxism.

Whereas the original vision of Dadaism (1915–1922) was to detonate the visions of desire evoked by art by smashing the art-forms they were imprisoned in, the Surrealists (1922–) tried to arm desire by subverting the realities which constrained it, investing life itself with the magic possibilities of art.

Situationists united these visions by preaching what they called the *supercession* of art. They wanted to create 'situations' within life with the fluid and unbounded possibilities of art.

Looking for the unstable margins of culture, its points of crisis, they hoped to insert their presence as catalysts for catastrophies so definitive they would 'make all retreat impossible'.

The Situationists offered no programme, no five-year plan. They stood only for unlimited social autonomy and unbridled self-gratification. Their favourite reading was *Alice in Wonderland* and the Marquis de Sade (who read correctly is an anti-Christian revolutionary rather than a pornographer). They refused to found or to lead a mass movement and considered the artist's only legitimate function was to catalyze repressed desires. 'Our ideas,' they announced, 'are already in everyone's heads.'

In 1966, a group of Situationist-inspired students captured the student union at Strasbourg University. They dismissed its welfare officer ('thought policeman'), disbanded the union, and spent the entire union funds on printing and distributing an outrageous Situationist pamphlet. They also plastered the city of Strasbourg with seditious/obscene comics.

At the climax of the ensuing court proceedings the judge denounced these

DE LA MISERE
EN MILIEU
ETUDIANT

considérée
sous ses aspects économique, politique, psychologique, sexuel et notamment intellectuel
et de quelques moyens pour y remédier

par
des membres de l'Internationale Situationniste
et des étudiants de Strasbourg

— 1967 —

deuxième édition - 20ᵉ mille

'adolescents' who had 'openly slandered their colleagues, professors, God, religion and the clergy, and every government and social system in the entire world'. Moreover, he continued, 'They have rejected all legal and moral restraint and cynically extolled the virtues of theft and the destruction of study, the suppression of work, and advocated total subversion and a global proletarian revolution in the name of "perpetual orgasm".'

The Situationists complimented the judge on his style and republished his tirade world-wide.

Then, in 1968, Situationism exploded like lava through the volcano of the Paris students' uprising and subsequent near-revolution. Situationist slogans were sprayed all over the buildings and metros of Paris.

LIVE WITHOUT RESTRICTIONS

OR DEAD TIME. CULTURE IS THE INVERSION OF LIFE. NEVER WORK. THE COMMODITY IS THE OPIUM OF THE PEOPLE. SCREAM, STEAL, EJACULATE YOUR DESIRES. THE MORE YOU CONSUME THE LESS YOU LIVE. THEY ARE BUYING YOUR HAPPINESS, STEAL IT. IT IS FORBIDDEN TO FORBID. KNOWLEDGE IS INSEPARABLE FROM THE USE TO WHICH IT IS PUT. BE CRUEL. DOWN WITH THE NAZARENE TOAD. I TAKE MY DESIRES FOR REALITY BECAUSE

I BELIEVE IN THE REALITY OF MY DESIRES. IMAGINATION TAKES POWER. EVEN IF GOD EXISTED WE WOULD HAVE TO SUPPRESS HIM. ART IS DEAD: DO NOT CONSUME ITS CORPSE.

But once famous, the Situationists fell into vicious internal disputes and were reduced to their founder member, Guy Debord. Debord eventually announced himself disgusted by his own celebrity and disbanded the movement in 1972.

In a sense the SI's project had fulfilled and played itself out by the early seventies. For from then on their ideas and attitudes were no longer peripheral to Left thinking but central to it. Jean Paul Sartre's journal, *Les Temps Modernes*, summarized the SI's achievement as its reinstatement of subjectivity to the revolutionary project – enthroning the needs of the self over such theoretical abstractions as class.

In May 1968 I (FV) was studying at the Sorbonne and got caught up in the events there. Wildly excited Malcolm made strenuous efforts to join me but was frustrated by the rail, sea and air strikes. Instead, Malcolm and Jamie Reid (who was to become the Sex Pistols' art director) fomented an acrimonious sit-in at Croydon Art College. I returned to London with some Situationist literature which fascinated Malcolm and which I translated for him. Jamie had meanwhile visited Paris as soon as he could after the events and made his own contacts with neo-anarchist and SI-influenced groups.[2]

But if the Sex Pistols stemmed from the SI, their particular twist of radical flash and burlesque rage was also mediated through a band of hooligan pedants based in the Notting Hill Gate area of London. This was King Mob. King Mob came about like this.

In the mid-sixties one of the few

British Situationists was Chris Grey, a quietly spoken, aristocratically mannered intellectual who lived with his dreamy-eyed woman in Cambridge Gardens, W10. In an idle moment, Chris boasted he could call on at least 30 trained and combat-hardened street-fighters in the Ladbroke Grove area alone.

Hearing of this exciting development, Guy Debord rushed across the Channel to inspect the troops. He was directed by an embarrassed Chris to the home of one Dave Wise and bursting in discovered Dave lying on a sofa watching Match Of The Day with a can of McEwan's Special Export.

Such idle truck with the State's one-way communication system (ie Dave's six-inch telly) annoyed Debord who became furious when Dave informed him that the guerrilla combat unit was him and his brother Stuart. Denouncing

Jamie Reid being arrested in June '77 after the Pistols Jubilee boat gig. Richard Branson brings up the rear.

THIS IS YOUR BUILDING

GO WHERE YOU WANT.

TELL YOUR SECURITY GUARD TO

FUCK OFF!

One of the milder posters put up during King Mob's 1969 occupation of the London School of Economics.

Dave's modest library as ideologically suspect and throwing books all over Dave's flat, Debord raged back to Paris. Chris Grey was duly expelled from the SI for the heinous political crime of lying – the SI insisted on complete transparency from its members and especially abominated fibs.

So then Chris and Dave and his brother Stuart (the Wise brothers were stocky Northerners and both art college lecturers) founded King Mob (after the eighteenth century Gordon Rioters), a band dedicated to anti-cultural activities like smashing up Wimpy bars, defacing the work of lickarse artists, and publicly celebrating Valerie Solanas's shooting of Andy Warhol.

They also supplied the muscle (and two sledge-hammers) to despatch the infamous LSE 'gates' (which the authorities had erected throughout the college to restrict access).

These were mostly highly educated people. Dave Wise could argue persuasively about the critique of art implicit in the aesthetic of the British Romantics. Or discourse learnedly on the subversive aspects of William Blake's poetry.

King Mob also announced that football hooligans were the avant-garde of the British working class, and they proselytized amongst Hells Angels, Piccadilly Circus junkies and skinheads. At its height King Mob mustered about 60 people.

So it was to King Mob that Malcolm and Jamie gravitated in the aftermath of '68. And it was with Chris Grey that Jamie published the influential first English collection of Situationist writings: *Leaving the Twentieth Century* (whose graphics clearly anticipate the Sex Pistols' imagery).

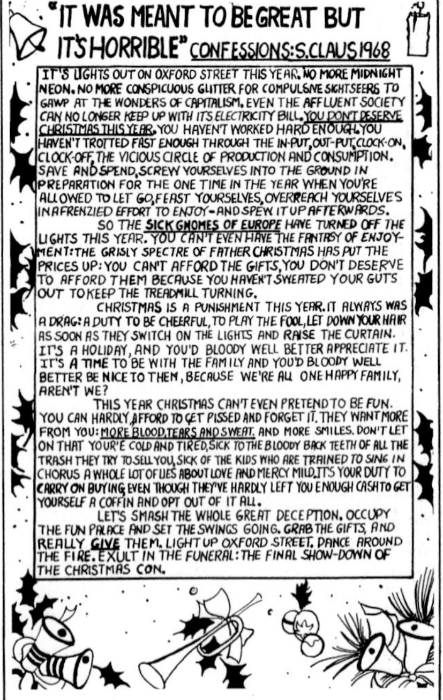

"IT WAS MEANT TO BE GREAT BUT IT'S HORRIBLE" CONFESSIONS: S. CLAUS 1968

IT'S LIGHTS OUT ON OXFORD STREET THIS YEAR. NO MORE MIDNIGHT NEON. NO MORE CONSPICUOUS GLITTER FOR COMPULSIVE SIGHTSEERS TO GAWP AT THE WONDERS OF CAPITALISM. EVEN THE AFFLUENT SOCIETY CAN NO LONGER KEEP UP WITH ITS ELECTRICITY BILL. YOU DON'T DESERVE CHRISTMAS THIS YEAR. YOU HAVEN'T WORKED HARD ENOUGH. YOU HAVEN'T TROTTED FAST ENOUGH THROUGH THE IN-PUT, OUT-PUT, CLOCK-ON, CLOCK-OFF, THE VICIOUS CIRCLE OF PRODUCTION AND CONSUMPTION. SAVE AND SPEND, SCREW YOURSELVES INTO THE GROUND IN PREPARATION FOR THE ONE TIME IN THE YEAR WHEN YOU'RE ALLOWED TO LET GO, FEAST YOURSELVES, OVERREACH YOURSELVES IN A FRENZIED EFFORT TO ENJOY - AND SPEW IT UP AFTERWARDS.

SO THE SICK GNOMES OF EUROPE HAVE TURNED OFF THE LIGHTS THIS YEAR. YOU CAN'T EVEN HAVE THE FANTASY OF ENJOYMENT: THE GRISLY SPECTRE OF FATHER CHRISTMAS HAS PUT THE PRICES UP: YOU CAN'T AFFORD THE GIFTS, YOU DON'T DESERVE TO AFFORD THEM BECAUSE YOU HAVEN'T SWEATED YOUR GUTS OUT TO KEEP THE TREADMILL TURNING.

CHRISTMAS IS A PUNISHMENT THIS YEAR. IT ALWAYS WAS A DRAG: A DUTY TO BE CHEERFUL, TO PLAY THE FOOL, LET DOWN YOUR HAIR AS SOON AS THEY SWITCH ON THE LIGHTS AND RAISE THE CURTAIN. IT'S A HOLIDAY, AND YOU'D BLOODY WELL BETTER APPRECIATE IT. IT'S A TIME TO BE WITH THE FAMILY AND YOU'D BLOODY WELL BETTER BE NICE TO THEM, BECAUSE WE'RE ALL ONE HAPPY FAMILY, AREN'T WE?

THIS YEAR CHRISTMAS CAN'T EVEN PRETEND TO BE FUN. YOU CAN HARDLY AFFORD TO GET PISSED AND FORGET IT. THEY WANT MORE FROM YOU: MORE BLOOD, TEARS AND SWEAT. AND MORE SMILES. DON'T LET ON THAT YOU'RE COLD AND TIRED, SICK TO THE BLOODY BACK TEETH OF ALL THE TRASH THEY TRY TO SELL YOU, SICK OF THE KIDS WHO ARE TRAINED TO SING IN CHORUS A WHOLE LOT OF LIES ABOUT LOVE AND MERCY MILD. IT'S YOUR DUTY TO CARRY ON BUYING, EVEN THOUGH THEY'VE HARDLY LEFT YOU ENOUGH CASH TO GET YOURSELF A COFFIN AND OPT OUT OF IT ALL.

LET'S SMASH THE WHOLE GREAT DECEPTION. OCCUPY THE FUN PALACE AND SET THE SWINGS GOING. GRAB THE GIFTS, AND REALLY GIVE THEM. LIGHT UP OXFORD STREET. DANCE AROUND THE FIRE. EXULT IN THE FUNERAL: THE FINAL SHOW-DOWN OF THE CHRISTMAS CON.

Leaflet issued during King Mob's Christmas 1968 occupation of Selfridges' toy department.

Such were the influences, ideas and attitudes, which, percolating through Malcolm's and Vivienne's boutique in the King's Road, gradually assumed the form of decor and clothes, and, eventually, of the Sex Pistols.

The transmutation was not deliberate and involved many people over several years, some of whom subsequently disappeared from the scene.

I suspect, too, that Malcolm didn't always take Situationist ideas as seriously as Jamie. But they *worked* so he carried them on. And so well did they work that in the end they carried *him* on, often despite himself and against Vivienne's (more commonsensical) judgement.

Malcolm has never been a thinker, but he is easily carried along by the force and inner logic of an idea.

And Situationism was one of the best ideas this century. [FV]

[1]Anyone interested in Situationist ideas should search out Ken Knabbs' excellent 1982 translation of the Situationist journal, *The Situationist International Anthology* (Bureau of Public Secrets, PO Box 1044, Berkeley, California 947070). Other essential reading is *The Society of the Spectacle* by Guy Debord (Buchet-Chastel, 1967), and Raoul Vaneigem's *Treatise of Savoir Vivre for the Young Generations* (Gallimard, 1967). Beware crappy and unauthorized translations! Bernard E. Brown's *Protest in Paris* (General Learning Press, New Jersey, 1974), pages 88 to 109, is easily the best account of Situationism by a non-believer. Greil Marcus is currently working on a major book around this subject and has already produced some striking reviews and think pieces. See, for exam-

ple, his review of the SI journal in *The Village Voice Literary Supplement*, No 7, May 1982 and 'The Cowboy Philosophers', *Artforum*, March 1986. I'd also personally recommend the novels of the late Alexander Trocchi, published by John Calder. Trocchi was really only an honorary Situationist, being too far gone on heroin to participate fully, but he was a close friend and inspiration to Guy Debord especially. Trocchi's elegant and fierce writings, particularly *Young Adam* (1954) and *Cain's Book* (1960), are the closest thing I know to Situationist novels.

[2]Julien Temple, the other Glitterbest mainstay, learned Situationism from the outside after he joined Glitterbest and cleverly turned it into a career ideology – eventually to ensconce himself in the jet/rock set as a pop star by default. When Julien married a beauty queen in '86, guess who came to the wedding. Mick Jagger and David Bowie – Punk's most despised figures.

DATA FILE
NEVER MIND
THE BOLLOCKS
HERE'S THE
YOUR
Sex
Pistols
Wanna
Be Me
Sex
Pistols
South Kensington

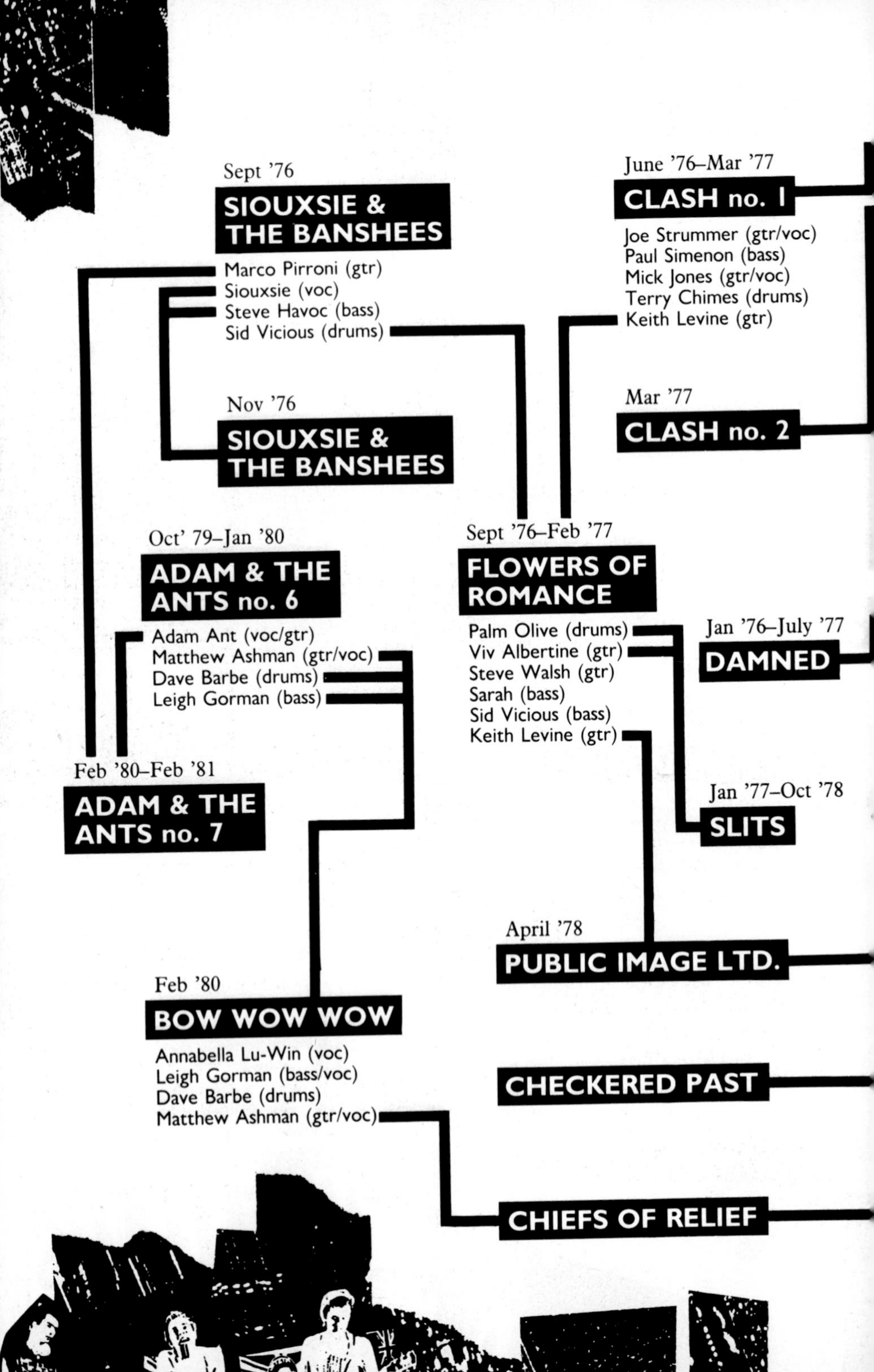

Sept '76
SIOUXSIE & THE BANSHEES
Marco Pirroni (gtr)
Siouxsie (voc)
Steve Havoc (bass)
Sid Vicious (drums)
June '76–Mar '77
CLASH no. 1
Joe Strummer (gtr/voc)
Paul Simenon (bass)
Mick Jones (gtr/voc)
Terry Chimes (drums)
Keith Levine (gtr)
Nov '76
SIOUXSIE & THE BANSHEES
Mar '77
CLASH no. 2
Oct' 79–Jan '80
ADAM & THE ANTS no. 6
Adam Ant (voc/gtr)
Matthew Ashman (gtr/voc)
Dave Barbe (drums)
Leigh Gorman (bass)
Sept '76–Feb '77
FLOWERS OF ROMANCE
Palm Olive (drums)
Viv Albertine (gtr)
Steve Walsh (gtr)
Sarah (bass)
Sid Vicious (bass)
Keith Levine (gtr)
Jan '76–July '77
DAMNED
Feb '80–Feb '81
ADAM & THE ANTS no. 7
Jan '77–Oct '78
SLITS
April '78
PUBLIC IMAGE LTD.
Feb '80
BOW WOW WOW
Annabella Lu-Win (voc)
Leigh Gorman (bass/voc)
Dave Barbe (drums)
Matthew Ashman (gtr/voc)
CHECKERED PAST
CHIEFS OF RELIEF

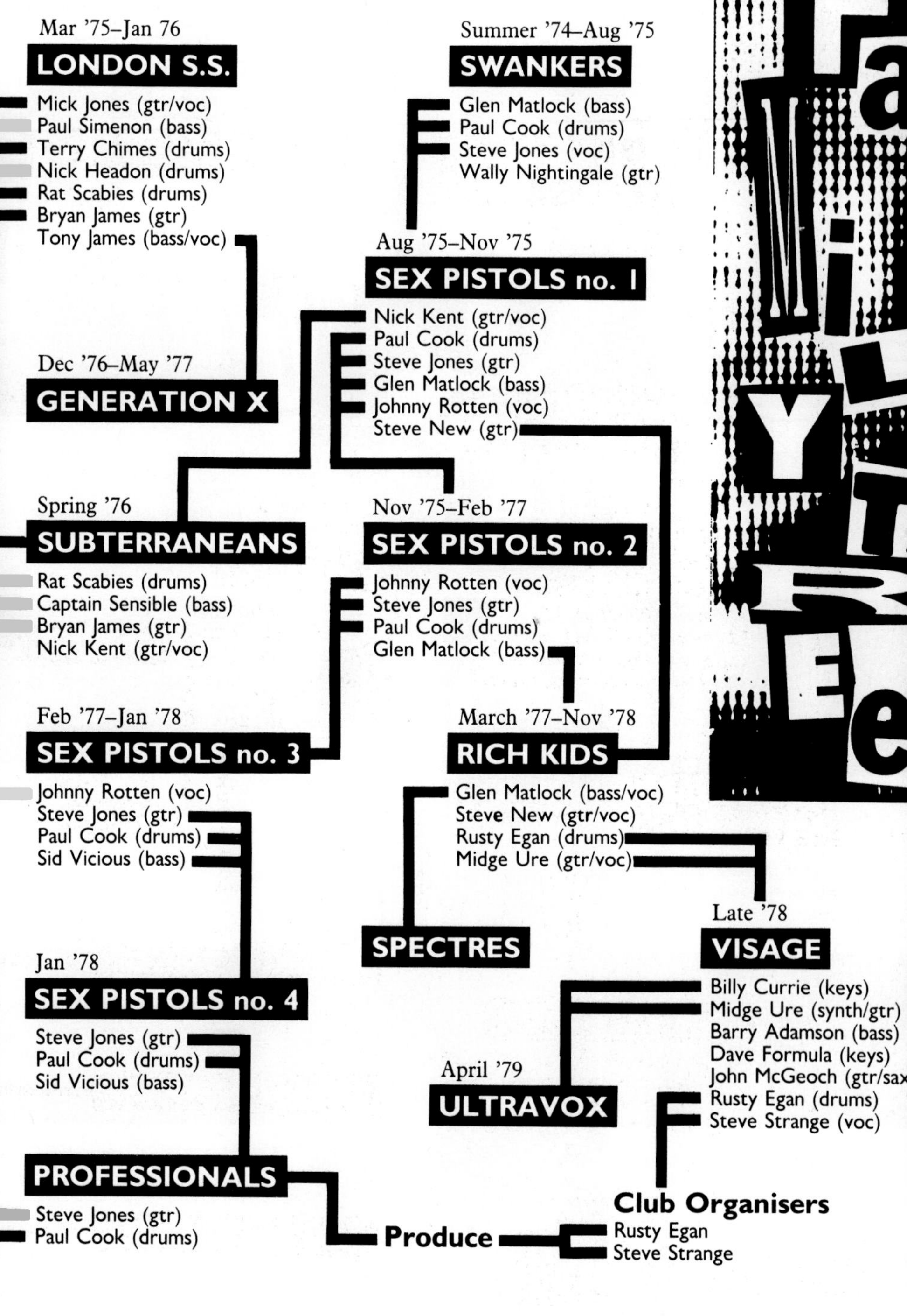
Family Tree
Mar '75–Jan 76
LONDON S.S.
Mick Jones (gtr/voc)
Paul Simenon (bass)
Terry Chimes (drums)
Nick Headon (drums)
Rat Scabies (drums)
Bryan James (gtr)
Tony James (bass/voc)
Summer '74–Aug '75
SWANKERS
Glen Matlock (bass)
Paul Cook (drums)
Steve Jones (voc)
Wally Nightingale (gtr)
Aug '75–Nov '75
SEX PISTOLS no. 1
Nick Kent (gtr/voc)
Paul Cook (drums)
Steve Jones (gtr)
Glen Matlock (bass)
Johnny Rotten (voc)
Steve New (gtr)
Dec '76–May '77
GENERATION X
Spring '76
SUBTERRANEANS
Rat Scabies (drums)
Captain Sensible (bass)
Bryan James (gtr)
Nick Kent (gtr/voc)
Nov '75–Feb '77
SEX PISTOLS no. 2
Johnny Rotten (voc)
Steve Jones (gtr)
Paul Cook (drums)
Glen Matlock (bass)
Feb '77–Jan '78
SEX PISTOLS no. 3
Johnny Rotten (voc)
Steve Jones (gtr)
Paul Cook (drums)
Sid Vicious (bass)
March '77–Nov '78
RICH KIDS
Glen Matlock (bass/voc)
Steve New (gtr/voc)
Rusty Egan (drums)
Midge Ure (gtr/voc)
SPECTRES
Late '78
VISAGE
Billy Currie (keys)
Midge Ure (synth/gtr)
Barry Adamson (bass)
Dave Formula (keys)
John McGeoch (gtr/sax)
Rusty Egan (drums)
Steve Strange (voc)
Jan '78
SEX PISTOLS no. 4
Steve Jones (gtr)
Paul Cook (drums)
Sid Vicious (bass)
April '79
ULTRAVOX
PROFESSIONALS
Steve Jones (gtr)
Paul Cook (drums)
Produce
Club Organisers
Rusty Egan
Steve Strange

DISCOGRAPHY

ANARCHY IN THE UK/I WANNA BE ME (EMI 2566) Nov 76
First pressing. Producer credit: Chris Thomas, A and B sides.

NEVER MIND THE BOLLOCKS HERE'S THE SEX PISTOLS (Virgin V2086) Oct 77
The first limited edition included a poster and a one-sided single Submission.

ANARCHY IN THE UK/I WANNA BE ME (EMI 2566)
Second pressing. Producer credit on B side changed to Dave Goodman. Almost immediately after release the r'cord was deleted and there were no more pressings.

SUBMISSION (Virgin VDJ24)
This one-sided single released with the Bollocks album became a collector's item.

GOD SAVE THE QUEEN/DID YOU NO WRONG (Virgin VS 181) May 77
(The A&M pressing with No Feelings on the B side is extremely rare.)

NO ONE IS INNOCENT/MY WAY (Virgin VS 220) Jun 78
Featuring the great train robber Ronald Biggs and 'Martin Borman'.

PRETTY VACANT/NO FUN (Virgin VS 184) Jul 77
(The B side is a Stooges number produced by Dave Goodman.)

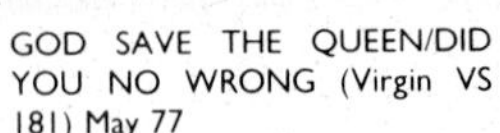

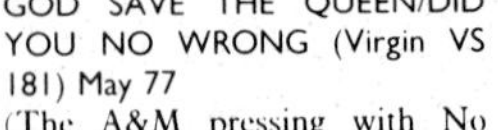

MY WAY/GOD SAVE THE SEX PISTOLS (Virgin VS 220)
The first of the 12″ singles with My Way as the B side (which became the A side on the 7″).

HOLIDAYS IN THE SUN/SATELLITE (Virgin VS 191) Oct 77
The record was almost immediately withdrawn when a firm of travel agents claimed the graphics on the record sleeve infringed their copyright. Sid Vicious contributed to the music on the A side.

NEVER MIND THE BOLLOCKS HERE'S THE SEX PISTOLS (Virgin VP 2086)
The first release after Johnny Rotten left the band. 12 songs including Submission.

SOMETHING ELSE/FRIGGIN' IN THE RIGGIN' (Virgin VS 240) Feb 79
Dedicated to Sid Vicious. Produced by Steve Jones.

SILLY THING/WHO KILLED BAMBI (Virgin VS 256) Mar 79
Ten Pole Tudor wrote the songs, Vivienne Westwood wrote the lyric for the B side.

THE GREAT ROCK 'N' ROLL SWINDLE (Virgin VD 2501) March 79
Double album. (McLaren's testament and the Pistols' swan-song.)

C'MON EVERYBODY, GOD SAVE THE QUEEN (symphonic version)/WHATCHA GONNA DO ABOUT IT (Virgin VS 272) June 79
The B side, the debut single of the Small Faces, sung by Johnny Rotten.

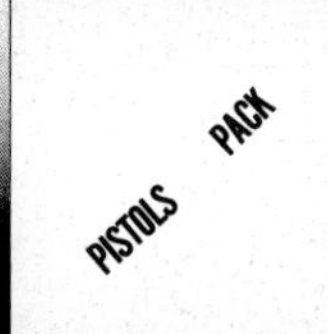

SOME PRODUCT (Virgin VR2) July 79
An interview album.

THE GREAT ROCK 'N' ROLL SWINDLE/ROCK AROUND THE CLOCK (Virgin VS 290) Oct 79
(Business as usual without the band.)

SID VICIOUS (Virgin OVED85) Dec 79
Poor quality album with out-takes of My Way.

THE VERY BEST OF THE SEX PISTOLS (YX 7247 AX) Dec 79
Only released in Japan. Including the previously unreleased Black Leather. Now deleted.

FLOGGING A DEAD HORSE (Virgin V 2142) Feb 80
A compilation of the best singles and tracks.

THE GREAT ROCK 'N' ROLL SWINDLE (Virgin V 2168) May 80
Film soundtrack with Who Killed Bambi (which was not included on the first album).

(I'M NOT YOUR) STEPPING STONE/PISTOLS PROPAGANDA (Virgin VS 399) Jun 80
A side a cover of the Monkeys song. (B side not worth listening to.)

PISTOLS PACK (Virgin SEX 1–6) Dec 80
Including limited edition of Black Leather.

ANARCHY IN THE UK/NO FUN (EMI/Virgin VS 609) 1983
Simultaneous release of original 7" tracks plus 12" version.

LAND OF HOPE AND GLORY/ THE FLOWERS OF ROMANESQUE
The Elgar classic played by the 'Ex Pistols' and produced by Dave Goodman. (Contrary to rumours assiduously spread by certain parties this record had nothing to do with the Sex Pistols and does not feature them in any shape or form.)

LAND OF HOPE AND GLORY/ THE FLOWERS OF ROMANESQUE
A limited edition picture disc.

NEVER TRUST A HIPPY (HIPPY 1)
This 'live' album is actually *worse* than the above UK 1!

SUBMISSION/ANARCHY IN THE UK (Chaos EXPORT 1)
Out-takes.

THE BEST OF THE SEX PISTOLS LIVE (Bondage BOND007)
A side from the time when Glen Matlock was with the Pistols. Listenable. B side: Dreadful quality and appalling performance.

SEX PISTOLS – MINI ALBUM (Chaos APO CA3)
Six tracks produced by Dave Goodman.

AFTER THE STORM (Receiver RRLP 102)
Four songs on the B side from the same take as Pistols Live. A side includes an out-take of the New York Dolls.

SUBMISSION/NO FEELINGS (Chaos DICK 1)
Two tracks from Mini Album.

WHERE WERE YOU IN '77 (77 Records)
Performance OK. Sound quality bad. In the early part of the album Sid Vicious is playing quite well.

PISTOLS LIVE (Receiver PRLP101) 85
First live independent release from recordings made in 76. Reasonable quality.

POWER OF THE PISTOLS (77 Records)
The first track on the B side is quite good. The rest dreadful.

LIVE WORLDWIDE (Chaos/ Connection KOMA 788017)
A live album containing several songs which have nothing to do with the Sex Pistols.

SEX PISTOLS LIMITED EDITION (PIC 007)
Picture disc of live Pistols' tracks. The B side is from the USA final tour.

ANARCHY IN THE UK LIVE (UK 1)
One of the worst quality indie live albums.

100 CLUB SEX PISTOLS PARTY (SP 3086-bootleg)
The quality isn't good but the performance is brilliant.

ST. ALBANS BASH 28TH JANUARY, 1976 (SEX 3523-bootleg)
The A side is the earliest recorded performance. The quality is very poor. B side recorded from TV performance.

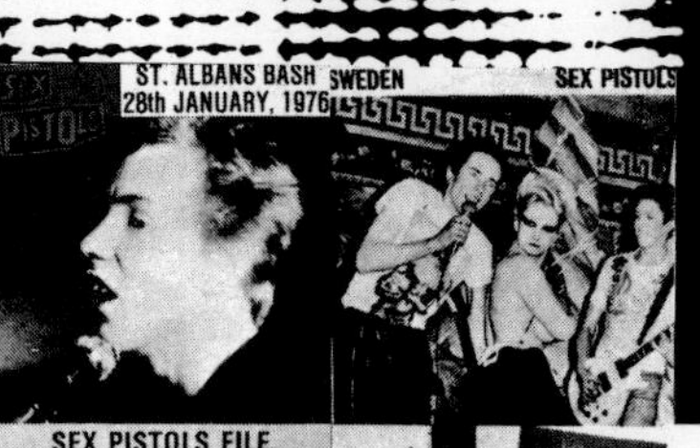

SWEDEN (bootleg)
Live double album of the '77 Scandinavian tour. Sound quality good.

SEX PISTOLS FILE 1976–1978
Four record box set. Includes the famous 'Spunk' bootleg and three-albums' worth of the 100 Club and US tour. Performance is good. Sound quality bad.

TOUR OF SCANDIVANIA (SP 3117-bootleg)
Average sound quality and performance.

COPY OF SPUNK BOOTLEG

ROCK-N-ROLL (Odd 2) 78
Live from Atlanta. Sound quality fair.

HOT OFF THE PRESS
Bootleg of a live '76 performance. Sound quality good.

GUN CONTROL (SP 2900)
Live from the Winterland gig during the US tour – 14 Jan 78. The last live recording. (Johnny Rotten going off his head.)

GREAT ROCK 'N' ROLL SWINDLE (VTM 12, VBM 12)
Video of Julien Temple directed semi-documentary movie. Supposed to be the Pistols' movie but really McLaren's.

ROCK REVOLUTION (TE-M344) 84
Video about punk and new wave produced in England featuring the Sex Pistols, Clash, Jam, Bob Marley, Talking Heads and others. Includes a performance of Anarchy In The Uk from Aug 76.

PUNK ROCK
Don Letts' movie. An 8mm film transferred to video. The quality not very good but the footage is unmissable.

D.O.A. (024V)
Documentary on film and video of the USA tour. Scheduled for 1986(?) release.

CHECKLIST OF CHARACTERS (Ages given as in 1977)

BOOGIE (John Tiberi): Pistols tour manager. Age 27. Father antique dealer, mother ex-schoolteacher. Grammar school. Left school at 16. Worked in photography for four years. Worked with 101ers and Clash. Took over from Nils Stevenson as Pistols roadie.

TONY BULLEY: Television director for Thames TV. Age 33. Lives in Teddington. Father retired marine engineer. Grammar school, college of art. Deck hand. Schoolteacher. Television graphic designer. Television director.

AL CLARK: Press officer Virgin Records. Born 1948 in Spain. Mother schoolteacher, father mining engineer. Left Spain aged nine to go to Scottish prep school. Then public school and university (Birmingham and Madrid). Worked at Virgin from 1974.

PAT COLLIER: Age 26. Grammar school. University. Labourer. Sound engineer, Decca. Ex-bass guitarist Vibrators. Left to run own studios and to form new group the Boyfriends.

PAUL COOK: B. 20/7/56. Brought up in Hammersmith area. Two sisters. Father carpenter and joiner, mother casual work. Comprehensive school. Qualified electrician. After the Pistols' break-up Paul and Steve stayed together. They tried to relaunch their careers several times without much success but kept their hands in as session musicians and around-town characters.

DEBBIE: Age 17. Comprehensive school. Left at 16. Worked at Seditionaries. Followed Pistols from the early days. Debbie subsequently became a prostitute working the notorious Shepherd's Market area of London. Her memoirs featured in *Men Only*. She then changed her ways and recanted in *19* magazine: 'I had my first punter when I was 14.'

ALAN EDWARDS: Age 23. Publicist for punk rock bands. Ex-freelance music journalist.

DANNY FRIEDMAN: Museum assistant, Theatre Museum, Victoria and Albert Museum. Born 1943 in Hampstead. Father psychoanalyst, mother electroencephalographist. Direct grant school. One year on organic farm in Wales: 'In other words I was a hippy.' School of Oriental and African Studies. Three years working at British Museum, then V&A.

DAVE GOODMAN: Producer of early Sex Pistols tracks and sound man on early tours. Age 26. Father toolmaker, mother matron. Left school at 16. Bass guitarist in band. Started PA company. First contact with Pistols through hiring them equipment. Since the band broke up Dave Goodman has released many live recordings of the Pistols on tour. These have been frequently criticized for poor quality. It should be remembered, however, that while Goodman was dropped as a producer once the Pistols made it, the 'wall of sound' he created with them in these first gigs (a sound he had pioneered with the proto-punk band Eater) was central to the Pistols' appeal.

DEREK GREEN: Managing Director of A&M Records. Age 32. Brought up in East End of London. Lives in South London suburb. Family man.

LAURIE HALL: Business Affairs Manager, EMI Records. Age 32. Lives in Herts. Grammar school. London University (law degree). Solicitor. EMI Records.

LESLIE HILL: Managing Director, EMI Records. Age 41. Lives in Buckinghamshire. Married with one son. Grammar school. Chartered accountant. Worked in publishing and music prior to EMI.

MICHAEL HOUSEGO: Studio producer, Thames Television. Age 33. Lives in Lancaster Gate. Father local government officer, mother Post Office worker. Public school – left at 15 with 13 'O' levels. Local and freelance journalism. Fleet Street. Thames TV.

STEVE JONES: B. 3/5/55. Brought up Shepherd's Bush and Hammersmith. Family later moved to Battersea. Only child. Father professional boxer, step-father makes gaskets for electric cookers, mother hairdresser. Comprehensive school. Remand centre. (See PAUL COOK for subsequent career.)

JACK LEWIS: Age 60. *Daily Mirror* showbiz reporter. First journalist to interview Sid Vicious.

MARCUS LIPTON, CBE: Labour MP Lambeth Central. Grammar school. MA Oxford. Known for his denunciations of punk. Died in 1978.

GLEN MATLOCK: B. 27/8/56. Parents live in semi-detached in Greenford, Middx. Father coach builder, mother accounts clerk with Gas Board. Grammar school. Art college. Had Saturday job in Malcolm's shop. Left Pistols to form the Rich Kids. Arranged the Pistols' songs for the 1986 movie *Sid and Nancy – Love Kills*.

MALCOLM McLAREN (original surname Edwards): Age 32. Brought up in North London. Mother and step-father successful clothing wholesalers. In and out of various art schools for about eight years, he was generally considered a brilliant but volatile and erratic student. During this time he also worked as a stage designer. While a student at Goldsmiths' College of Art helped organize a subversive arts festival which ended in tumult. Started a shop with Vivienne Westwood at 430 King's Road which specialized in 1950s' and Teddy boy objects and clothes. He then suddenly switched to fetishistic clothing, suitably altering the shop's decor, and its name to 'Sex'. He managed the New York Dolls for a while in the USA and on returning to GB became involved with the Sex Pistols.

Starred in *The Great Rock 'n' Roll Swindle*. Subsequently lost control of his Glitterbest management company to the Official Receiver. Launched the ultimately unsuccessful Bow Wow Wow in 1980. Left Vivienne Westwood – she kicked him out of their Clapham flat for cavorting with a German groupie (this was actually after a misguided suggestion from FV that if Malcolm confessed Vivienne would 'understand' – sorry about that!). Started a successful solo pop career as a performer. Then moved to Hollywood to pursue his dream of film-making and set up home with Hollywood actress Lauren Hutton. Was signed and then ditched by Paramount. In 1985 McLaren lost all rights to the Sex Pistols in a legal suit originally brought by John Lydon. [And see The (Early) Life and Crimes of Malcolm McLaren.]

MARK P (Mark Perry): Ex-bank clerk. Ex-editor *Sniffin' Glue* fanzine. Well-known punk spokesman. Director Step-Forward Records. Vocalist in Alternative TV.

JOHN PEEL (John Robert Parker Ravenscroft): Age 38. Lives Suffolk. Father Liverpool cotton broker. Shrewsbury public school. 1960–67 worked in radio in US. 10 years with BBC radio; first enthusiast of punk.

JAMIE REID: Art director for Sex Pistols. Was living with Sophie throughout the Pistols' career. Age 30. Brought up in Croydon. Father journalist, mother housewife. Grammar school. Croydon Art College. Semi-professional footballer. Demolition worker. Landscape gardener. Edited *Suburban Press* with Sophie. Since the Pistols has collaborated with the Dead Kennedys and others and established his own reputation. In 1981 the Victoria and Albert Museum bought Jamie's collection of Sex Pistols graphics and artwork for £1,000.

BERNIE RHODES: Designed and printed T-shirts for McLaren and Westwood. Helped with management of Pistols in early stages. Managed the Clash up to their first bust-up (and intermittently since). In an idle moment gave Malcolm McLaren and hence Adam Ant the idea for the Barundi beat (which he himself nicked off a forgotten sixties' single). Successfully launched Dexy's Midnight Runners: 'I wanted to make the unfashionable fashionable' – Bernard is nothing if not cryptic.

JOHNNY ROTTEN (John Joseph Lydon): B. 31/1/56. Three younger brothers. Father mini-cab/lorry driver, mother barmaid. RC comprehensive, FE college. After leaving the Pistols reverted to his real name, John Lydon. He founded Public Image Ltd which after a disappointing first album (dubbed by Simon Frith as 'a dull, dark claim to artistic significance') has put out increasingly interesting and commercial material.

SOPHIE (Sophie Richmond): Secretary and office manager to Malcolm McLaren and Sex Pistols. Age 26. Lived with Jamie during Pistols' life span. Father diplomat. Educated abroad, RC convent school, university. Printing and publishing. *Suburban Press* with Jamie. Sophie has now retired from the scene to raise her baby daughter.

TERRY SLATER: Creative Director, EMI Music. Age 35. Londoner living in Surrey. Left school at 14. Played in rock 'n' roll band. Worked in US as a performer and songwriter. Returned to England 1970. First to sign Sex Pistols.

JULIEN TEMPLE: Glitterbest employee and director of *The Great Rock 'n' Roll Swindle*. Brought up on council estate in St John's Wood, London. Mother schoolteacher, father travel agent for Intourist. Grammar school. Kings College, Cambridge (1972–75). National Film School. Post-Pistols Julien went into pop video production and hit the jackpot with his videos for Bowie's 'Blue Jean' and the Rolling Stones' 'Undercover'. Went on to direct the pop musical *Absolute Beginners*.

TRACIE: One of the first Pistols fans. Age 18. Father former bus driver now minds his children at home, mother left home. Grammar school. London College of Fashion. Shop assistant. SS claimant. Worked for Westwood in 'Seditionaries'. Tracie died suddenly in 1978. McLaren arranged a wreath emblazoned 'NEVER MIND THE BOLLOCKS TRACIE', and a film crew to record the funeral. Much to the family's consternation. (This was one of the many never-used sequences for *The Swindle*).

SID VICIOUS (John Simon Ritchie a.k.a. John Beverley): B. 10/5/57. Brought up in East London. Comprehensive school. FE college. Drummer for Siouxsie and the Banshees. Took over from Glen Matlock as bass player for Pistols. Arrested for the murder of his girlfriend Nancy Spungen in October '78. Died in February '79 of a heroin overdose.

RON WATTS: 100 Club promoter. Lives High Wycombe. 'The godfather of punk.'

VIVIENNE WESTWOOD: Age 36. Parents retired shopkeepers. Grammar school. Teacher training college. Viv met Malcolm about 10 years ago and left her husband for him. She has two boys, one by Malcolm. Was a primary school teacher until she began working full-time in the shop which she subsequently ran alone. After then dissociating from Malcolm businesswise, Vivienne began a solo career as an independent fashion designer based in Paris and Milan. [More information on Vivienne is in The Life and Crimes of Malcolm McLaren].

ACKNOWLEDGEMENTS

First of all Sophie, for her diary, and for much help and advice; then John, Paul, Sid and Steve; and Glen Matlock; the mothers: Mrs Cook, Mrs Jones and Mrs Lydon; to Malcolm McLaren for incalculable help and inside information, Vivienne Westwood the same, Jamie Reid ditto; thanks also to EMI, A&M and Virgin Records (especially Al Clark), Julien Temple for his invaluable overview of the last days, and to everyone else who generously gave their time to our questions; for permission to reproduce articles: Associated Press, *Daily Mirror, Daily Mail, Evening Standard, Daily Express, Evening News, Daily Telegraph, Guardian, Sun, Music Week, Sounds, News of the World,* Virgin Records; permission from Oxford University Press to quote from Iona and Peter Opie's *The Lore and Language of Schoolchildren*, 1959; Capital Radio and Tommy Vance; our thanks also to Graham Greene for the quotations from *Brighton Rock*; the anonymous editors of *No Future*; and many thanks to all the fans – those who contributed and those who wanted to.

SEX PISTOLS CASSETTE

If you have enjoyed this book you may like to hear *Sex Pistols – The Heyday,* Judy Vermorel's interview cassette first released by Factory Records, featuring John Rotten, Sid Vicious, Paul Cook and Steve Jones. It runs for approximately 60 minutes and costs £3.99 (including postage and packing). Cheques and postal orders should be made payable to SPDC and sent to Mindopal Ltd, 57 Duke Street, Grosvenor Square, London W1M 5DH.

GOD